A
PARTISAN
VIEW

A PARTISAN VIEW

Five Decades of the Literary Life

William Phillips

STEIN AND DAY/*Publishers*/New York

First published in 1983
Copyright © 1983 by William Phillips
All rights reserved, Stein and Day, Incorporated
Designed by Louis A. Ditizio
Printed in the United States of America
STEIN AND DAY/*Publishers*
Scarborough House
Briarcliff Manor, N.Y. 10510

Library of Congress Cataloging in Publication Data

Phillips, William, date
  A partisan view.

  Includes index.
  1. Phillips, William, date. 2. Editors
—United States—Biography. 3. Partisan review (New
York, N.Y.: 1934)
4. Partisan review (New York, N.Y.: 1936) I. Title.
PN149.9.P44A37 1983   070.4′1′0924 [B]   83-42828
ISBN 0-8128-2931-X

Acknowledgments

For this memoir, thanks are due—for different reasons—to many people. I was fortunate early on in working with an unusually brilliant, vain, quarrelsome community of writers and thinkers. And it is to this extraordinary community with whom I grew up that I must acknowledge an intellectual debt. Most of them are in this book, playing their flamboyant roles, telling the resonating stories of their lives and works.

I also want to thank several people for reading the manuscript and giving me more work to do with their suggestions: Steven Marcus, who urged me to be tough-minded; Kay Agena, who almost spread her enthusiasm to me; Edith Kurzweil, who, in addition to goading me to write the book, reread and made me redo many parts; Daniel Bell, whose total recall had me correct some of my facts; Edna Phillips, who was at once sympathetic and critical; and Joan Daly, who read the manuscript through a microscope.

I am grateful, too, to Dr. Yela Lowenfeld, who tried to impress on me that being up is better than down, to Robert H. Montgomery, Jr., to Joan Schwartz, and to Joanna Rose and my other friends on the Advisory Board of *Partisan Review* for helping to make the whole thing possible.

I must also thank the Guggenheim Foundation, the National Endowment for the Humanities, and the Rockefeller Foundation, for generous grants that kept me away from teaching.

The rest, for better or worse, is my own doing.

Contents

A PARTISAN VIEW

1

HISTORY REMADE

AS a participant in many of the literary and political events now being disputed, I have thought for some time of adding my own account of what happened in those fateful decades to the so-called historical record. But I have held back until now because of some doubts about the general meaning of my own experiences—doubts that might be described more technically as methodological scruples. At first, I wondered how typical my experience was. In the thirties, my literary and political world certainly seemed marginal to what was popularly thought to be the mainstream. We were not only young; we thought of ourselves as alienated, against the grain, radical, outside the system. And though our arrogance led us to believe we were intelligent, gifted, and superior to our elders, it never occurred to me that our history would some day be considered important. In fact, as I look back, it seems to me we underestimated each other. For all our vanity, our self-confidence, we felt like pygmies in comparison with not only the literary and intellectual figures of the more distant past, but with those who came just before us.

And while our concerns were nothing short of global, it always seemed to me we were pompously—and incestuously—talking to ourselves, like school boys and girls addressing the big issues and the basic philosophical questions. Our conversation about a new socialist society to repair the injustices of the one we lived in sounded like the inbred, self-intoxicating discussions within a political sect. To tell the truth, even in the depths of the depression and the height of the revolutionary zeal among New York intellectuals, the notion of a large socialist movement in America, not to speak of the revolution, struck me as a kind of political psychosis, that is, as the fantasy of people who acted as though they were living in Russia.

Who could have dreamt that in the eighties everyone would want to know what happened in those early decades? Who could have conceived that the disheveled dissidents of the thirties would be expected now, like elder statesmen, to write the history of that period—or that others would write about them? Every student learns that the young rebels of one generation become the establishment of succeeding generations; but this is one of those generalizations so commonplace that while it appears to be true of all time, never seems entirely applicable to any specific one.

So why have I finally succumbed to both internal and external pressures to write a kind of intellectual memoir? I am not sure I have a precise answer. One reason seems to me that a time comes when one does what one always thought to be impossible because it suddenly becomes necessary. Another, less personal, reason is the belated recognition that a memoir is a recollection that shapes past events, and that its claims to truth, which are based on the force of one's experience, are just as great as those of presumably objective accounts, following the prescribed methods of historical research. After all, what is history but the sorting out of conflicting testimonies, memories, and records?

This is particularly true in our age of revisionism. For we tend to revise history almost as soon as it has been made. So rapidly have all our ideas been changing, and so quickly have we forgotten what we once believed, that the past has been dissolving into the present. The period from the thirties through the sixties has been particularly vulnerable to reinterpretation and misinterpretation. It is as though it had lost its own history—a victim of intellectual amnesia.

The revision has been mostly from the left, which has placed the guilt for the cold war on the United States and has been castigating American society and the American government for being repressive and reactionary. It has distorted the role of individuals and institutions. But the right has also done its share of revising in playing up the menace of the left and playing down the weaknesses of American society. Norman Podhoretz's book, *Breaking Ranks,* is an example of the confident revisionism that celebrates the wisdom of the new conservatism and makes liberal and left opinion responsible for all our failures. It also invents a history for a number of people, including Lionel Trilling, Irving Howe, Norman Mailer, myself, and other writers associated with *Partisan Review.* Podhoretz's general thesis is that we did not go all the way in our anti-communism out of fear of criticism by liberals and radicals. (Podhoretz's views are discussed more fully later in this memoir, but the memoir itself is in part a reply to his version of the past.)

More recently in *The Truants,* William Barrett has written a more detailed account of an earlier period. He, too, depicted the time he was dealing with it differently than I remembered it, partly for personal reasons and partly from an ideological frame of reference. The main figures he discusses—Lionel Trilling, Philip Rahv, Delmore Schwartz, and myself—are revised in order to fit a picture of the rise of neoconservatism and the ebb of liberalism. Hence his emphasis on those elements of *Partisan Review* that he thinks led to neoconservatism and his neglect of its other aspects. There is also a certain amount of distortion of the role of the leading actors in order to designate some as "representative" figures, in keeping with his overall political and psychological scheme.

I plan to tell the story of that part of literary and intellectual life in which I was directly engaged. Most of it was in New York. And much of it had to do with those trends and circles that were affected by the radicalization sweeping over Europe and America in the thirties, the reaction setting in later in the forties and fifties, and the new turns in the seventies and eighties. There were other currents and other people with whom I had little or nothing to do, but I think the world I knew has turned out to be central to the large forces and the enormous changes of those years. To some extent, *Partisan Review* was in the middle of things; and though I do not intend to write the history of the magazine in this book, it does serve as a frame for a more personal account.

As we know, decades are arbitrary and often misleading divisions of an epoch, as are all divisions. But I have found it convenient to break up my account into the thirties, forties, fifties, sixties, and seventies, since these decades are already associated with certain kinds of moods and events. The thirties, for example, are never anything but the radical thirties, the forties are the gray years of transition to the fifties, which have been historicized as a time of reaction. The sixties, of course, are the heyday of the new left and the counterculture. But they also mark the solidification of a neoconservatism in reaction to the infantilisms of the left and the celebration of self-realization, self-expression, and self-indulgence. The seventies saw a reshuffling of ideas. As for the eighties, I will go out on a limb and make some tentative assessments, mostly of a pessimistic nature. As I see them now, they appear to be a time of growing intellectual confusion and political disillusion. Are we witnessing in the last few decades an example of Henry Adams's law of entropy?

It goes without saying that these essentially political tags for the last few decades are useful only for broad identification and characterization. Beyond that, one has to get into the intellectual texture of the times, for what we are involved in is nothing less than the vast political contradictions, the enormous complexities of the arts, and the critical thinking of the modern period.

2

THE CENTER
AND THE FRINGES

LITERARY publications, unlike journals of opinion
that reflect the changing intellectual climate, usually have their
moments of glory, after which, if they survive, they carry on like old
soldiers. For literary magazines, like writers, come out of a time and a
place, out of some literary current or sensibility. Thus *Partisan Review*
was born in the thirties—actually twice-born—and originally bore the
stamp of that era. If it has not been restricted by its origins, if it has
defied all the pressures of a time and country that have celebrated
youth, novelty, and escape from traditions, I think it is mainly because
of the continuity between the thirties and the following decades, and
because the traditions *Partisan Review* both inherited and helped
form have continued to be pertinent.

Of course, when *Partisan Review* was started in the thirties, first as
an organ of the John Reed Club, then as an independent journal, the
concept of the future was nothing more than a personal and a historical abstraction to me. None of us thought of the magazine as anything
but an instrument for dealing with the pressing literary and political
problems of the time; and we never dreamt that *Partisan Review*

would not only have an influence on writing and thinking but would also set a pattern for literary publications in the following decades.

It is impossible to reduce editorial policy to a simple definition. But, in retrospect, it can now be seen that our idea of the magazine provided a way of responding to new situations as well as a response to the immediate one. Essentially, our aim was to reconcile the modernist spirit, which was often conservative and antihistorical, with a political consciousness that emphasized the historical dimensions of art. Since the thirties, definitions of literary modernism have been shifting, as has our political thinking, but the fate of modernism, and the relation of writing to the pressures of the culture as a whole, have been key questions throughout. Of course, our prime concern was with literary quality, new talent, and new ideas. But the criteria for judging originality as well as accomplishment obviously have to do as much with literary direction as with taste.

To be sure, we were part of the swing away from the doctrinaire left positions of the thirties. As I look back, it would appear that we swung too far, though I must say that we always distinguished ourselves from the ultraconservative anti-Communists, and the magazine always remained critical of the commercial and ruling politics of the country. In fact, as the temper of the country became more and more conservative, the magazine became more critical of the adjustments to the new political and literary mood. Yet we never abandoned our anti-Stalinism and our distaste for both the corrupt and the foolish left.

During this period we published most of the serious writers who were either already established or who became known later, but always in a context that indicated the policies of the magazine.

In the fifties, the divisions that were tearing apart the earliest coalition were becoming clearer and sharper. The new conservatism was in full swing, as former radicals began to sing the praises of the country and the culture. The conservative anti-Communists, unlike the radical anti-Communists, didn't regard the Soviet Union as an obstacle to socialism and a threat to democratic values; the defects of the existing system were forgotten and its virtues inflated. The new conservatives mounted a high-powered attack not only on Marxism but on all other forms of radicalism. Some of these attacks were justified, but the impulse was also polemical, not simply one of intellectual inquiry.

The fifties, which have become the favorite arena for revisionist

16

history, were, of course, memorable for the exploitation of the anti-Communist position by reactionary and chauvinistic ideologues, once restrained by radical opponents of Stalinism. The culmination was reached in the wild, irresponsible, and pathological campaign of Senator Joseph McCarthy who, besides persecuting innocent as well as guilty people, succeeded in distorting the issue of communism. *Partisan Review* again, in this muddled and unsavory situation, saw its task as that of opposing both the demagoguery on the right and on the left.

Culturally, the spirit of retrenchment showed itself in a turn against experiment and avant-garde attitudes in the arts, and in a general reaction against the idea of modernism. It meant, too, that the mass media were looked at more indulgently; conventional writing became more acceptable; and academicism became the dominant mood, particularly in poetry and criticism.

And though the magazine had addressed itself earlier to these questions, most notably in Clement Greenberg's famous 1939 essay on "Avant-Garde and Kitsch," it was now felt necessary to emphasize the old distinctions that separate entertainment and literary packaging from the less popular forms of serious writing. One of the more forceful essays on this subject was Dwight Macdonald's "Mass Cult and Mid-Cult." Ironically, it should be added, the populist strain in the vulgar Marxism of the thirties helped to prepare the ground for the later reconciliation with the commercial pressures of the mass market and its need for more conventional forms of art.

In fact, *Partisan Review* was also swayed by these powerful currents, but I think only in a small way. The main effort of the magazine was to resist the conservative push, without, however, giving in to those radicals in politics and in the arts who had swung to a sectarian extreme. The problem was further complicated by the radical-conservative polarization that affected writing as well as politics, though it might be said that in the fifties the culture was still mostly on the side of tradition. At this time, for example, we published an assault on the new conservatism by Irving Howe, which—excessively I think—also accused the magazine of giving in to it. At the same time I wrote several pieces critical of the move to the right, politically and culturally, one of which had a title, "A Portrait of the Artist as a Middle-Aged Man," that clearly indicated our bias.

But it was the sixties that brought the earlier tendencies to a head—

and sharpened the dilemmas of the magazine. The blossoming of the new left and the counterculture not only drove the conservatives more to the right, but further splintered the remnants of the left. And the hostility of the new left to the so-called old left further complicated the role of the magazine. Politically, the problem boiled down to steering a course that, on the one hand, recognized the innocence and idealism of the youth, who were trying to escape from the system without getting caught in the rigid ideologies of the Communists, and, on the other hand, was critical of the counterculture and the new left for converting their ignorance, their petulance, their self-indulgence into an infantile left politics and pop culture that managed to be both alienated and modish. Culturally, the polarization tended to highlight the celebration of experience, sexual freedom, and half-cocked experiments at one extreme, and a devotion to order, rationality, tradition at the other. But there was a good deal of sanity and talent in between that was ignored by the obsessive polemics on both sides. And *Partisan Review*, acting on the assumption, borne out by cultural history, that ideological extremes play themselves out and that in the long run only talent and genuine ideas survive, tried to foster the kind of writing that was not affected by either conservative or radical postures. To be sure, this was not easy, since distinctions are not so clearcut in practice as in theory, and I must admit the magazine was swayed by the crosswinds as it tried to stay on its cultural course. But in the overheated atmosphere of the sixties, the magazine got it from both sides as it was accused both of swinging with the youth and of holding the line with the old guard.

3

GROWING OUT
OF THE TWENTIES

PARTISAN *Review* was born in the thirties, in the decade that some look back on with so much curiosity, nostalgia, misunderstanding. It seems so long ago, especially when one considers what has happened since: Hitler, Mussolini, the Holocaust, World War II, Vietnam, two Israeli-Arab wars, Watergate, China, women's liberation, several sexual and cultural revolutions, nuclear armament. But, despite these enormous changes, many of the questions that haunt us today are updated versions of the questions I grew up with earlier. And if the time since then appears foreshortened, it is because of the peculiar sense of contemporaneity that makes the whole modern period seem of a piece.

Intellectually speaking, I, too, was born in the thirties. Perhaps it is too egocentric to identify one's formative years with the beginnings of this era. But I think it can be said that the thirties were the cradle of our entire epoch, and that we are all living out the unsolved problems—intellectual as well as political—first posed at that time. For what we think of as the contemporary mind had its origins in the profoundly traumatic shift of consciousness that took place in the thirties.

A Partisan View

It can be said that the twentieth century began not in 1900 but in the thirties. The first two decades were a warm-up time. The twenties solidified the modernist movement in the arts, but the following decades saw a steady erosion of the spirit and the accomplishments of modernism. At first, the radicalism of the thirties, especially the vulgar Marxism of the Stalinists, countered the modernist sensibility with a populist view of the arts, and, in the name of democracy, promoted the idea of naturalism, with its emphasis on content, particularly in literature. What the radical ethos left undone, the popular media finished off, by enlisting the concept of democracy in the service of the profit motive.

My own development—and my literary biases—happened to coincide with the tension between the experimentalism and the intense explorations of consciousness of the modern sensibility and the wider social range of a historical perspective. So that while my views matured in the thirties, my cultural attitudes were first formed in the twenties, and though one could discuss the forces and events that shaped our time with an objectivity transcending one's own history, existentialism, which has become a chic catchword, has at least taught us one thing: that observations cannot be separated from the history of the observer.

Although I was born in Manhattan, on Madison Avenue at 106th Street, my own history actually began inauspiciously in the East Bronx, the dumping ground then for European immigrants, as it is now for blacks and Puerto Ricans.

Both my parents came from Russia, my mother from Kiev in her twenties, my father from Odessa in his teens. My father was given a new name by some friends (the old one, Litvinsky, was not considered suitable for his new life in America). He went off to Oregon to live for a time in an Owenite colony, then came back to New York, where he was advised, I gather, to become a lawyer—of all the possible occupations, the one he was least fit for. My parents separated when I was one year old, and my mother took me to Kiev, where we lived with her mother and her family, consisting of what seemed like an unusually large number of uncles and aunts and cousins, until I was four, when we came back to New York. One of my earliest recollections was running away from my father, that strange man, who met us at the dock. We lived for a few years on Wilkins Avenue in the Bronx, then moved for two years to Rockaway because someone planted the fantasy in my father's head that he would become a judge there. All that happened was that my father lost what little law practice he had had in the Bronx. The only benefit was that I learned to swim in the bay, where I was forbidden to go. Back in the Bronx, again on Wilkins Avenue, then to Crotona Park East, on the fourth floor of a walk-up where we stayed, precariously, often unable to pay the rent, until I got out of college.

The Bronx was then predominantly Jewish, as was Morris High School, which I went to, and which produced some distinguished professional people. Trotsky was said to have lived a block away on Stebbins Avenue when I was growing up and learning to play football and baseball in Crotona Park and fighting with sticks and bottles the Italian gangs who came from further east in the Bronx, looking for some soft Jewish victories. But if I was not very tough, many of my blockmates and teammates, who never went beyond high school, and some of whom, I suspected, became gangsters, were tough enough to send the Italian invaders back where they came from.

My mother and my father combined an abysmal provinciality, which took the form mostly of an inability to fit into American ways, with the cultural heritage Europeans are born into, and which they held onto unconsciously. As a result, they had an admirable but unsophisticated snobbery toward the concern for status, money, and social climbing they saw all around them. Their contempt for their more successful friends and neighbors was only heightened by my father's failure as a "provider," as the head of the family was then called. I do not know which was cause and which effect, but my father's decline as a money-maker—he was a totally unsuccessful lawyer—was paralleled by a psychological and intellectual decline and a steady removal from the world, from friends, from relatives, and even from those normal activities that took one out of the house. According to my mother, he had been more worldly when she first knew him—he was chairman of a local school board on the lower East Side and an officer of a Jewish fraternal organization. Her first shock came when he brought his belongings, a suitcase full of shoe trees, to his new home. After the marriage, my mother said, he began to shed his friends and retire from all activities. And as my father became more withdrawn and less able to "make a living," my mother became more demanding, more hysterical, and more hypochondriacal.

In fact, withdrawal became my father's mode of existence. At first he spent nights and weekends laboriously poring over books of philosophy by Plato and Aristotle, which he barely understood but converted to his own needs, and later Herbert Spencer, who became his favorite thinker (I never knew why), while my grandmother, who lived with us when she had not moved out because of a fight with my father, would walk around mumbling that he wasted his time reading books instead of making a living. So far as I could make out, what my father got from the philosophy he read was some kind of idealism and spirituality, which he counterposed to the bitter realities of the life he knew, and which supplied some meaning for an otherwise meaningless existence. He even found the same kind of solace in popular poetry—particularly in Longfellow's homilies—which he used to declaim out loud like some ritual prayer.

But serious philosophy and literature had a limited usefulness, as one might expect, for coping with the world or making it more bearable. So he soon took up with the standard varieties of therapy or palliation. In this my father was ahead of his time. Long before Yoga became fashionable, my father was a devout follower. And unlike most current use of Yoga for casual relaxation, my father practiced Yoga to free himself from the grubby materialism of the world. Yoga took the place of Plato, and night after night my father would sink into himself for deep contemplation. But no spiritual support could last very long, for it could not provide the satisfactions my father could not get from his own life. So he went from one nostrum to another. After Yoga it was dematerialization. He would sit or lie for hours in a trance that was somewhere between meditating and sleeping, literally believing that he was dematerializing his body. After that came Couéism, which was less rigorous. All he had to do was to repeat at every spare moment that every day in every way he was getting better and better. Then came Fletcherizing, which was simply a way of chewing one's food to a mush. At every meal, my father would lead us all in chewing. Like a priest conducting a prayer for his flock, my father would count fifty chews on one side, fifty on the other, with the rest of us devoutly counting and chewing our cud, though my grandmother, who had badly fitting dentures, was not much of a chewer, nor did she have much use for activities that did not have practical results. After this came mesmerizing and exerting one's will to influence people and objects. Thus we would move such early equivalents of Ouija boards as tables and chairs, and I learned to sway people by putting my hands on their backs and coercing them to move backward or forward. So carried away was I by this idea of inflicting one's will that I believed I could affect people and events. I recall willing that World War I would end on my birthday, and I was assured of my powers by the fact that I missed by only three days. Also, when I was fourteen or fifteen, I believed that if I walked along certain streets I could bump into a ravishing girl in my class, with a Mediterranean face and the up-to-date name of Bozzie, whom I did not have the courage to phone.

At the end, my father became a Christian Scientist. So unbearable must have been his life that only a religion like Christian Science that attended to worldly and physical matters as well as spiritual ones could have given him some comfort. In fact, it did give him some kind of primitive strength to endure and survive, for when he had a stroke that partially paralyzed him and affected his speech, he refused to see a doctor, claiming that he could cure himself. Of course he could not, and a doctor had to be called. But in less grave situations he could deceive himself. He believed he could make his white hair black, and he would triumphantly point to a few black hairs at the back of his head. He also thought he could cure his hernia, which he said he got carrying my mother over the threshold after their marriage, and for a time he stopped wearing his truss. But the evidence could never be examined, for he was a firm believer in inactivity, never lifting anything or doing anything that required physical effort. It was only much later that I became aware that this appearance of strength—just like its opposite, hypochondria—was actually a lack of a sense of reality.

My mother's search for another world took the form of mysterious illnesses and a feverish pursuit of quack doctors who prescribed exotic cures. She had all kinds of nervous pains and paralyses that occupied her the way other people are occupied with jobs and professions. She went to Michigan for mud cures, to one hospital after another for traction, for manipulations, for tests. She went through a succession of diets, from tomatoes to raw bacon, starting each one with fresh expectations—though it was not always clear what she was to be cured of—but with apparently no recollection of the unsuccessful treatments she had already been through. And when all these diversions had failed to ease either her pains or her discontents, then she would break down and completely space out. At the time I was probably too young, certainly too removed, to grasp the nature of what doctors later referred to as my mother's episodes. All I knew was that each time my mother took to bed the house was converted into a hospital, and my father's meditations were temporarily extended to include my mother's condition, with his own spacing out, representing itself as a cure, actually merging with hers. But, of course, nothing helped; nothing helped to pay the bills or to bring my father back to earth or lift my mother out of her depressions. Then my mother would threaten suicide. They were idle threats, but my father, my grandmother, and I acted as though they were genuine—how else, with no psychiatric advice available, could we act? Though I must say that I learned early to cut out, to turn into myself, as though what was going on was a psychodrama in which I was a suffering spectator, a victim, and about which I could do nothing.

One day, after I was married and no longer living at home, it seemed real. My father phoned to tell me in a thin, frightened voice, that my mother had said she was going to turn on the gas. "Come quick." Edna and I drove up to the Bronx as fast as we could, to find my mother and grandmother playing casino.

My father had no friends. My mother had a few, whom she visited, or who came occasionally to have tea and jelly in the dining room (there was no living room), and to whom my father awkwardly tried to relate. My father had two sisters in Canada, and a brother living in Chicago, who, I was told, owned a department store, though I suspect it was a dry goods store. I saw them several times as a child when they visited us on Wilkins Avenue, but they stopped coming soon after, and, so far as I know, my father had no further contact with them. When I asked my mother about this years later, she said she was ashamed to have them visit, for we were too poor to entertain them properly. "How could you feed your family and have guests on eight dollars a week?" she said. When I asked why she didn't take a job, she said it didn't look good for the wife of a professional man to work. It would have been better than scrounging and not being able to pay the rent, I thought, but there was no way I could know the truth or her motives.

What the relation between my mother and my father was I could never figure out. On my father's side, it seemed to be a kind of nervous, frustrated, abstract devotion. She was part of his fate. As for my mother, it must have been a combination of hate, fear, father substitution, and a variety of conventional attitudes. She once told my wife that she had no sex after I was born. She used to say my father was "a clean man," but what she meant was not clear. He bathed and took an enema once a week, as did my mother, "to clean themselves out." They seemed to think of their insides as a network of plumbing that had to be flushed regularly. My father also changed his union suit once a week. But my mother may have had something sexual in her mind when she spoke of cleanliness, for she regarded sex as a form of dirt, like germs.

After my father died a few men courted her, but she acted as though they were making obscene advances. One man wanted to take her to the movies. When I said, "Why don't you go?" she looked at me with disgust.

My mother must have had a witty unconscious, at least in her attitude to sex. She had a few severe depressions in her seventies and eighties. In desperation, I took her to a psychiatrist, the only one I could find who was willing to treat her. After the first session, I asked her how it went. "He must be crazy," she said. "Why?" I asked, assuming the pot was characterizing the kettle. "He's crazy," she repeated; "he asked me about my sex life." Maybe she had some mad instinct about the psychiatrist, for on her next breakdown, when I called him again, he said to me brutally, "Put her in a cab, and take her to Rockland State Hospital." I did not take his advice.

Who knows what they felt about me? They were certainly not ordinary parents. My mother must have cast me in the role of substitute husband. To her last days—she was ninety-six when she died— she was constantly making demands on me that only a neurotic wife could make. She would go in for paranoid scenes, accusing me of not loving her, not caring what happened to her, not respecting her. And she had a canny, almost supernatural perceptiveness, underneath her disordered ideas and feelings, that permitted her to catch anything that might justify her wild charges. If she had not been torn by her

25

fears, and had not had such a miserable life, she might have developed into a woman of remarkable gifts and intelligence. Even in her turmoiled existence, she managed to write a novel, which, I am sorry to say, I could not bring myself to read. She was also a person with some social ideals and principles, which, again, were distorted in her unbalanced psyche. One incident illustrates the sad combination of hope and suffering that twisted her life. She phoned me one morning, and in the ominous tone I had become accustomed to when she was in one of her agitated states, she said she wanted me to come right over. I assumed she had decided for the hundredth time that she had cancer, and I said I was working and would come later. No, I must come immediately, otherwise something terrible would happen. So, angry at being a prisoner of her manias, I went. She had done something awful, she said, and I must promise not to tell anyone. What was it? What crime had she committed? She had signed the Stockholm Peace Pledge. Relieved, I said is that all. I thought it was a front for other political aims, but if she wanted to support it, that was her business. "You don't understand," she said, "I signed it three times." "O.K.," I said, "so what?" "But I used a different name each time." I could not help laughing and told her it was silly but not illegal. But why did you do it, I asked. Well, she said, if it would help maintain peace, I thought signing it three times would be three times as effective.

My father had the opposite attitude toward me. I was some distant object, and his main interest in me seemed to be in my role as someone who could humor and take care of my mother, to keep the domestic situation from boiling over. He had no idea of my interests or ambitions. When I was in my twenties, just before he died, I showed him the first essay I had published. His only comment was that it was too complicated for people to read. What people he had in mind other than himself, I could not fathom.

If my father was the luftmensch and my mother the self-made victim, my grandmother was the demon of the family. She was short and squat, like a Jewish peasant, with a plebeian style and charm. But she came of a professional family, and she had the cunning, drive, and willfulness of a frustrated middle-class woman. She came to this country from Kiev when I was six, to live with her daughter, who had made a supposedly successful marriage to a lawyer. There was some vague expectation of her learning English, but the prospect was dim, so I learned Yiddish in order to speak with her. She seemed to hate my father, although it was not clear to me whether it was out of malevolence, a need to dominate the family, or because he was a failure. I had not yet learned to use Freud for facile analyses of motives; besides, it was obviously more comfortable for me not to see too clearly what was going on. My mother told me that my grandmother had kicked her husband out—why I never discovered—and tyrannized over her daughter. According to my mother, it was my grandmother who pushed her into marriage with my father, but I had learned early that my mother's account of her life was not very reliable. However, there were stories about my grandmother's powerful character that made her out to be an old female Jewish Robespierre; she was said to have organized a revolt on the ship that brought her to America to protest the bad food. And I myself had seen enough evidence of her ability to stir up trouble, to turn my mother against my father when my mother's own dissatisfaction waned, particularly when my grandmother could not have her way or was not the star of the family. When my father died, she had her victory at last: as I came in the door she greeted me with the moans she felt appropriate to indicate her grief to the neighbors, but immediately took me aside and whispered, "We finally got rid of him."

Education, in the late twenties as well as now—at least for me— meant going to school. It was the quiet twenties, before dropouts, drugs, and delinquency for the middle class. Still, high school and most of college—where else but at City College, the poor boy's steppingstone to the world—was like a routinized trance. Before then, I had floated through P.S. 40, on Prospect Avenue, at the top of my class, but sleepwalking most of the time. The only thing I remember was a teacher in my fourth grade, Mr. Tuphor, who had us sing daily: "Two four, two four, who the heck are we for, Tuphor, Tuphor." I had been an A student, brooding but with no pronounced intellectual curiosities, until my senior year at Morris High School, when I lapsed into a state where I was no longer with it. My grades zoomed down, so that I lost a state scholarship that had seemed a certainty until then. I would sit as though I were stoned in class, clenching my fists, dreaming of athletic accomplishments, physical powers, girls, aware of my body as some nervous, tense, multi-limbed and orificed object that belonged to me but had a detached existence. It was mostly in this period that I began to go in heavily for athletics—football, cross-country running, wrestling, swimming, water polo—continuing into college, partly to take my mind off my mind, partly as a compensation for being younger and smaller than my classmates. In those days good marks were rewarded by skipped grades, as a result of which I never learned certain arithmetical processes, and I always felt like a little kid among older and bigger boys, and girls with bodies bursting into womanhood, which distanced them from me.

Only in my last year at college did I come awake, and that was not my professors' doing, though I had an amateur preacher as an English instructor who pepped me up by telling me I had some slumbering gifts. The great figure on the campus was Morris Raphael Cohen—in fact the only distinguished professor in the humanities. But he was essentially a logician, and his influence was largely methodological, not substantive. He taught several generations of students to think, sharply, clearly, and, above all, skeptically. He gave weekly talks on Thursday at noon, as alternatives to going to chapel, and these talks became an intellectual institution. He would speak for about an hour, usually raising doubts about accepted ideas, his long, thin, Semitic face symbolizing for us the ironic skepticism of his thinking. Then there would be a short session of questions and arguments, after which a core of dedicated student dialectitians would follow Cohen to a smaller room where the discussion would rage for hours. I recall one of his irreverent ideas that shook me up. It was an assault on the concept of the survival of the fittest, which he claimed was just a tautology, for the definition of fitness involved survival. He illustrated this by pointing out that his own survival was based on weakness and hypochondria, since he was ailing and was forced to take extra measures to take care of himself.

Actually, my first real education came from fellow students, and it turned out to be my introduction to modernism. I had gotten to know some of the more literary and more ambitious students, one of whom was Jules Henry, a stubborn, narrow, and somewhat bizarre frustrated poet, who became an anthropologist. He and Herbert Ferber, the sculptor, who has been my oldest friend, and I formed an intellectual trio. But one day I was talking in the famous alcoves to an older, bearded student—my first contact with what I later came to know as a Village, or bohemian, character—who was spouting some strange and fascinating notions about art and criticism of a kind I had never heard before. I asked him whether the ideas he was presenting were solely his own or existed in any written form. Sure, he said, and gave me the name of a writer, T. S. Eliot, and the title of one of his works, a collection of essays called *The Sacred Wood*. I rushed to the library, and for several years afterward, including my tour of duty in graduate school, I was swimming in the exotic waters of modernism and pondering the new, complex questions of criticism.

By the time I was at graduate school at New York University as a part-time instructor, I was reading all the moderns: Baudelaire, Mallarmé, Hopkins, Joyce, Mann, Eliot, Pound, educating my eyes with Mondrian, Picasso, Klee, Kandinsky, and soaking up all the criticism and aesthetics I could lay my hands on. Everything I had learned and thought about was poured later into an essay that was printed in *The Symposium* (my first published piece), under the weighty intellectual title, "Categories for Criticism." I had submitted it to *Hound and Horn*, and after several months I got back a letter saying they could not understand the essay but thought it had something, and were taking the liberty of sending it on to *The Symposium*. After another wait, *The Symposium* wrote me, saying they were accepting the piece and would pay me fifty dollars. Though the essay contained some original speculations, I must say it was full of heavy thinking and a heavy prose, which had an air of technical expertness, to go with it. But it impressed some people. Years later, I came upon a review of American periodicals in T. S. Eliot's magazine *The Criterion* by H. S. D. (April, 1933), which singled out my piece as representing a breakthrough that was forging a new critical language. Forging or not, the prose reflected the youth of the writer.

By that time the great depression had hit us. My father, who had barely made it in better times, was now completely down. Unable to cope or to understand what was happening, his spirit, which had been held up by the therapies that served as artificial stimulants, was broken. Yet I drew no political conclusions from what surely looked like the collapse of the system. Perhaps it was because I had never expected anything from the system; perhaps it was because my own head was in the clouds, too, but in intellectual clouds, not in hypnotic therapies, like my father. Perhaps the whole esthetic of modernism

29

served as an insulation against political reality. Ironically, I discovered the left not through the cataclysmic events of the time, though they obviously provided the setting, but in the cloisters of the academy. I had done some of my graduate work in philosophy, and one of my teachers in the early thirties was Sidney Hook, who was already an anti-Communist but still a maverick Marxist. Hook had an enormous influence on bright students, one of whom was Delmore Schwartz, who told snide but admiring stories about Hook's running duels with his young adversaries. At that time, Hook had not yet channeled a good deal of his enormous talents into politics, and his sharpness, his range, his concern for his students, and his love of genuine argument were impressive and endearing. But my move to the left was also academically self-impelled. I was teaching an elementary course at N.Y.U. in which we had to read some essays to learn something called expository writing. The standard text, however, was so bad, so pointless, so banal, while pretending to be popular in the way only academic collections can be, that I decided to use the political weeklies *The Nation* and *The New Republic* as texts, for, whatever their shortcomings, they were at least not manufactured to supply the common denominator for some imaginary student need. Anyway, in the process of reading and discussing the topical coverage of these magazines as they came out religiously every Tuesday, both teacher and students became not only politicized but radicalized—though I should add immediately that by radicalized I mean becoming aware of a changing world outside literature and the arts, aware of politics and the problems of society.

In the last year of college I began to realize that literature, criticism, and the world of ideas lay beyond the history of literature that one learned at school. It was only after I was out of college that I came near the fringes of literary and intellectual life.

While teaching at N.Y.U. I became aware of Greenwich Village. It was at this time that I met Edna, who had a number of bohemian, semi-intellectual friends. Somehow the story arose that Edna had been a student of mine, and I have not bothered to correct it. The truth is that I met her at a small party in New Rochelle, where I had gone with Herbert Ferber and Jules Rosner, a handsome, athletic, serious but not intellectual, former classmate at Morris High School. It was at the home of Rose Kaplan, who later married Will Olson, a member of the English department at N.Y.U., who later was dropped in an academic purge of Communists and fellow travelers. Will Olson was almost a caricature of the English instructor at that time: tall, athletic, slow-speaking and thinking, outwardly sensitive, and contemptuous of the fast-talking New York intellectual whom he referred to as the City College type. I recall only one other person at Rose's house, Frieda, who married a Communist functionary. Frieda struck me as clever but too bouncy. Rose had the kind of scatter-shot brightness that you know will never go very deep. Edna was not very talkative but clearly more sensitive and more intelligent than the others. Frieda was chubby and Rose full-blown, but Edna was skinny and had a sharply defined, thin face, like an Indian. We talked quietly and ruminatingly, the way students do who are searching to define themselves intellectually. One of my main fears was that she was older than I was —she was certainly more mature—but I was soon relieved to find that that was not so. Edna was majoring in English and philosophy at New York University and expected to go on to graduate work and university teaching, but she was warned by her professors that as a Jew and a woman, her chances were so slight that it was scarcely worth trying. One of the ground rules at N.Y.U. was that only Anglo-Saxons could teach English literature.

The academy was also, in those prehistoric times, thoroughly male chauvinist. There was a club at University Heights (the uptown branch of N.Y.U.), the Andiron Club, to which members of the faculty were invited for special occasions. Once when I was asked, I had to sit outside in the corridor listening to the proceedings, presumably because I was a newcomer. But Margaret Schlauch, professor of linguistics at Washington Square, who later exiled herself to Poland, also sat outside, because she was a woman.

The circle in the Village on whose fringes I found myself was made up mostly of non-academics, passionately interested in the arts, but not writing or painting themselves, except in an amateurish or, at most, semiprofessional way. Most of them became Communists shortly after, and indeed they were typical of a generation, in New York at least, of high-minded, idealistic, educated aesthetes, without an intellectual profession and floundering in their beliefs and tastes. All they needed was a depression to throw them off balance completely, and a new cause, like Communism, to provide them with a philosophic approach to all problems, an absorbing political activity, and a social life that made them feel part of something bigger than themselves. I say I remained on the fringe of this group because I sensed a basic dilettantism in their thinking, although I cannot say that I was formed or mature enough to understand completely what was wrong with them or what was the right approach to serious work. They were all bright and decent people, bright enough to pick up the advanced aesthetic jargon of the time. I began to see less of them as I became more involved in writing and editing and became friendly with people who were professionally engaged in the arts, and not long after we broke completely for political reasons. Obviously, we cannot have a culture without such enlightened amateurs, but at the same time these are the people who, because they are not anchored to a medium or a tradition, move en masse with every new movement or fad.

4

THE THIRTIES

THE thirties are often thought of as a revolutionary decade. But this was not so, at least not in the United States. Very few people, even Communists, believed that a revolution would actually come to America. Nor did one simply lose faith in the system; one lost faith in the idea of the future. What the depression did was to destroy the notion of progress, of orderly progression from youth to adulthood, from school to job or profession. It brought an air of uncertainty, restlessness, and drift.

I knew I would be—or wanted to be—a writer. But one's beliefs were so shaken that the normal continuity of literary development was upset. I had been stirred by the new Marxist ideas and could no longer go on with the attitudes I had built up and the questions that had seemed important, as though nothing had changed.

It was about 1934 that I first heard of the John Reed Club, a left-wing organization of writers and painters, associated more closely with the Communist party than I realized at the time. I began to go to its meetings. Like most political associations connected with the arts, its literary and intellectual level was not the highest. Nevertheless, one gets sucked in—something that people who have never been involved in political movements cannot understand—by the spirit and ostensible goals of the organization, and by the zeitgeist. What I mean is that despite one's awareness of the stupidities of the organization or the cause, one is sucked in by some reformist zeal that places the end above the means and leads one to believe the means could be purified. One thing led to another, for politics has a logic of its own, and soon I became secretary of the John Reed Writers Club which, in the Communist hierarchies, is the top post. At the same time as I was becoming deeply involved, I was also becoming more and more opposed to the crude literary positions and corrupt politics of the Communists who dominated the John Reed Club and the literary left generally—a dual process typical of the history of Communists who either ended up as cynical organization men or broke completely and took one of the various roads open to anti-Communists.

The John Reed Club occupied two floors in an old loft building at 430 Sixth Avenue between Tenth and Eleventh streets, which has since been torn down and replaced. The writers occupied a lower floor, the artists the floor above. It was decrepit and barely furnished, but its dingy decor fit its proletarian spirit. One of the attractions of these headquarters of social justice was that across the street was a women's jail, now upgraded into a public library, where the inmates exhibited themselves and thrust their breasts through the small openings in the barred windows.

One incident at the John Reed Club summarized the literary crudity and the political indoctrination found in cultural circles close to the Communists. It was the time of the famous Scottsboro case, which involved the arrest of several young black men accused of raping two white girls. At a meeting of the club a letter from one of the blacks was read, which sounded like this: "I din't jazz no girls. I din't jazz nobody. Nobody jazzed no girls," etc., for two or three pages. When the reading was over, one John Reed Club member jumped up and announced, "This is literature."

Disillusioned, what did I do? I dreamt of a magazine to express my views and to mobilize a group of writers looking for a similar direction. It was about this time that I met Philip Rahv, who had drifted in from the West Coast. He was more politicized than I was, having come directly to the left without going through a modernist phase as

34

I had. My first non-Marxist publication was in *The Symposium,* while he had started out writing in *The New Masses.* He was unsophisticated, but very intelligent and endowed with a shrewd political sense. I knew little more about him, and I learned little more about his past in all the years we worked together, for he was very secretive and self-protective, as though he were in a permanent underground.

I also started to write for *The New Masses* and other left publications, but I was increasingly appalled by the sectarian orthodoxy that prevailed in circles connected with the Communists. Still, I was not entirely aware that the vulgarities of the politics as well as the approach to the arts was not an intellectual aberration but was grounded in the monolithic structure and thinking of the Communists. Rahv and I still had the illusion that a new literary publication could be an organ for those radical writers who had no use for the party-line aesthetics of *The New Masses,* and that it could be open to talent, regardless of politics. We had no experience in putting out a magazine, no sense of what it involved, no notion of how to raise the necessary money. We were cocky kids, driven by a grandiose idea of launching a new literary movement, combining older with younger talents, and the best of the new radicalism with the innovative energy of modernism. But we could not envision anything beyond an organ of the John Reed Club, which at least provided the base for such a publication. The only trouble was that there was no money, not at the John Reed Club, nor indeed anywhere else.

Only a miracle could produce a magazine. But only miracles have sustained *Partisan Review* throughout its life. Miracles, however, are often man-made, and the first miracle arrived in the form of an urbane Englishman, John Strachey, just turned left, who was coming to New York and who agreed to give a talk—on literature and dialectical materialism—for the benefit of the John Reed Club. We hired a hall, sold tickets, publicized the event—all quite amateurishly, for entrepreneurial professionalism had not yet invaded the realms of serious or radical culture. Nevertheless, the lecture turned out to be a smash hit; people were begging for tickets and trying to crash the gate. It was a Sunday night, and Rahv and I and our wives left the hall with our pockets stuffed with bills, scared of losing them or of being robbed before we could get to the bank the next morning.

We had raised the unbelievable sum of eight hundred dollars, enough to run a little magazine for a year in a collapsed economy. We had no rent, no salaries, nobody to phone, and printing costs made the depression seem like a literary utopia. There was no financial support from the John Reed Club, or from any other source, but we were able to supplement the original windfall through lectures and other affairs, run under the auspices of the club. In fact, we were so enterprising that the John Reed Club became known for having the best dance floor in the city. But we knew we had finally made it when we were arrested for "charging admission at a party" and "selling drinks without a license."

It happened one Saturday evening at a party for the German composer, Hans Eisler, who had been prominent in Communist activities and had just arrived in the United States. The affair had been going full swing when a man approached me as I was standing next to the table where the punch was being sold and asked me the price of a drink. (I realized later he was waiting to trap me near the table.) I told him it was twenty-five cents, and he asked whether I would pour one for him. I did and dropped the quarter he had ostentatiously given me in a box full of money on the table. He then asked me to step outside with him, informed me he was a cop, and said that I had violated the ABC law—selling liquor without a license—a serious offense. Apparently another cop had taken Rahv outside, too, and told him he was running an affair without a license. They took us to a nearby police station, where they said we could explain things to the captain and then be free to leave. We quickly received our first lesson in police methods and promises. As soon as we got there they frisked us and locked us in a cell for the night—a double room with twin sleeping benches—at the same time assuring us we could be released on bail in the morning while awaiting trial. I was permitted to call my wife, but it was impossible to raise the bail money on Sunday. However, with remarkable resourcefulness she managed to find a friend who put up a Soviet bond as bail.

I thought I would make the best of it by trying, in the meantime, to get some sleep. But even if I could have slept on one of the hard benches in the cell, I would have been kept up all night by Rahv's stalking back and forth as though he were in a cage, cursing one by one, with all the petulant and fulsome rhetoric he could sputter out, all those members of the John Reed Club who were not in jail and who were probably having a good time at the party.

At the trial several months later we were defended by a lawyer for the International Labor Defense League, a Communist-dominated organization, which meant his primary duty was to carry the class struggle into the courtroom. Only secondarily, and as a fringe benefit, as it were, was he concerned with what happened to Rahv and myself.

The trial was a farce. Since I could be made to look more respectable than Rahv, I became the featured defendant. Much was made of the fact that I was a college instructor, and before long the judge began to address me as Professor Phillips. Our attorney kept piling copies of things that I had written on the judge's desk and pushing them under his nose, while the judge kept pushing them away, obviously irritated at this crude attempt to build up my "character" in a way that clearly had nothing to do with the charges. And though we were finally found not guilty, the judge told us later he had almost sentenced us out of sheer desperation and annoyance at the noisy antics of our lawyer. In the end, apparently what saved us was that the ensnaring and careless tactics of the cops in arresting us ultimately outweighed the provocative and ideological ineptness of our defense.

Partisan Review began as a monthly and as the organ of the John Reed Club. But it was understood from the beginning that Rahv and I were the main force behind the magazine and its chief editors. Since the magazine was sponsored by the John Reed Club, however, it had to have the kind of editorial representation all organizations— especially political ones—demand. Hence the masthead of the first issue looked like a showcase of participatory democracy.

This first phase of the magazine, which should really be called the "old *Partisan Review*," was short-lived. It lasted for a bit over two years, through nine issues. At the same time the editorial board kept shrinking, until at the end there were only three editors, Rahv, I, and Alan Calmer, a sensible, intelligent, self-effacing functionary of the John Reed Club, who slept on a cot at the club and seemed to have no home and no visible private life. The last two issues, in fact, were put out independently, and did not mention the John Reed Club on the masthead. (There was a short period when *Partisan Review* merged with *Anvil*, Jack Conroy's magazine in the Midwest. But the marriage did not last as the differences between us were too great—Conroy was too populist and anti-intellectual—and *PR* decided to go it alone again.) All this time Rahv and I were becoming increasingly fed up with the literary politics of the Communists, with their manipulation of theories, slogans, and writers, and we were coming to the conclusion that an independent literary movement could not exist within the orbit of the official Communist party. Hence we suspended publication until we could regroup and find new sources of support.

In the meantime, we were told, the Communists were trying to appropriate *Partisan Review*. We could not verify it, but we were informed by several people that Alexander Trachtenberg, the party's cultural commissar, had tried to get Alan Calmer to put out an issue of the magazine quickly so that we would lose our claims to it. We were told that Alan Calmer refused to do it, which corroborated my sense of Calmer as a principled man. The last I heard of Calmer, he apparently had broken with the Communists and was writing a book on American literature.

Alexander Trachtenberg was the head of International Publishers, the Communist publishing house, but he was rumored to have other, more mysterious duties. Short and portly, he looked like a European businessman and patriarch, except for the enormous mustache that flowed up his cheeks, and gave him the face of a Turkish conspirator. He also had the reflexes of a functionary.

He always spoke cryptically and cautiously and was a master of political double-talk, which meant he could always land on the right side of any question. Only occasionally, when he apparently felt safe, was he able to relax, and then, late in the afternoon in his office alone with Rahv and me, he would tell stories of his early revolutionary days, referring to Stalin as the Old Man. A few times he even let go and talked admiringly about Trotsky as a brilliant and inspiring figure.

It is hard to reconstruct the atmosphere of literary and political life in the thirties, at least in those circles affected by the general radicalization of the time and by the influence of the Communist party. For this atmosphere was not simply a matter of extremes, as sometimes pictured by biased observers: it was neither a fool's paradise of Utopian beliefs and hopes nor a wasteland of disillusionment and cynicism. To simplify this atmosphere is to fail to explain how so many people were both attracted to and tortured by the false promises of the Communists, how so many careers, particularly abroad, were made and destroyed, and how so many lives were broken by doubts and fears and by the processes of conversion and deconversion. It was a complex of contradictions, which I tried to summarize in a piece I wrote for *Commentary* in the sixties.

The going version of the story [of what happened in the thirties] is that the radical spirit ruled the 30's while the 40's and 50's were dedicated to conservatism, philistinism, and chauvinism, and that now the pendulum is swinging once more to the Left. This picture is really too simple, and comes out of the sentimental association of radicalism with purity. It ignores the unsavory side of the radical movement, brought mostly by the Communists, just as it leaves out the legitimate distaste for party-line thinking that originally led many people to break with the ideas and organizations linked to the Communists.

Still, despite all the illusions and duplicities of the thirties, it was a time when human aims seemed more attractive than national goals and when articulate people talked more about the hope for an ideal society than the benefits of the existing one. It was a time when responsibility meant responsibility to ideas and convictions, justice seemed more important than expediency, the greater good meant more than the lesser evil, dreams seemed more cogent than reality.

Mostly the thirties was a period of contradictions. It was a time of sense and nonsense, idealism and cynicism, morality and immorality, disinterest and power drive, and it was a time when it was possible to believe simultaneously in democracy and dictatorship, in an anti-human abstraction called History and in a moral idea of man usually regarded as unhistorical. It seemed possible to believe in everything and its opposite; and a theory of dialectics along with a policy of practicality and activism were used to rationalize the untenable and to justify the reprehensible.

But we must decide whether the radicalism of the thirties was an aberration or a movement in the main line of history, or both, and whether the anti-radical mood that followed was a reaction against being taken in or a reconciliation with things as they are. What we think of these things has as much to do with the future as with the past. . . .

This is an abstract and backward look, but it does correspond to the situation that I lived through. For the short period I was connected with the John Reed Club, it seems to me I was constantly debating with myself, and with those who had abdicated before what they thought was history but was only the bureaucratized ideology of the Communist party, whether the evils of the party outweighed its contributions to the socialist cause. It is still true and still one of the major dilemmas of radicalism that there are almost no democratic socialist movements anywhere strong enough to challenge the virtual monopoly of the Communists on the left. (Recently, the Socialists in Spain and France have become much stronger, though it remains to be seen whether they can break the hold of the Communists on radical thinking.) But it was even truer—and more disheartening—in the thirties that if one split with the Communists, one had to retire from effective, radical organized politics. Hence their stranglehold on those people who could not make more than one decisive political choice in their lives.

There were, of course, the Socialists, the Trotskyites, the Lovestoneites, and various other political sects. But it seemed to me that aside from exposing the Communists, which was useful, they spent all their time bickering and attacking each other, and they never gave any indication that they were capable of—or even interested in—coping with larger national issues and becoming a mass party. Behind the Trotskyites there was the grand figure of Trotsky, but the local leaders were absorbed in the minutiae of Communist party history, like rabbinical scholars studying the Old Testament. I recall, for example, telling Max Schachtman, one of the two top officials of the Trotskyites, that they should be involved more in such things as how to get more milk for poor babies than in the obsessive investigation of the factional quarrels of the various Communist groups. As for the Socialists, we had a kind of abstract respect for them, but none of us ever took them seriously as a political force. A common question of disillusioned Communists was, "But if we break, where do we go?"

The Thirties

The relation of the party with its intellectual fellow-travelers is worth noting, particularly since there seems to be some parallel to the relation of the Russian intelligentsia with the Soviet government. Despite most accepted notions, there was no intellectual reign of terror, at least not within the fold, so to speak, and not at the upper levels, though the treatment of outside opposition was ruthless. On the contrary, there was a kind of cynical acceptance of disaffection and even criticism of the party by writers, so long as it was not made public or generalized into a fundamental condemnation of the Soviet regime and its satellite parties. And such, I understand, is the position of intellectuals in the Soviet Union, who apparently are permitted to speak freely to each other about the party and the government, and are persecuted for the most part only when they insist on airing their views outside elite circles. But, though such latitude kept cynical writers in bounds, it was only another sign of corruption and personal manipulation to those of us who were young enough to be mobile and who were genuinely interested in the political dimensions of literature and not in its controls. Still, I should emphasize again that breaking was not easy for anyone, and for some it was traumatic—which is one of the reasons why so many writers moved so far to the right after disengaging from the Communist left.

The Communists were experts at maintaining a fraternal atmosphere that distinguished sharply between insider and outsider.

One couldn't just leave; one had to be expelled. And expulsion from the tribe brought into motion a machinery calculated to make the expelled one a complete pariah. Party members were forbidden to talk to the ex-Communist, and a campaign of vilification was unleashed whose intensity varied according to the importance of the expelled person. At the very least, however, anyone who left the Communists was accused of being an informer, a lackey of capitalism and imperialism, an enemy of the working class, and, worst of all, a Trotskyite. For the Communists, a Trotskyite had nothing to do with the beliefs of Trotsky or his followers; it was a catch-all term for anybody opposed to the Communists from the left. The fact is that the Communists were more opposed to and more afraid of liberal and Marxist critics than they were of conservatives—and perhaps rightly so, for a challenge from the left tended to cut the ground from under

41

their radical claims and pretensions while one from the right made them feel politically more virtuous. Thus they used to refer to John Chamberlain when he was most sympathetic to them as an enemy, on the ground that those who were closest to them were the main enemy. Of course, to maintain a rank-and-file membership at this level of naivete and faith was no small accomplishment, particularly when you consider that most party members started out with an enormous reserve of honesty and idealism.

I had never joined the Communist party, but for some reason—perhaps not entirely favorable to me—I had access to Communist circles and occasionally was permitted to attend meetings in the inner sanctum. Once, for example, I was asked to come to the ninth floor, the top floor of the building that housed the Communist party, to discuss my too open criticism of the party. The "ninth floor" was a term that had a symbolic significance somewhat like Kafka's castle, for that was where all the offices of the leading functionaries were. My interrogator, David Ramsey, the editor of the theoretical organ of the party, told me I could say anything I wanted to people on the inside like himself, but that he had heard I had been talking freely to ordinary members and supporters of the party who were too naive to be subjected to sophisticated arguments.

I recall a big hush-hush meeting called to discuss the "change of line" on the cultural front, to keep step with the new popular front political policy. The importance of the meeting was indicated by the presence of a representative of the Communist International, a tall, bearded, phlegmatic man, with a strong accent. A Communist writer and editor spoke for the new line, his hand significantly patting his pocket, which, according to another Communist writer, Joseph Freeman, a shrewd and vain conformist in public and nonconformist in private, contained nothing but a letter from Moscow. The trouble with understanding and accepting the new line was that it meant abandoning all the old sectarian notions about proletarian literature and art being a weapon in the class struggle, and trying to win back all the writers who had been attacked previously for not being left enough—and nobody knew how far to go in the new direction.

Alexander Trachtenberg kept summarizing the arguments for partial against complete change—nobody dared defend the old line—and unable to make up his mind shuttled back and forth with an "on the one hand" and an "on the other hand," which was not an uncommon tactic in such situations, and was often referred to as thinking dialectically. Finally, another writer, Joshua Kunitz, a clever expert on Soviet literature, could not stand the indecision and blurted out, "We know, Trachtie, on the one hand and on the other hand, what we want to know is which hand."

At another such meeting to keep writers in tow, the same expert talked on the effect of the change of line on Soviet writers to reassure confused American Communists that the adjustments were simple and smooth in the Soviet Union. Everyone, except Rahv and me, accepted without question the official explanations, with that mixture of cynicism and belief in the wisdom of the party that characterized most of the bureaucrats I had met. When Rahv and I plied the speaker with skeptical questions we were denounced as disrupters and under the influence of Trotskyism. After the meeting was over, we went out for drinks with the speaker of the evening and continued to talk about the situation in Moscow, this time informally, without the orthodoxies of a formal session, and by three in the morning we were told that, of course, we were right. It was assumed that we could talk this way among ourselves but not publicly or at official meetings, or with the "rank and file," the sacred constituency of the party that was kept in a state of permanent ignorance and enthusiasm.

When we broke we were called every dirty name in the Communist political lexicon, Rahv even more than I, because he had had more to do with the Communist party than I did. *The Daily Worker* called us Trotskyites, counterrevolutionaries, literary snakes, agents of imperialism. Party hacks like Mike Gold joined in the vulgar diatribes that reflected the general level of Communist polemics. People we had known for years stopped talking to us; when we met them on the street they looked the other way.

A word should be said about our Trotskyism, a charge that was picked up by a number of fellow-travelers and liberals who were in the habit of having the party do their thinking for them at that time. I had, of course, been reading Trotsky and other critics of Stalinism as well as the opposition press, particularly the Trotskyists and Lovestoneite publications. This was something few party members and fellow-travelers did. I was shocked to discover that not even the functionaries read Trotsky or someone as harmless as Norman

Thomas—obviously to keep their minds pure and free of any doubts or questions. But while the opposition press alerted one to the lies of the Communists, it offered little more than other forms of sectarianism. Trotsky, however, was a transcendent figure, one who had to have an enormous influence on anybody on the left who still had any pretensions to thinking.

For me, as I am sure for others, Trotsky, aside, of course, from his enormous talents as a writer, a historian, and a polemicist, opened the prospect of a condemnation of the Soviet system without abandoning Marxism. It was Trotsky who made one finally realize why the Communists were the main obstacle to the realization of democratic socialism.

But I was never a Trotskyite, nor were most of the people who later wrote for or were associated with *Partisan Review*. For it was clear from the beginning that the Trotskyites were the guardians of their own orthodoxies and that in many respects they were like the Stalinists but without power. Dwight Macdonald and James Burnham, two writers on the board of *PR*, later became Trotskyites, but only briefly, and both had many disagreements with them. I suspect the reason Macdonald and Burnham became Trotskyites was that it was a phase they had to go through as neither had been a Stalinist.

As for the relation with Trotsky, he wrote several things for the magazine, but we had a running quarrel with him, mainly on the question of the relation of writers and periodicals to a revolutionary party. We kept asserting our belief in total independence while Trotsky wrote a rather bitter polemic against us in which he seemed to be nurturing the illusion that writers and intellectuals splitting off from the Stalinists should naturally become his disciples and followers. When they kept their distance, Trotsky ascribed this to their inability to remain revolutionaries after having been burned by Stalinism.

One of the most insidious things about being a Communist, perhaps about belonging to any Marxist party, has been the simultaneous inflation of one's intellectual pretensions and the shrinking of one's capacities. Marxism, used properly as a source of historical insight, can be a useful system of knowledge. But because Marxism lays claim to being a global philosophy, Marxists frequently have acted as experts in fields in which they were ignorant, producing tracts on

44

everything from aesthetics to science on the level of adult education. And there was a period for me, too, when Marxism took the place of a specific discipline. Thus I once wrote for a Communist theoretical journal a very knowing piece, full of Marxist generalities, on the principles of indeterminacy and other related philosophical and scientific questions, an area in which I had had some, but not sufficient, training. A recent example of this kind of thinking was Althusser, the French party philosopher, who brandished old Marxist terms and categories—like theory and practice, the dialectic, science versus humanism, historical materialism—as though they were fresh ideas. The reason Althusser cannot be taken seriously as a philosopher is that he was operating within prescribed limits and assumptions set by the Communist party, even though he made at least a partial break in 1978. In fact, the party has usually nurtured theorists who were part of the ruling apparatus, to insure reliable thinking.

Against this kind of homemade thinking raised to the point of official theory, Sidney Hook, especially in his younger days, was an effective antidote. Indeed, many of us learned a good deal from Hook. I remember in his graduate class one day—as in his earlier writing—a sharp and concrete discussion of the meaninglessness of dialectics as applied to science. When he read my amateurish piece on indeterminancy he said to me, with the concern and authority of a good teacher, that I had a very good mind but that I would ruin it if I continued to mistake Marxist clichés for thinking. I replied that he might be right but that I would have to find out for myself—which I did shortly afterward.

5

NEW PARTISAN REVIEW

IT was about this time that I met Fred Dupee, who was then the literary editor of *The New Masses*. I told him how we felt about the Communists and that we wanted to publish a magazine that was free to criticize them, but that we had no money. Dupee was not an ideologue, nor very responsive to abstract political arguments, but he was a person of great sensibility and taste: hence, he was aware of the political atmosphere around the *New Masses* and he had no difficulty in grasping its ultimately corrupting effect on all literary activity. Besides, he had just come from more romantic radical work on the waterfront and he was not really at home in the rigid, bureaucratic setup of *The New Masses*. He said he had a friend whom he wanted us to meet, Dwight Macdonald, a classmate at Yale, now a writer for *Fortune*, who was moving left rapidly, in the direction of the Communist party. We arranged to get together at my house one Sunday—which became known as "Bloody Sunday." (I lived then on East Twelfth Street between Fifth Avenue and University Place, uncomfortably near the Communist headquarters and across the street from a firehouse, which woke us every night.) As I recall, we were at it all day long; and I still have in my mind a picture of Rahv and myself backing Macdonald up against a wall, knocking down his arguments, firing unanswerable questions without giving him time to answer, and constantly outshouting him. Now if anyone has ever argued with Dwight Macdonald, he knows that it was not easy to outtalk him, even on theoretical questions, which was not where his main talents lay. All I can say is that we were fired up sufficiently with the rightness of our position to keep banging away, and Dwight was just uncertain enough—and new to the intricacies of left politics—to listen, with the result that at the end of the day we were all agreed we should revive *Partisan Review* as an independent literary journal. As for money, Dwight and Fred had a friend, George Morris, a gifted abstract painter, also a classmate at Yale, who, they thought, might be interested and could help finance it. The sum we needed for a year, according to our modest calculations, was fifteen hundred dollars.

Mary McCarthy, another friend of Dupee and Macdonald, also joined our group, and the first issue of the new *Partisan Review* came out in December 1937. The new board was, as I look back, remarkably aggressive and varied, so aggressive and varied that one had to wonder how we were able to work together for so long. Besides myself, the board consisted of Fred Dupee, a man, as I have indicated, of great taste and literary sensibility, with a wry wit and an almost British gift for undercutting people's pretensions; Dwight Macdonald, possessed of an enormous bustling energy, stubborn, opinionated, argumentative, full of convictions in all areas, an excellent journalist and polemicist; Mary McCarthy, remarkably intelligent and astute, a first-rate prose talent, utterly committed to what she thought was right and honest regardless of the consequences, but with a weakness for Utopian politics; George L. K. Morris, shy and modest, but firm in his ideas about modern art; Rahv, intellectually alert and arrogant, ruthless, ready to steamroller any opposition with an endless stream of heavy but wild and original rhetoric. Rahv and I, partly because of our political experience, partly by temperament, supplied the theoretical base of the magazine and tended to restrain the more adventurous instincts of some of the others. Perhaps we tended too much toward sobriety, but at a time when we were in an almost constant state of siege, it seemed necessary to be aware of the literary and political consequences of our acts. For, as expected, the Communists and the writers and editors under their influence kept up a steady attack and used every means to discredit and undermine us.

Much has been made of the persecution of liberals and radicals, particularly in the McCarthy era. And it was, indeed, a shameful episode in the treatment of dissent in this country. Liberals and anti-Communist radicals were lumped haphazardly with Communists in a campaign that merged McCarthy's personal ambitions with various reactionary forces. However, the Communists did not play an exemplary role, for they added to the general confusion by denying for the most part that they were in fact Communists, thus dissolving the principle of intellectual freedom in the right to conceal one's opinions. The Communists also assisted McCarthy in confusing political beliefs with espionage—a confusion that is particularly destructive because it fails to distinguish between dissent and a new form of nationalism, service to a foreign state.

McCarthyism has not suffered from lack of publicity, but the other side of the equation, the vilification and persecution of anti-Communist liberals and radicals by the Communists has been played down. It may be difficult to realize now how much influence the Communists had in literary and intellectual circles in the thirties. The issue is often muddled by talking about the political size and power of the party on the national scene, which was tiny. But the penetration of the party, and even more important, the appeal of the cause it claimed to represent, was inordinately large in publishing houses, in magazines like *The Nation* and the *New Republic*, a few liberal newspapers like *PM*, the *Post*, and a few eastern colleges. And this was the world in which we lived. Hence, in starting the new *Partisan Review*, we had to buck not only the traditional right but also the monopoly on the left that the Communists had fashioned. Naturally, since the Communists and fellow-travelers did not have state power, their hostility mostly took the form of unprincipled attacks and subtle, underground sabotage and slander.

Rahv and I, having known at first hand how the Communists treat not only those who have broken with them but also the left opposition generally, were not eager to take on the Communists in their own territory. But Mary McCarthy and Dwight Macdonald, being perhaps bolder, more interested in excitement, more quixotic, insisted that we attend a meeting of the League of American Writers and challenge both their literary line and their political control. The League of American Writers, like all Communist fronts, was run by a small Communist faction, but it had just enough innocents and seemingly unaffiliated writers to serve as window dressing and to permit the organization to claim it was a broad association of liberal and left writers. All the sensible arguments Rahv and I could muster about how futile and disagreeable it would be to try to present a minority view at the meeting could not dissuade McCarthy and Macdonald and had the effect only of making us look like cowards and political pussyfooters. A position based on reason and caution is always bound to look like weakness, and this was not the only round I lost against the forces of morality and forthrightness. Anyway, Eleanor Clark, another brave but politically inexperienced writer, joined our little band of oppositionists, and we five crusaders went to the meeting in New York to challenge several hundred faithful followers of the party line, many not knowing what the political or the literary conflict was all about, but knowing where their allegiance lay and knowing that anyone who questioned the policies of the League of American Writers was a "Trotskyite disrupter." (Years later, when everyone should have known better, Kenneth Burke, at a taped round-table discussion of the thirties under the auspices of the *American Scholar,* spoke of Mary McCarthy as a disruptive publicity seeker. And more recently Garry Wills, in an introduction to Lillian Hellman's *Scoundrel Time,* referred sarcastically to McCarthy's and Macdonald's opposition to another Communist-sponsored Waldorf Conference as a fake exercise in the cause of intellectual freedom. (Obviously, the Waldorf Conference was a triumph of liberty.)

Mary and Eleanor and Dwight got up to speak against the narrow interpretations of literature and politics and the factional control of the organization. Though immeasurably more talented and intelligent, they were no match for the infighting skills of their opponents who were old hands at this kind of polemic. Loyalists like Joseph Freeman, Joshua Kunitz, and Granville Hicks, all veteran public debaters, managed to confuse the issues and at the same time appeal to the prejudices of the hand-picked audience. Rahv and I, who were more familiar with the jargon and pseudo-arguments of the Communists, tried at the end to bail out our fellow dissidents, but our heart was not in it and we could not make much headway against a stacked meeting.

But we had no such constraints in the magazine itself, whose role we saw as being open, forthright, and aggressive. Stalinist lies and shenanigans were exposed constantly, as were double-talking liberals, nor were Trotsky and the Trotskyites spared any criticism. At the same time, our opposition to conservatives was always clear. It was evident, for example, that we did not accept the unhistorical approach of the New Critics, even though we published them and acknowledged their talents and their contribution to critical method. False literary reputations were cut down, particularly by such uncompromising critics as McCarthy, Macdonald, Lionel Abel, and, later, Randall Jarrell. On the whole, the magazine was raucous, impious, and intransigent.

Some of the contents of the first issue of the new *Partisan Review* are worth noting because in its variety as well as in its direction it set the tone for the future of the magazine. The issue included Delmore Schwartz's famous story, "In Dreams Begin Responsibilities," poems by Wallace Stevens and James Agee, essays by Edmund Wilson and Lionel Abel, reviews by Sidney Hook, Lionel Trilling, Arthur Mizener, and William Troy, and a long editorial stating the aims of the magazine.

This statement was not free of the ponderous rhetoric of the period. But it did, I believe, introduce for the first time the combination of social concern and literary standards that guided a new creative and critical movement. And it would be interesting to quote from it at length, if only to see how well its formulations have stood up:

> As our readers know, the tradition of aestheticism has given way to a literature which, for its origin and final justification, looks beyond itself and deep into the historic process. But the forms of literary editorship, at once exacting and adventurous, which characterized the magazines of the aesthetic revolt, were of definite cultural value; and these forms *Partisan Review* will wish to adapt to the literature of the new period. . . .
>
> But *Partisan Review* aspires to represent a new and dissident generation in American letters; it will not be dislodged from its inde-

pendent position by any political campaign against it. And without ignoring the importance of the official movement, as a sign of the times, we shall know how to estimate its authority in literature. But we shall also distinguish, wherever possible, between the tendencies of this faction itself and the work of writers associated with it. For our editorial accent falls chiefly on culture and its broader social determinants. Conformity to a given social ideology or to a prescribed attitude or technique will not be asked of our writers. On the contrary, our pages will be open to any tendency which is relevant to literature in our time. Marxism in culture, we think, is first of all an instrument of analysis and evaluation; and if, in the last instance, it prevails over other disciplines, it does so through the medium of democratic controversy. Such is the medium that *Partisan Review* will want to provide in its pages.

The range and the direction of the magazine were indicated by the variety of the subjects and contributors in the early issues. The list is more than a roster of well-known figures and younger writers who have since become well known. It indicates a bringing together of diverse talents, but more than that, a bringing together of writers, committed to modernism and literary innovation, and radical social and political thinkers, most of whom were either non-Communist or anti-Communist. This was the first time in this country that such an idea of intellectual community had been forged, and perhaps the last time, for since then there has been a wholesale dispersal of writing and thinking. There have been many reasons for this intellectual decentralization, but the principal ones seem to me to come from the brain drain by the mass media, from the drifting of writers across the country, mostly to universities that have tended to set up at least the appearance of intellectual foci, from the large and varied geography of the country, and from the confusion of chic with advanced art and thought. And it is hard to say whether it is a cause or consequence, but the breakup of this community has been accompanied by a breakdown of old beliefs and assumptions in both politics and the arts and an enormous diversification of ideas, styles, and goals. Those who are pleased with this state of affairs refer to it benignly as pluralism; those who take a negative view think of it as a collapse of values and standards. In any case, both responses might be exaggerated, for as we know, the past always looks more cohesive in retrospect.

But for those who are especially troubled by the lack of a center today, it might throw some light on the differences between the thirties and the present situation to consider why it was possible in the infancy of *Partisan Review* to assemble in one magazine so many of the gifted and adventurous minds of the time. For one thing, it cannot be emphasized too strongly that the commercial publications, particularly those in the middle range of culture, had not yet thought of coopting writers by offering fees—and the illusion of an audience—of a size only a purist or a madman could refuse. In addition, the time was ripe for intellectual fusion. Modernist and experimental writers were looking for a social base; and writers who had acquired historical consciousness were both sufficiently disillusioned with the Communists and sufficiently loyal to their radical experience to feel a kinship with each other. It was a time when literature and politics were able to coexist, without either one trying to absorb or destroy the other.

6

WRITERS ON
THE LEFT

INTELLECTUAL communities are held together generally by their disagreements as well as their agreements—that is, by the feeling that these disagreements are important enough to pursue, and that, however difficult they may be to define, they stem from common aims and premises. However, the New York intellectual community that was created in the thirties was particularly quarrelsome and torn by personal and political differences—by vanity, temperament, and conviction. With some notable exceptions, it was also not known for its loyalties. Compared, for example, with the New Critics and the writers associated with them, who were always praising each other and who, when they disagreed, did so with the utmost gentleness and gentility, the New York writers often acted as though they were in a primitive struggle for survival. One can only speculate about the forces that added a jungle morality to a sense of community. But two factors stand out. For one thing, the core of this community was political; not only was its thinking political, but it grew out of the idealistic impulses, the factional wars, and the disillusionments of the radical movement. And political groups are notoriously sustained by infighting and ruthless competition. In addition, much of this community was made up of newcomers, of second-generation Americans who had not yet acquired the gentilities that come with the security of a long tradition and were overconcerned with the idea of making it. When one thinks of the divisions and the quarrels, one is tempted to call the idea of a community a myth; still, one would have to say it was a myth that worked, and one that has been endowed with a historic reality by critics and historians of the thirties and forties.

It goes without saying that aging improves the past. Still it does seem to be a fact that an extraordinary number of gifted writers emerged in the late thirties and early forties. Moreover, their talent was of a cohesive and generalizing nature, unlike most contemporary talent, which appears to have no center, with fiction dispersing in many directions and literary and social criticism gravitating toward professional specialization or journalistic performances for the more popular media. Having left behind their political commitments, these writers had not yet discovered the appeals of money or the new power groups. Fiction and poetry had not yet been conceived of as vehicles for feminists, or blacks, or gay liberationists, or the counter-culture. In fact, the writing of the post-Stalinist period in this country was largely a reaction against the politicization of literature promoted by the sectarian Marxism of the Communists. In any case, it is a common complaint of people who recall the larger perspectives and the abundance of theoretical writing of the earlier period that there is a paucity of people today who can write about the central literary and social issues in a way that transcends academic study and factional or parochial interests. It would seem that as our problems have become bigger and more complex our approach to them has become narrower and more superficial.

On the other hand, most of the writers I knew and worked with were, after breaking with the Communists, much abler, more tough-minded, less fuzzy than those who stuck with the Communists at the time. The only fellow-traveling poets I recall whose minds were not predictable were Sol Funaroff, an unorthodox personality who died young, and Kenneth Fearing, a cynical figure, who managed to act as though there were no political constraints on him even while supporting the Communists. Of the fiction writers, Josephine Herbst seemed to have the greatest capacity for independence, but I suspect that her passionate convictions tended to overwhelm her intellectual and political judgment. Most of the others were either veteran party-liners or soft-headed fellow-travelers. Joseph Freeman, who edited *The New Masses*, and Joshua Kunitz, who wrote about Russian literature, were, perhaps, the saddest victims of their politics, for both were shrewd and forced by their intelligence into a cynical acceptance of their roles. Privately they knew everything; publicly they knew nothing. Then there were the writers who had converted themselves into hacks. One wondered whether they really believed in the crude and literal-minded orthodoxies they professed or whether they had simply excluded from their minds the kind of thought that leads to questioning. Perhaps there were personal fears of all sorts; perhaps they did not have the courage to start a new career; perhaps they could not bear to leave their wives or husbands or friends, even if they themselves had doubts. Some were just not smart enough to look into their own lives. There were, for example, Isidor Schneider, a writer of some talent—who knows how much—who got caught in the web, and Michael Gold, a writer of very limited intellectual capacity, though his early novel, *Jews Without Money,* had a certain primitive force. He must have enjoyed the spotlight he was given by the party and probably began to believe in the praise fed him by the party regulars.

On the whole, I think the Communist intellectuals ran the gamut from the natural or induced innocence of the rank-and-file mentality to the professional cynicism of those who knew what they were doing. A primitive example of an intellectual who succeeded in lowering his consciousness was Edwin Berry Burgum, a critic and teacher at N.Y.U. I met him when I began teaching and doing graduate work there, and I must confess I was largely responsible for his shift to the left, which was not difficult, for he offered little resistance to my efforts. He was not made for outstanding literary criticism, but he seemed worldly and sophisticated enough not to have fallen for the crudities of the then current Marxist fashions. Yet he quickly went beyond what was expected of a radicalized intellectual, swallowing all the official doctrines, and he was soon writing essays demonstrating that Proust was a bourgeois decadent and Kafka a nascent fascist. He also believed, apparently with his whole being, in the idea of proletarian literature, which only the most orthodox or simple-minded party critics took seriously.

The almost masochistic nature of Burgum's thinking came out spontaneously one day in an argument about proletarian literature. (It was before I had broken and he had stopped talking to me.) When I asked Burgum why he believed in something without even listening to the theoretical implications or the facts, he replied that he had faith in the party, and, like someone looking to be overpowered by a masculine force, he added that he wanted to be led by a longshoreman. Aside from his personal fantasies, he was obviously parroting the myth that the party was the instrument of the working class. I have often wondered whether, in addition to the political meaning, the mystique of the working class did not contain, as it did for D. H. Lawrence, an element of abnegation before the image of potency of the strong worker.

Figures like Granville Hicks, who was part of the inner circle, and Malcolm Cowley and Kenneth Burke, who were fellow-travelers, seemed more reasonable in their literary politics, and all broke eventually, but in one way or another they danced to the Communist tunes. Hicks at least had a literary education, though his early book, *The Great Tradition,* was a reductive exercise in Marxist criticism. The section on Henry James, for example, which makes him out to be a spokesman for the bourgeoisie, sounds like a parody of the historical method. Still, Hicks was an intelligent and honorable man, and the reason, I think, for his having succumbed to the vulgarities of the movement is to be found in his moral earnestness and rigidities and in the fervor of his commitments. Malcolm Cowley was something else. A graduate of the bohemianism of the twenties, he took too easily to the orthodoxies governing the League of American Writers, where he officiated for years in the thirties and early forties.

I recall Cowley being at a farm I visited in Connecticut, in the early thirties, before he had been politicized. Hart Crane, who was a friend of his, and other lesser literary figures were also there. In my innocence I expected to be overwhelmed by literary talk, but instead Crane spent hours trying to get a male dog to mount a tomcat, which was not easy, as animals, too, seem to have been affected by the contemporary emphasis on identity. Cowley had written earlier an interesting account of literary life and sensibility in the twenties, in *Exile's Return*, but I suspect that his transformation into a left critic with factional political responsibilities came about largely because he was able to adapt without too much difficulty to the requirements of the times.

Kenneth Burke was a more complicated and adventurous critic, and in his case two incidents I recall make me believe that his use by the party served as a kind of anchor for him, a way of making a luftmensch feel his feet were on the ground. The first is an extraordinary example, almost too good to be true, of the self-hypnosis of intellectuals determined to believe in something they were not fitted by nature to believe. It was at a May Day parade, in the early thirties, and Kenneth Burke, who was marching with the writers' contingent, was yelling in a raspy, brittle voice, "We write for the working class." None of his fellow marchers seemed to think it odd that someone whom even trained readers found hard to understand should think his writing had any relation to the working class. One kind observer said maybe Burke meant he wrote in the interests of the working class, though it would appear difficult to stretch such esoteric ideas as "symbolic action" or "perspective by incongruity" into revolutionary weapons. On another, more private, occasion, he indicated a disturbing caution involving his relations with the party. I had stayed late one day and was alone in the *Partisan Review* office when Kenneth Burke arrived unexpectedly. We had just printed a critical review by Sidney Hook of a recent book by Burke. And Burke had apparently come in to complain about it. We argued a bit but got nowhere, for Burke wanted some kind of restitution. All I could do was to suggest he write a reply, which we would print. He thought for a few minutes, then said he didn't think "they" would like his appearing in any form in *PR*. "They," so far as I could make out, referred to the editors of *The New Masses*.

As for Burke's critical writing, it has had a number of admirers, mostly among academic and esoteric critics. To my taste, his best work was his first, *Counter-Statement*, a relatively simple and straightforward discussion of a number of classic writers and of some theoretical questions. His later work became increasingly complicated and remote from what I conceive to be the proper concerns of the literary and critical imagination. And though Burke, no doubt, had a subtle and inventive mind, it was used more and more to create odd and abstruse associations, paradoxes, definitions, and combinations of ideas. Using criticism as a vehicle for covering the whole range of modern thought, he tried to bring together such diverse intellectual forces as psychoanalysis, Marxism, and the New Criticism. But, however brilliant and agile his theoretical excursions might have been, his thinking seems to me to have the quality of inspired intellectual improvisation.

Two writers who did not remain in the Stalinist orbit were Horace Gregory and James T. Farrell. Farrell broke in the middle thirties, at about the time the new *PR* was organized. Gregory stayed longer, not, I assume, out of conviction, but because he did not have the toughness and the physical resources to hold his own against the expected assault by the Communists. Gregory was a spastic, and the fact that he was able to function as well as he did at teaching and writing was a tribute to his enormous will and courage. We met at the John Reed Club in the thirties, where he gave a talk stressing quality in reading and writing. (Gregory later reminded me that he was criticized for this and that I defended him.) I was impressed by his energy and his dedication to the literary life, but taken aback by his fixation on reviewing and other aspects of the reputation-making process in literary history. Gregory and his wife, Marya Zaturenskaya, also a poet, kept up a steady recital of who said what about whom, favorable or unfavorable, that can be described only as a continuous record of literary opinion. Nevertheless, I respected his literary instincts, and we remained friendly until in 1937 he asked Rahv and me to write a piece for a literary annual, *New Letters in America,* he was putting out. He liked the essay, which was called "Literature in a Political Decade." But when *The New Masses* ran a typically Stalinist putdown of it in an unfavorable review of the book, Gregory made no attempt to defend it in his reply. For a few years after that we had little to do with each other. But early in the forties, Horace Gregory and his wife were invited to a *PR* party at my house on West Ninth Street on the theory that there should be a statute of limitations on literary and political feuds that did not involve life and death questions or utterly unforgivable behavior. It was a typical bash of the time, when prices were so low that anyone could afford whiskey and food for a hundred people. Late in the evening, when I was drunk enough to raise buried questions, I said to Marya that I had found it difficult to forgive Horace his failure to defend the piece in his annual. Marya said very sadly that Horace had been worried about his job. (He taught at the time at Sarah Lawrence.) I remembered that Marya did not work and that they had a son and a daughter, and I answered just as sadly that I could not put myself in the position of prescribing how far another man was to go in sacrificing his livelihood for his beliefs. Anyway, we decided to bury the past, and Gregory became a frequent and valued contributor to the magazine. He was, of course, a distinguished poet, and his sensitivity to mundane but odd experience enabled him to relate in an original way to the mood of the time.

James T. Farrell came from a rougher strain. Brought up, just as Studs Lonigan was, in the streets of Chicago, Farrell enjoyed a good brawl, though unlike many writers he fought not out of vanity or self-aggrandizement but for his opinions and principles.

His natural skepticism and contentiousness made him a bad risk for orthodoxy, and, like Rahv and myself, he soon became impatient with the doctrinaire and simplified Marxism of the Stalinists, which he exposed in an early critical book, *A Note on Literary Criticism*. A section of *Studs Lonigan* appeared in the first issue of the John Reed Club *Partisan Review*, and he continued for some years to write for us.

Unfortunately, we began to drift apart in the fifties, as we moved in different literary directions. Still, Farrell was obviously a novelist of great power, and I always admired his critical spirit and his personal and political honesty. He was constantly on the alert for sham and pomposity. In a sharp but good-natured way, he loved to cut phonies down to size. There was no shortage of them; so Farrell rarely ran out of subjects. His uncoordinated walk was disturbing—it gave him an air of unpredictability—and because he was very nearsighted, his mischievous eyes appeared to be constantly staring through one. Yet he was very sweet and gentle, and, compared to most writers I have known, almost without rancor or malice.

What stood out mostly, however, was his remarkable memory, a seemingly total recall of names, faces, incidents, and conversations that defined not only his person but his entire literary personality. Unlike most writers interested in sports, who are football freaks, he was a baseball freak: he knew every name, every statistic, every incident in baseball history. His memory was his method, the core of what has been called his naturalism. And though it marked his contribution to modern fiction, which helped to rescue the social novel from its ideological fetters in the thirties and restore it to its nineteenth-century dimensions—no small accomplishment—still his mastery of realism was removed from the concern with modernism and experiment that many of us were drawn to at the time.

As I have suggested, both the demands of the media and the new doctrines of the left, which connected social awareness and responsibility with "realistic" structures, actually served to sanction for both writers and readers an art for the marketplace. Naturalism and realism, as we know, have been much misused terms, having been applied to a wide variety of writers, from Zola to Joyce, as well as to the Ashcan School of painting, to popular novels, and to TV entertainment. But outside the stricter definitions of literary criticism, the terms have been given a kind of honorific value to sanctify more salable writing and to endow it with the requisite certificate of seriousness. It is by now a commonplace of criticism that genuine naturalism or realism is itself a highly stylized form, for there is no accepted version of reality to which realistic fiction is faithful. (The "realism" of contemporary pop painting, for example, is an illustration of a conceptual art utilizing the photographic image.) And though, as editors of *Partisan Review*, we did not rule out any approach to writing, one of our concerns was to resist the pressures that tended to obliterate the distinction between serious and commercial art and to promote the new realism. In painting, the distinctions were clearer—this was long before the pop scene—and our biases were indicated in the art criticism we published in the early years of the magazine by Clement Greenberg, James Johnson Sweeney, George L. K. Morris, and Robert Motherwell.

Though we felt some continuity with the spirit of the twenties and early thirties when we started the new *Partisan Review*, we were actually representing—or creating—a new intellectual atmosphere. Except for a few older writers, it was a young group, with all the energy, drive, and sense of beginning of writers who think of themselves as part of a new spirit. In contrast with the left writers I had known and worked with before, those who gathered around the new *PR* not only seemed sharper and more gifted, but they had the sustained intensity, the curiosity, and the pride in their work that mark the professional.

Of the established figures who associated themselves with us, the one whom we respected most was Edmund Wilson, a strange, remote, impressive figure. A man of immense literary scholarship, he was making an effort to master Marxist theory and radical politics. I recall long talks with him about Marx and Marxist aesthetics, when my awe of his reputation and knowledge was tempered by the realization that I knew more about radical theory and the movement of the left then he did. But I really felt legitimized only when he praised something I had written, for that meant recognition by some-one noted for his critical sense and his prose. Wilson was actually at his best in capturing the mood of a work or the life of a writer, as in *Axel's Castle*, which, despite its flaws as historical criticism, is a masterpiece of re-creation of the world of the Symbolists. In the many essays about individual writers he wove together a narrative and critical style to reconstruct their lives and works, like that of the great literary historians and essayists, such as Taine and St. Beuve. But some of his judgments were parochial, like his dispraise of Kafka, or his excessive praise of William Saroyan and John O'Hara. Wilson was at his weak-est, however, when he ventured into literary or political theory, and in this respect was typical of an older generation of critics who had not been trained in literary analysis and who were more concerned with sensibility than with method. Thus Wilson's view, for example, of the psychology of art in *The Wound and the Bow* seems superficial, and his reading of Marx and Lenin in *To the Finland Station*, a work of wide and imaginative scholarship, actually converted their doctrines into an epic poem.

Edmund Wilson (he was "Bunny" to his friends) always seemed to me an austere figure to whom it was impossible to get close. I had heard stories that after he married Mary McCarthy he wanted to keep both of them away from the magazine, for reasons one could not imagine, unless they arose out of some kind of jealousy involving his young bride. I had also heard that he often referred to the magazine as Partisansky Review, even though three of the five editors—or four of six, if you include Mary McCarthy—were not Jewish.

7

THE NEW TALENT

THE younger writers who, with the editors of *Partisan Review*, formed the core of the new group, included Clement Greenberg, Harold Rosenberg, Meyer Schapiro, Lionel Abel, Delmore Schwartz, Sidney Hook. We were friends, but I think we were held together less by friendship than by a sense of common values and purpose. I was closer at the beginning to Clement Greenberg, and later to Delmore Schwartz, but the demands of Delmore's psyche were such that I could describe the relationship only as difficult and intermittent.

It is painful for me to write about my relation with Clem, as everyone called him, because I found myself quite suddenly, years later, in a maze of psychological misunderstandings that I still do not entirely comprehend. As Clem became well known and a power in art circles, he grew more self-assured and impatient, but generally he did not change much. When I first knew him, I was struck by his enormous confidence and will. He had, I felt, what used to be known as a strong character—definitely stronger than mine. He seemed more sure of his opinions than most of us, certainly more than I was, though what some people referred to as his dogmatism was often concealed behind a polite, almost stammering manner. His dogmatism seemed to me mostly a matter of strong convictions, to which I was accustomed, for few of the writers I knew and worked with could be accused of reticence or modesty. Besides, Greenberg usually knew what he was talking about, and firm opinions seemed preferable to temporizing or double-talk. Perhaps I am unduly sympathetic to such an assertive personality, but that may be because I, too, have often been charged with being dogmatic when it seemed to me I was only stressing something I was sure of—and with people who are equally assertive and sometimes uninformed. (Matthew Arnold is reputed to have said: Yes, I am dogmatic, but I am right.) Besides, Greenberg was highhanded mainly in the fields of painting and sculpture where, after all, he did create a language and a set of values for a generation of art critics.

It has been said that Greenberg was sometimes too arbitrary in his judgments, and that his method was too formal. In giving the new painting a plastic definition, much like the textual definition of poetry by the New Criticism, Greenberg established the formal image of the New York School. But, like the New Critics, Greenberg did not go into the question of how personal and social meanings were translated into visual terms, a method more historically minded critics regard as one-sided. Criticism as a whole has not yet found a method for describing how non-plastic ideas and feelings mesh with the medium. The closest approach to such a method has been developed in the writings of Meyer Schapiro. What has been called Greenberg's formalism was not the basis for the early opposition to his writings, some of which came from the painters themselves, who were divided (often for private reasons or because of what he had said about them) in their feelings about Greenberg and unhappy about his designation of Pollock and Smith as the outstanding younger artists. Most of the opposition came from resistance to a new, strident voice and to the art he was promoting. Even among the editors and advisory editors of *Partisan Review*, which first printed some of Greenberg's most important essays, there was a certain amount of coolness and irritability when his name came up. And frequently in the forties, when the question of his continuing as our art critic was discussed, I had to argue with Rahv and James Johnson Sweeney, who was on our advisory board at the time. Rahv, in fact, was skeptical of the new art, for which he had no eye and in which he had little interest, though his opposition was usually expressed in discreet and indirect ways. He was always putting Clem down as an art critic, insisting that he became one because he figured out this was the best way to get ahead quickly.

I cannot say much about our clash in the late fifties, except that it came unexpectedly and at a bad time in Greenberg's life. Suddenly, he became enraged at me. The immediate cause was ostensibly that he had just broken up with Helen Frankenthaler and he was annoyed that Edna and I had seen Helen without telling him. He seemed to be angry not only with me, but with everyone else. Though he was known to be domineering, he accused me of trying to dominate him, and of having been disloyal. We talked about it several times, but I could not find the key to his anger. I can only assume this was one of those moments when, because of some personal crisis, everything in a relation gets out of hand, for I have never known him to be disloyal or malicious either before or after this incident.

Harold Rosenberg was too much of a maverick and too wrapped up in his own cocoon to be a reliable member of an inner core. But his intellectual style makes one think of him as a charter member of the New York literary community. My first impression of him was that of a larger, gaunter, darker, more genial Ezra Pound. Because of a stiff leg, he was usually to be seen sitting, and my earliest recollection of Rosenberg is of him in a chair in the middle of a large room in an apartment so laid out that one had to go through the room he occupied to get to any other room. There he sat, holding court, as it were, talking to everyone who passed through. He was one of the great talkers of our time, at the beginning more of a talker than a writer, though later his verbal gifts became more and more evident in his writing. Sylvia Marlowe, the harpsichordist, once said Rosenberg was a verbal magician, which was not a reference to a prose style but to a phenomenal articulateness. I rarely saw Rosenberg in a conversation he did not dominate in some way, by doing most of the talking, or designating the subject, or setting the tone. Unless crossed, he was always genial and witty. He seemingly enjoyed drinking and eating as much as talking, though all these activities appeared to be inseparable.

Rosenberg's ego was as large as his body. He always thought issues of *Partisan Review* that contained something by him were particularly good. In the forties, Harold wanted to be an editor of the magazine, and he tried to persuade me by saying that it was not fulfilling its cultural mission, which it could do only if he were an editor. The assumptions were overbearing, the manner genial. One day I brought these proposals to an end by suggesting that with his editorial vision he could start his own magazine, which would immediately outshine all others.

Rosenberg's mind could be described as literary, the common designation of minds that are not primarily analytical, orderly, systematic. But it might better be described as being in the French tradition, given to a rhetoric of free association, startling contrasts, and witty parallels. It is the kind of mind that makes one think of what would happen if someone on an analytic couch indulged in a free association of ideas instead of a free association of personal feelings and memories. For this reason, Rosenberg has often been dismissed as an ideological critic of painting, one whose theories were stronger than his observations. And I have heard it said by his rivals that actual paintings interfered with his ideas about them. But I think it should be pointed out that there are different kinds of criticism. Though Rosenberg cannot be classed as a formal critic, his writing about the arts has often been brilliant and original. His early description of the new painting as action painting, did not really explain the evolution of the medium, and, as Mary McCarthy pointed out in an otherwise sympathetic review, the concept of painting as a form of action leaves unanswered all the questions about quality and direction. It provides no means of distinguishing between one type of action—or painting—and another, between, say, Pollock and a pop artist. Before he died, however, Rosenberg had indicated he was aware of this problem of criteria and differentiation by his dismissal of most of the pop scene as a degeneration of the earlier abstract expressionist movement and a sign of the collapse of the idea of the avant-garde.

But despite its removal of painting from the accepted canons of criticism, what I think was most interesting about Rosenberg's theory of painting as an act was that even though it may not have sufficed as a definition of the painting, it was a remarkably suggestive characterization of the spirit animating the artistic community at the time. As an indication of Rosenberg's intellectual affinities, it might also be interesting to note that the idea of art as action had some currency in France, particularly in the writings of Sartre, who probably picked it up from Blaise Cendrars.

Meyer Schapiro, who was more or less at the outer edge of the inner circle, mainly, I suppose, because he was preoccupied with his own thinking and research, had all the formal characteristics of genius. Endowed with a phenomenal memory—Sidney Hook once said the trouble with Schapiro was that he could never forget anything—he acquired a mastery of almost every field of human knowledge. Perhaps experts in any one field would find gaps in his knowledge of their subject, but to most literary intellectuals who were not specialists but who themselves had a broad range of learning, Schapiro's erudition was staggering. It was also occasionally embarrassing and resented, as in an incident in the late forties.

Schapiro, Richard Blackmur, and I were lunching in a small Jewish delicatessen on Eighth Street. At one point Schapiro asked Dick Blackmur, who was then teaching at Princeton, what he was writing. Blackmur said he was working on a study of Henry Adams, which, in fact, he had been doing for about ten years, and for which he had received a Guggenheim fellowship some time back. Schapiro said he had not read Adams for a number of years, and then proceeded to give Blackmur a lecture on the subject, with exact textual references, page numbers, dates, and interpretations. Blackmur, who was a slow-speaking, pipe-smoking cross between a New England writer and a professor, became more and more uncomfortable and could barely conceal the anger behind his waspish restraint. Finally he said to Schapiro, with a glance at me, "You intellectuals in New York use your minds too much," to which Schapiro answered without any hesitation, "You know, Dick, when you use your mind, you do not use it up."

Schapiro's talents were so overwhelmingly verbal and so wrapped up in the forms and substance of scholarship that they often acted as a barrier to personal exchange. When one talked to Schapiro, whether it was on the phone, in one's house, or at a chance meeting on the street, one usually talked about abstract or objective things. I was never sure, however, whether this was his doing or whether one fell into this kind of talk because of the image one had of Schapiro. He was the nearest thing to a superb intellectual machine that I have ever met—one of the highest order, combining erudition with incisive thinking. Rahv once said that after an hour's phone conversation with Schapiro one could get a Ph.D.

One day he dropped in at my house. After he left, I said to my mother that she had seen the closest thing to a genius she would ever see—by which I meant that his mind had all the attributes of genius. All she could say was to ask how much money he made.

Though Schapiro was not very tolerant of loose or sham thinking, he was a very sweet man, humanly generous, never malicious, and almost impervious to gossip. He was born with the face of a saint—a Jewish saint—which might have been a handicap. He had the drawn, tragic look of a man groping with all the problems of knowledge and morality.

Schapiro was at his best when he was lecturing. I have heard he is still a marvelous teacher and lecturer. But the public talks that he gave in the forties were like intellectual séances. Even though the subjects were often esoteric—some were on a remote or little-known aspect of medieval art—one was anesthetized into a trance-like appreciation of the wide learning, the deft analyses, the startling associations, the bold generalizations. Unfortunately, if one was out of his field one remembered the virtuousity of the performance more than the substance of the lecture.

Schapiro's critical writing is unique in its fusion of scholarship with the accents of criticism. His method was essentially to bring the entire cultural context to bear on individual works and the development of specific styles and schools.

Lionel Trilling was a complex figure, and one's relation with him had to be complex. Though there were disagreements on many political and literary questions, one had respect for his enormous ability and grace.

Trilling wrote frequently for the early issues of *PR*. But he was a marginal member of the original group, mainly, I have always assumed, because he usually kept his distance from associations that would circumscribe his thinking. And though he was friendly and gracious, he had an enormous reserve, which amounted almost to a wall around him, and I had the feeling that he did not like the exaggerated expressions of intimacy common at the time. He called many people his friends, but there must have been degrees—or kinds—of friendship. In all the years I knew Lionel Trilling, I was not disposed to talk about personal things, which, as I reflect on it, was probably mostly my own doing. This is not to say he was ever unsympathetic or unconcerned.

It has occurred to me that Trilling was able to preserve his working self by dissociating himself from the draining and time-consuming entanglements of human relations—a trait, by the way, I admired and envied.

Oddly, or maybe naturally, Diana Trilling was just the opposite: she seemed more interested than Lionel in people's lives and was usually available for help and advice.

Lionel was much more controlled and abstracted than Diana not only in his writing but in ordinary conversation—which, in part, would account, incidentally, for some of the uncertainty and disagreements about his views both in literature and in politics. But only in part, for he has been a prime subject of the new revisionism.

I met Lionel Trilling in the late thirties. Several of us—I forget who, though I think Fred Dupee was there—had lunch with Trilling to discuss what he might write for *PR*. He looked then very much the way he did shortly before he died. He was jaunty but low-keyed, classically handsome, very much like the aristocratic portraits of the seventeenth century, with soft but defined features, modest but assured in his manner, in the way only someone who sensed his own gifts could be.

I do not recall what we talked about; all I remember is that Lionel struck me from the beginning as a man interested in ideas but soaking them up like feelings and impressions. This, of course, was the dominant tone of his thinking to the end of his life. Like all of us, he went through many phases in his beliefs, but they were merged with his tastes so that they appeared often as intellectual moods rather than clearly defined positions. In this respect, Lionel Trilling was almost a prototype of what has become known as the literary imagination, and though in some matters he had very positive political opinions, they were usually subordinated to his sense of cultural style and intellectual ambiguity. This was one of the reasons, I believe, why he was able to remain friendly with people of divergent views and, in turn, was liked and admired by many who disagreed strongly with the tenor of his thinking. Another reason is that he did not embroil himself in most of the political controversies of the period. When he did make political statements, they were often so modulated by the indirection of his prose and by his almost courtly recognition of opposing views that they were regarded as a minor part of his complex thinking and were overshadowed by his views on literary and cultural matters.

Still, in both literature and politics Trilling was a liberal. Like many of us who were anti-Communist, he often appeared to be somewhat conservative because he distinguished himself from the pro-Communist liberals. Culturally, too, his distaste for pseudo-radical stances emphasized the more moderate element in his thinking. Even though he was often attracted to extreme ideas, particularly to extreme personalities, Lionel Trilling was nevertheless wary of the writing or fashionable way of life in this period that pushed toward the edge of existence. The essay on Howells, for example, made clear Trilling's preference for the more balanced literary figures and the more stable forms. Throughout his writing, Trilling indicated that despite his admiration for such figures as Kafka, or Rimbaud, or Dostoevsky, or Beckett, who have been identified with avant-garde attitudes and underground experience, he did not feel an affinity with them. How conscious Trilling was of his predilections or his contradictions I do not know. Certainly, they were built into his style and into the very process of his thinking—in his conversation as well as his writing. When he talked, a favorite word that came up constantly was "complicated." "It's very *complicated*," he would say of most problems and ideas.

An incident one evening many years ago indicated the strength of his convictions. It was just after he had sent in his piece on Howells. Edna and I were having a quiet dinner at the Trillings' house. It started out as one of those warm evenings with a seeming excess of good feeling on everyone's part. At one point Lionel said quite benignly that he hoped I wouldn't mind if he made some criticism of a story I had just written. The gist of his criticism was that I should have more thematic complication in my fiction. His tone was appropriately friendly, and I took it in that spirit, even thinking he might be right. In fact, it seemed to me this might be a proper occasion for some observations about his recent writing that I had hesitated to make before. So after the necessary apologies and qualifications, I said as gently as I could that I had been wanting to tell him he was being read as a conservative thinker, which was all right if that was the way he wanted to be seen, but if not, I suggested he might be more aware of the inflection of his writing. This all seemed mild and muted enough and in keeping with what I thought was the license that the friendly mood of the evening permitted. But that was not the way Lionel took it. He became agitated and indignant, and in an angry voice I had rarely heard him use, he insisted that he wrote what he believed and didn't care what people thought. Of course, we did not get anywhere mainly because, as I saw it, what Lionel was saying was opposed to what I always thought to be the basic quality of his mind: its ability to accommodate to the modulations and contradictions of current thinking. He normally presented himself in the way he would have liked to behave, and in my long association with him this was an unusual incident. As I recall, only two other times did I see Lionel lose his calm. One was at a party at my house, when he almost hit Alfred Kazin during an argument in which Kazin asked him when he would repudiate Diana's politics. The other was at the Podhoretz's, before Norman's shift to the right. I forget the immediate cause, but at one point Trilling began to scold Podhoretz for his fashionable radical views. Since I was sympathetic to Norman, though I knew Lionel to be right in some respects, and perhaps because I, too, was influenced more than I realized by the left atmosphere, I felt awkward trying to defend Norman and act as a buffer between him and Lionel. It was not easy, for Lionel's distaste for what he thought of as mindless and his apparent irritation at the defection of someone who had been a disciple were so great that he could not be diverted easily.

Lionel's relation, in general, with Midge and Norman Podhoretz seemed to be that of a teacher as well as a friend—as it was with Steven Marcus—alternating between pride and disappointment, and exhibiting a mixture of affection and irritation.

And politics was mixed up with personal matters. Once at the Trillings, this complex relation led to a tense and bizarre scene. There were a few people besides the Podhoretzes and Edna and me, but they were mostly spectators. In the middle of the evening, Lionel suddenly said to Norman that he felt *Commentary* was too fixed in its politics. Diana joined in. I could see Midge and Norman were trying to stay cool. But the tension was palpable, partly because not all the issues were out in the open. The argument seemed to be over strategy and appearances, for Norman and Midge had assumed that their views could not be that far from those of Lionel and Diana. I stayed out of the cross-fire, but I was pulled in when Diana suddenly switched to me and said that the criticism of *Commentary* was not to be taken as a political approval of *PR*. I was so taken aback by Diana's sudden shift in my direction that I hardly knew what to say. Midge even became momentarily sympathetic to me, although I was further from her views than Diana and Lionel were. However, I assumed that Diana was trying, by turning on me too, to lessen the assault on Norman and to indicate she had not suddenly swung way over to the left.

The next morning Diana phoned me to explain that she wanted to divert the attack from *Commentary* and to praise me for my admirable restraint. This incident, of course, had more to do with the Podhoretzes than with me, and in the light of Podhoretz's later criticism of Trilling as a defector from the conservative ranks, it takes on a greater interest.

By treating Trilling's outbursts as untypical, I seem to be emphasizing his urbanity and dislike of confrontation. And, in fact, his usual manner was gracious, even courtly. But this side can be exaggerated, as I think Alfred Kazin does in *New York Jew*, where he says Trilling played down his Jewishness, presumably more than other Jewish writers at the time. This, I think, is a misunderstanding of Trilling, who never denied his Jewishness nor concealed his strong support of Israel, but whose relation to his Jewish origins was set in an earlier period, when one thought less of one's ethnicity than of one's internationalism and concerns for humanity as a whole. We thought of literature and our literary profession not as Jews, but as heirs to the Western tradition. Certainly, this was the feeling of all of us who considered ourselves to be socialists. It was only with the decline of Marxism and after the Holocaust that one's Jewish consciousness was given primacy, as it were, over one's human consciousness. And for people like Lionel, as for me, it was still never felt to be appropriate to wear one's star on one's sleeve. Only recently has it become intellectually fashionable to parade one's Jewishness. And if any of us is to be accused of playing down his Jewishness, then surely Hannah Arendt, one of Kazin's heroines, should have been criticized by him. For not only did she subordinate her Jewishness to her human and philosophic interests, but she was also open in her opposition to the state of Israel; and she continued to hold these views long after Hitler had made it almost necessary to assert one's Jewishness.

Except for occasional displays of personal or political anger, Lionel Trilling's person was very much like his writing: orderly, graceful, flexible, modulated, appearing to be constantly in control. This is not the place to evaluate Trilling as a writer; in any case, he defies easy definition. He was not the kind of critic who aggressively pushed a single idea or method or cause. He was a historically minded critic, but his main contribution was in his interweaving of literary modes with social and political forces. He was, I think, our most accomplished essayist, and his writing was distinguished by a unique tone of urbanity and cultural awareness that combined sound scholarship with a knowledge of the more sophisticated methods of criticism and a sense of political and social issues. I do think his dislike of avantgarde attitudes and of the more raucous trends in the contemporary scene tended to put him among those who would conserve rather than forge new traditions. But, like Matthew Arnold in an earlier period, what he wanted to conserve was nothing less than the best of our cultural heritage, which he felt was being eroded by the Stalinization of the liberal mind. He was not a propagandist for fashionably new values like Paul Goodman or Norman O. Brown, or for novel critical approaches like Harold Bloom or the deconstructionists, but, more important, he stood for intellectual sanity and an intricate but balanced view of literary and cultural matters. Far from being a forerunner of neoconservatism, as William Barrett claims in *The Truants*, Trilling stood for moderation and was against fanaticism of any kind.

If any writer could be singled out as the most extreme representative of the new intellectual grouping, it would be Delmore Schwartz. He was neither the most central nor the most typical, but he did embody most of the strains that came together during this period. Trained in philosophy, an accomplished critic as well as a writer of fiction and poetry, sensitive to political ideas, with the uncanny intelligence that only functioning paranoids seem to have, he possessed all the equipment for a modern sensibility and a miserable life. Like so many talented but warped and frustrated writers, he has become a legend, and the legend has overshadowed the achievements, though this may be partly a compensation for the fact that he never fully realized his talents. Recently, however, the pendulum has swung the other way, as it always does, often out of perversity, and underestimating Schwartz's work has become fashionable.

I met Delmore in 1937. He had written something for *New Directions* that caught my attention, and I wrote asking him to contribute to the new *Partisan Review*. He sent the story "In Dreams Begin Responsibilities," which has since become a little underground classic. We met soon afterward, and the immediate impression was the one that lasted to the end of his life, though his whole person, physical and mental, became progressively more disheveled. One felt immediately one was in the presence of a strange and possessed being, endowed with some extraordinary nervous and intellectual energy. His head was unusually large, his voice stuttering but insistent, his movements uncoordinated. His face had the pallor and his body the restlessness of an addict. He was always moving, twitching, talking, intense, and excited, his eyes looking for your response to him. Yet he was affable and friendly, almost ingratiating, with a kind of clumsy and persistent charm.

I was as close to Delmore as you could become with someone who was always demanding something from you and always suspecting you of turning against him. Being too close to Delmore meant not only being put in a kind of protective, almost paternal, position, but it meant also an endless struggle against becoming too entangled with one of the most active egos I have known. His strong mind, his weak but avid psyche, his awkward, stubborn body were constantly reaching out and wrapping themselves around an idea, a person, a compulsion. He enveloped you with his feelings and his ideas, even though you knew he was always satisfying his needs, not yours.

Delmore was one of the most natively intelligent writers and probably the most tortured writer I have known. (In the matter of suffering, John Berryman was perhaps not far behind him, and Robert Lowell was certainly well endowed with anguish as well as talent.) His intelligence was of that instantaneous, luminous variety one associates with an unusual mind; whatever the field, he seemed to be able to grasp its essence immediately, and, unlike those writers who pay homage to the cult of the creative by nurturing their own ignorance and narrowness, Delmore Schwartz was just as much at home with ideas as with purely literary matters.

But the truth is Delmore was being destroyed by psychic disorders, by alcohol, and by sleeping pills, and as he got older his torments spread.

I do not know what the clinical analysis would be. He was probably psychotic. He seemed to be manic-depressive and paranoid, and though he functioned better as a writer than as a person, it was a limited functioning. In his life it was clear that he was barely making it, though a native cunning enabled him to cope with situations when he was psychologically incapacitated. He was usually able to trade on his friendships with men and on his helpless relations with women, who, I suspect, were awed by his talents and intrigued by his wildness, to carry on the basic routines of living.

Even when he was younger, his charm, his intelligence, and his exuberance were clouded by his delusions and suspicions. But in his last years his paranoia took almost complete possession of him, though unlike most writers who feel persecuted he was sensitive about the way people treated him, and not about what they thought of his work. There were never too many friends: earlier the most loyal were William Barrett, Robert Lowell, Anatole Broyard, Milton Klonsky, and Oscar Handlin; later Dwight Macdonald, Meyer Schapiro, and myself, and of course, his wives, Gertrude Buckman and Elizabeth Pollet, and after them his women friends.

At the end he wore all of us out; though, as I recall, Dwight and Meyer seemed able to cope with him longer than I could, and I saw little of him just before he died. One had to have almost a professional, self-effacing tolerance—and we all had our own problems—to take the rages, the demands, the recriminations, the fantasies, mostly about money, but often about being betrayed by those few people who stuck to him and tried to help him.

The last time I saw him, a few years before he died, he was literally out of his head. He had come to see me, but because Edna and I were out, he went upstairs, where my sister-in-law and brother-in-law lived, to wait for me. He kept raving about the plot to kill him, insisting that some fruit on the table had been poisoned by "little children," and he would not leave. When I got home I brought him down to my apartment, which he also did not want to leave, and he went on screaming about the little children, apparently in heaven, for he kept pointing to the sky, who were out to poison him. When I finally was able to walk him to the hotel he was staying at on Washington Place, he continued to rant about the conspiracies against him, and in fits of anger he would bang on the nearest parked car. When we came to a traffic light, he would look up and say the red was a signal from God to stop, and when it turned to green, then God said it was safe to go on.

Now, despite the lessening of interest in his writing, a legend is growing up around Delmore Schwartz, partly because he lends himself to the myth of the unworldly, suffering artist, and people who had no use for him are getting in on the act. I think it would be more fitting and a nicer testimonial to his memory if we recalled him as he was and as we felt about him. His large, sprawling, perhaps unrealized talent, his intelligence, his enthusiasm for literary exchange, were of a piece with what made him so difficult, with all the things that destroyed him. But when he was at his best, at his most ingratiating, I can remember the excitement of his wildly animated talk, his shirt half out of his pants, smelling of whiskey and cigarettes, telling endless stories, and scoring loud, rhetorical points, long into the night. He claimed he slept only half the night, which made him twice as old as he was, having actually lived twice as much as if he had slept normally. Artificially old and sleepless, he was so strong, however, I thought he would never die. He was always ailing, but never seemed to be sick. My doctor, to whom I sent him once, said he had the constitution of a peasant.

I do not know what Schwartz was like as a child, for from the time I first met him, when he was in his twenties, his psychic distortions were full-grown. From his own stories he had an unusually morbid relation with his parents: he acted as though he hated his mother, refusing to see her or even to talk to her. What her crimes were was never made clear. He admired, somewhat grudgingly, his father's success as a real-estate operator, though he talked about him as if he were a distant, mythical figure. I cannot say when he officially became an alcoholic, but he always drank heavily, with the intensity of one who relied on it. He also took sleeping pills to get to sleep and pep pills to wake up. Most of the time he was distracted and unfocused, and seemingly unable to function. One wonders how he managed to

78

write, though the one time we wrote something together—the editorial statement that introduced the symposium on "Our Country and Our Culture"—he was sharp and efficient. (He insisted we write the statement because he wanted to avoid what he felt was Rahv's clumsy and ostentatious prose.) But when it came to the more mundane activities that are demanded from most of us he became helpless. He claimed he could not make tea or coffee, much less cook any food. His mind wandered at the thought of any simple editorial work, though he did read manuscripts acutely. I had even heard that when he taught at various universities he was often speechless and paralyzed. When he did perform, it was said that he held his students by telling funny and odd literary stories.

I recall several incidents that dramatize his adjustments of his mode of living to his incapacities. One day in the forties, Delmore and I were walking up Fourth Avenue just below Fourteenth Street when we ran into his ex-wife, Gertrude Buckman, whom he had apparently not seen for several years. He had barely said "Hello, how are you?" when he blurted out at her, "What size shirts and shorts do I wear?" I was so stunned, and I must say outraged, by this show of helplessness taking the form of machismo, that I screamed at Delmore that it is possible to be a poet, even a good one, and still know the size of one's shirts. I am sure I was not acting out of any sympathy for the lot of women—Gertrude Buckman seemed to be able to take care of herself—but out of an embarrassment at his having gone beyond the limits of selfishness.

Another time, some years later, Edna and I visited Delmore and his new wife, Elizabeth Pollet, on their newly acquired farm in Frenchtown, New Jersey, where he had decided to live. What insanity brought this coddled man who could survive only in a city where services and sympathy were always immediately available, and who saw nature mainly as a literary myth, to move to the country where (unless one is very rich) half one's life is a battle against nature—what brought him to the shabby flatlands of New Jersey, which certainly were not the natural habitat for a spoiled writer from New York, I cannot imagine. Anyway, there was a severe drought at the time, which we knew all about because our own well, in our country place in Long Valley, New Jersey, had run dry, and this was the major subject of conversation for the entire countryside. When we got to the

Schwartz rural retreat, I asked Delmore how they managed the water problem. "No trouble," he said. "How about dishes and baths?" He shrugged as though he couldn't understand why I even raised the question. Later, when I spoke to Elizabeth about the water, she said she filled two milk cans with water each morning at the spring of a neighboring farmer and that Delmore did not even know about it. I also discovered that the heating system was inadequate for the house, as is often the case with old farmhouses that have not been modernized, and that the temperature in the house was in the forties most of the winter. But of this, too, Delmore was oblivious, though Elizabeth, I was told, almost got tuberculosis.

Anything touching on money and work seemed to set off the paranoia that was always just under the surface. The magazine had recently received a subsidy, not large by ordinary publication standards but enough to permit it to take a bigger office midtown and to hire a modest staff. I had agreed to give Delmore Schwartz and William Barrett, the two associate editors at the time, the staggering sum of fifteen hundred dollars each as a yearly salary. Philip Rahv objected to their getting anything, certainly not fifteen hundred dollars, insisting they did not do enough work to justify any payment. We had a knockdown fight, during which all the conceivable moral and practical considerations were aired, though my main arguments were that Schwartz and Barrett should not have been kept as associate editors if they were useless, and that it was humiliating to put them in a special category that maintained their positions as associate editors but denied their usefulness.

Now it is very difficult to assess exactly what Delmore was able to do. He read manuscripts, gave opinions, made suggestions, though he could not work on manuscripts or handle any of the practical problems that fill the life of a magazine. He soon fell into one of his slumps, and, though he came to the office almost every day, he would often sit or wander about dreamily—as if he were intent on proving that Rahv was right about him. I must confess I did nothing to get him to work more, partly out of sympathy for his state, partly out of a feeling of helplessness in dealing with what was obviously a psychic disorder. One day, however, William Barrett complained to me that he was doing Schwartz's work in addition to his own and asked me to speak to Schwartz about it. Instead of telling Barrett it was his problem, without thinking I walked into the tiger's cage. Indeed, it was a tiger I tried to reason with in his apartment on Perry Street. Delmore snarled and screamed at me, his main argument being that it was none of my business, as he shrewdly hit the weakness of my position and kept yelling that Barrett should have talked to him himself. I granted this and tried to talk about the issue, but I soon realized that I could make no headway with pathology. I had no way of knowing how conscious it was, but his barrage had the effect of probing for my weak spots by trying to beat me down with vague threats and all kinds of ominous insinuations. I left not only with the feeling that I had been foolish as well as unsuccessful, but also completely shaken by the encounter with madness and with a will that would stop at nothing to get its way. Nor did it help to say to myself that I was so disturbed because it was a throwback to my mother's real or simulated fits of madness.

Once more, near the end of our relation and not long before Delmore's death, he broke out into an animal rage, this time again over something involving money. A small group, including Saul Bellow, Dwight Macdonald, Meyer Schapiro, Catherine Carver, our managing editor, and I raised some money to pay for psychiatric treatment for Delmore. As I recall, Catherine Carver was informally in charge of the project. Delmore apparently was not ready to go to a psychiatrist, but he wanted to get the money. He phoned me early in the morning when I was trying to work and ranted about how he needed the money and how nobody had the right to withhold money raised explicitly for him. I must say that I was sympathetic with his plight, even though he did not stick to his end of the agreement, but I told him I had no authority to give him the money, as I was only one member of the committee. I felt no guilt, but dealings of this kind with Delmore always left one shaken and with the feeling that however great was his suffering or need, friendship had been strained beyond its normal limits.

Sometimes Delmore Schwartz's irrationality took absurd or charming forms. Once he talked me into taking a plane to New York after I had visited him in Boston, where he was then teaching at Harvard. I had been scared of flying, but he persuaded me that it was safer, quicker, more comfortable, and saner to fly. It turned out to be a bad flight in a rainstorm, and as we kept circling over La Guardia, the woman next to me went on chatting nervously about recent plane crashes. Some years later, when he was going back to Boston from New York, he said he was taking the train. When I reminded him that earlier he had been an advocate of flying, he said that at that time he did not mind dying, but that now he did.

Then there were the times he became paranoid about having his wife stolen. These episodes were traumatic for Delmore and his friends but were so absurd as to make them almost as funny as sad. The first time involved his publisher and friend at New Directions, Jay Laughlin. One morning Delmore called and I heard a frantic voice at the other end of the phone sputtering something I could not understand about Laughlin and his wife. Finally, I grasped that Delmore was charging Laughlin with having an affair with his wife. I said it did not make sense to me and I did not believe it, and when I asked what evidence he had he only shrieked louder at me for questioning him. Trying to find some way of ending this pointless exchange, I asked him what reason he had to believe that Laughlin wanted such an involvement. He said it was because Laughlin was rich and wanted to display his power. "He has eight million dollars," I heard him say. "I don't see what having eight million dollars has to do with it," I said. "Eighty million, not eight million," he screamed back at me. This ended it; I do not know why, but perhaps the utter insanity of the logic put an end to the whole question.

The last time I saw Delmore when he was still moderately rational was just before he went to teach at Syracuse. He phoned one day and said he would like to come over with the girl he was going to marry. She was eighteen and lovely, but one had to wonder what these two—who looked as though they came from different planets—could possibly have to do with each other. She was small, soft, round-faced, and with her schoolgirl bun and pink skin, she had not yet lost the aggressive innocence of youth. She was self-possessed and peppy though inarticulate, very much like the young girls who used to flock to the White Horse Tavern to see the writers they had heard about at school and read in the little magazines. Delmore was back in form, drinking, talking, shouting, laughing, moving his body and his hands like a fighter looking for an opening. Most of the time he ignored her, presumably having brought her only to be looked at, as he reminisced about the past—a time that obviously excluded her. The high point of the evening came as he was standing, leaning against the fireplace, stoking his memory, when he suddenly blurted, "I don't know why I'm getting married, I can't fuck anymore." Then he went back without a break to the past. We all acted as though we had not heard it; perhaps Edna and she did not hear it. I kept quiet, stunned by Delmore's telling things nobody wants to hear.

Unlike his disordered existence, Delmore Schwartz's writing had an almost classic composure, though its themes came out of the conflicts and ironies of contemporary life. I like his fiction and essays better than most of his poems, but in the more successful poems, usually the shorter ones, as in the stories and articles, Delmore was able from the beginning to strike an assured and commanding tone and to sustain it to the end. The long poems always seemed endless and mechanically drawn out, but many of the shorter lyric poems had a combination of grace and intensity and a wide-ranging consciousness. And in stories like "In Dreams Begin Responsibilities" and "The Statues," Schwartz immediately created an atmosphere that in an old-fashioned sense established the touch of literary authority and mastery of the medium one finds only in the best writers. The essays, too, had the relaxed air and the easy combination of generalization and concrete observation that characterizes distinguished criticism.

It is difficult to classify Schwartz's writing. He was neither an experimental writer nor a popular one, nor did he create a style that influenced other writers. It was certainly not a style one can connect in any way with the jagged and quick rhythms of much contemporary writing. It had a kind of detachment and nervous serenity; and I suppose one could speculate that it was Schwartz's way of transcending the disorder of his life. I have often thought of Delmore Schwartz as a kind of second-generation T. S. Eliot, who brought a Jewish irony and rootlessness to the world-weary sensibility of the heir of the culture of the past.

How much better a writer Delmore might have been had he not been so wracked by alcohol, drugs, and his psychic state, we have no way of knowing and, in fact, it may be a false question. Perhaps, as with so many writers, his talent was tied to his disabilities, and what emerged as his style or mode of perceiving things was a combination of the two.

8

THE PAINTERS

MOST writers have not been sensitive to painting and sculpture, perhaps because they cannot relate to media that are not verbal. To be sure, there have been notable exceptions, from Baudelaire and Ruskin to more recently, Greenberg, Rosenberg, Ashbery, and Frank O'Hara. The French would seem to be an exception, but one wonders whether there was some kind of national aesthetic ego that led them to appropriate Cézanne and Picasso and Braque and Léger. Or it might be that the French critical idiom is at once so abstract and deceptively concrete that it seems to take in the plastic arts even when the experience is remote. American writers, however, being closer to their direct experience, have usually responded more to painting with a literary content, and while they have eventually accepted almost as a part of art history the achievement of the abstract expressionists and the New York School, they originally had no idea of the importance—or the advances—of figures like Gorky, Pollock, Motherwell, de Kooning, Rothko, Gottlieb, and the others. The fact is that most writers at first were either indifferent to or scoffed at the New York abstractionists. The story is told, for example, that Rahv once said to Rosenberg that Rothko was just a house painter, to which Rosenberg replied, "Isn't it interesting that a house painter should paint such pictures?"

I am not sure why, but I was aware of the new art almost from the beginning, and consequently, despite Rahv's passive resistance, *Partisan Review* was the only literary publication to ally itself with the new movement. Perhaps, by some personal quirk, I had an eye for the plastic arts, or, because of my need for aesthetic consistency, I was fed up with the old realistic painting, particularly that of the so-called Ashcan School, which was nourished by the Communists. (Clement Greenberg insisted I could paint, so one day he gave me a palette, brush, paints, etc. The result was that I became nauseated before we could test my talents.) Or it might have been because some of the artists and art critics like Ferber, Greenberg, Rosenberg, and later, Gottlieb, Frankenthaler, Motherwell, and Newman, were friends of mine. Herbert Ferber and I grew up together in the Bronx—the only instance I know of a relation that went back that far and lasted so long. Herbert had wanted to be a sculptor, but his strong-willed mother, a Rumanian with that old-world shrewdness that dominated poor immigrant families, made him go to dental school so he could be armed with a respectable and lucrative profession. However, Herbert continued to sculpt and went to art schools in the evening. In the thirties, when a feeling of restlessness in the arts as well as in politics filled the air, we were talking one evening, and Ferber asked me what I thought would be the next phase in painting and sculpture. Up to then he had been doing strong, slightly bulky, awkwardly stylized naturalistic carvings in wood and stone. I said, without thinking, and with that omniscience that sometimes comes with innocence, that the next step would probably be some fusion of abstraction with surrealism, that is, an abstraction that was personal, lyrical, and expressive. But, of course, when the new style came, I was not prepared for it, for what was in my mind was an idea, not a painting. I still recall having to get used to Pollock, though I did not resist. Clem Greenberg had to persuade me, not by argument, but by the example of criticism and his enthusiasm, that here was a new style of important painting.

Gorky, who was the transition figure, was easier to appreciate. Even Pollock, despite the novelty of his canvases, could be assimilated, perhaps because of his lyrical tone and because the magic of his

The Painters

seemingly wild and spontaneous method was so overwhelming. Motherwell, too, was not difficult to grasp, for he was very traditional in mood, almost French, and his main appeal was in the softness and sureness of his composition. But the others were not so easy.

Frankenthaler, Gottlieb in his later work, Kline, and, above all, Rothko and Newman, in the boldness and arbitrariness of their images, raised questions in one's mind, instead of evoking the immediate recognition one is accustomed to in literary works. One was almost forced to react as amateurs do to new forms by asking what Rothko and Newman did that any slightly talented painter could not do. True, Mondrian had done something like it before, perhaps more simply and more authoritatively, but the basic, expressively geometric shapes of the later Newman and the use of color as shape in Rothko seemed almost too easy. And though my painter friends insisted my eye was too untrained to catch the marvelous gradations of color in Rothko and line in Newman, I have felt that Rothko, at least, was inflated by the momentum of the entire movement. Still, the new school represented a dazzling array of talent. And as one looks back at the paintings now, they exhibit, despite the differences between the painters, differences that later grew larger, a common direction and a daring and innovative drive that was harnessed to a traditional control of the medium.

As for the later figures, my visual education apparently was slowed down, as all generational aesthetic experiences are. Hence there was no longer the feeling of excitement created by the artists of the thirties and forties. Painters like Louis, Noland, Stella, Oldenberg, Rosenquist, Olitski, who came later, did not seem so impressive as the earlier ground-breaking figures. And the more recent "conceptual" and "realistic" schools strike me as popular and perverse exploitations of the interest aroused by the abstract expressionists. The new realism, particularly, appears to be an accommodation of the more serious traditions of painting and sculpture to popular taste and to the current fashionableness of photography. We have come a long way from the great modernist turn at the early part of the century. The thrill of first encountering Picasso, Mondrian, Braque, Léger, Kandinsky, the Objectivists, all the equivalents, roughly, of the literary modernists, was part of the discovery of the new sensibility, and the feeling that developments in the arts and in criticism were of a piece and enveloped one's whole being. Perhaps young people feel something like that today, but it must be more in the nature of having a common sense of aesthetic freedom, of being able to go in any direction, in any style.

In the beginning, the painters were a closed circle, like a band of revolutionaries, or upstarts, trying to put over a strange, new, indigestible style. The museums, the centers of power in the arts, the media— all had no use for them. They felt that if they were to get anywhere they had to stick together. But this solidarity had to be artificial and strained, for it held together some of the most diverse, wild, egomaniacal figures.

Jackson Pollock, for example, was a loner, a heavy drinker, almost an American stereotype of the inarticulate genius, the nonintellectual craftsman. Yet he was shrewd and uncannily observant and sharp, particularly about painting. Like many people endowed with special abilities, he could spot instantly a phony idea or person. Through the haze of alcohol and slow midwestern talk, he would, in his artistic vernacular, come out with the most devastating remarks. He was built like a fullback, with a large, blondish head, hulking shoulders, and arms like tree trunks. One evening, at a small dinner party at Pollock's studio, with about eight people, including Lee Krasner, Pollock's wife, Clement Greenberg and a friend of his, Sue Mitchell, Edna and myself, I had a glimpse of the wild, tortured inner life of Jackson Pollock. Before dinner, we were sitting around and drinking when Jackson, who seemed already high, picked up a shoe that Sue had taken off and left on the floor. Pollock began to twist and break the tiny shoe with his strong hands, muttering, as he bent it, "I love women. I love women." At dinner he was at my left, and making conversation was not easy, as Pollock was either silent or talking into space. At one point, I thought we had a gambit. He said he was being analyzed by a "young woman." "That's nice," I said, "to be analyzed by a young woman. Is she attractive?" "A Jungian woman, not a young woman," he snapped. Since I had no faith in Jungian analyses, I said nothing. Finally, Pollock got so drunk he could not walk straight, and Clem and I had to half carry him down the stairs and over to his apartment. It was like dragging a tree.

Robert Motherwell was just the opposite. Outgoing, sociable, talkative, he stood apart from the other painters. He was articulate, almost

The Painters

to the point of an ingratiating eloquence. Motherwell had a large head
and a large body, but, unlike Pollock, he looked more like a cosmopolitan intellectual. He was trained in philosophy, wrote extensively,
was interested in living well, in well-appointed houses, in gourmet
cooking. When he was married to Helen Frankenthaler they made a
worldly couple, for she, too, was interested in high styles of living,
though with a touch of plainness.

Helen was actually much more shy and much less articulate. Her
verbal gift was a sharp and cynical but good-natured wit, slightly
Jewish in its irony and irreverence. She was also enormously attractive, with an earthy charm. I first met her through Clem Greenberg,
when she came down to New York from Bennington.

Matta was also very articulate, charming, and sophisticated. But he
was not American. The only other American painter I knew who was
a big talker was Barney Newman. His talk was freewheeling and
undisciplined, as though he were trying to channel his fantasies. He
was stocky, with a flowing European mustache. He dressed (usually
in black), talked (of odd things), and acted (he was an anarchist and
once ran for mayor of New York) eccentrically. He was generally
sweet-tempered but combative toward powerful institutions and
enterprises; for example, he was frequently involved in hassles with
department stores. He himself told the story about how he was
watching the World Series one day when an account executive of a
department store called to remind him that he had not paid his bill. He
screamed at him that they were uncivilized, and were interfering with
his life by calling during the World Series.

Adolph Gottlieb, whom I got to know well, was also articulate, but
in a simple, straightforward manner. He always gave the impression
of having his feet on the ground; he and Ferber were the most rational
and most sensible of all the painters and sculptors. Adolph had a
dapper mustache and, in later years, a ruddy face. He always spoke
slowly in a measured rhythm, as though he were looking for clarity
and understanding, which was very different from the common style
of aesthetic mystification.

And there was Mark Rothko, a big talker, too, but extravagant and
wide-ranging, with a homemade brand of wit and wisdom, very
Jewish in flavor. He was heavy, and he usually dressed carelessly,
often sloppily. He loved to eat and talk and drink. But he was always,

89

at least when I saw him, edgy and suspicious, frequently to the point of seeming paranoid. Tensions soon developed, because, so far as I could make out, he disliked critics and criticism—a dislike that included a number of art critics, including Clement Greenberg. In a sense his life was a parable of the fate of the whole movement with which he was associated: he catapulted from poverty and lack of recognition to fame and incredible wealth, but he could never fully adjust. To the end, when he committed suicide, he acted as though he were still poor, and he did not trust either the world that made him famous or his own powers.

Though I often complained that, unlike writers, the painters never criticized each other, one had to be impressed by the élan of the group, which came closer than anything this country had ever seen to the movements that spurred the arts in Europe. It was like a well-bred family that never squabbled in public, although the differences between them were often considerable and, in later years, more clearly seen.

There was Philip Guston, a charming, well-read, sophisticated painter, who later moved away from abstraction into social themes. Willem de Kooning was considered a part of the movement though he always had his own distinct style. Elaine de Kooning, his ex-wife, was sharp, intense, incredibly responsive to mood and tone. Lee Pollock was patient, strong-minded, very intelligent, and herself a pioneer in the method of painting that Jackson became more famous for. William Baziotes, a very good painter who, sadly, died young, exemplified the spirit of the New York School in the primitivism of his personal style and talk. Bradley Tomlin, an underrated painter who also died young, was gentle, sweet, a maverick in his almost courtly manner. Then there was Theodore Roszak, who was outside the pack. He was always a loner, whether out of strength or suspicion of a group I do not know. But he carried with him the modern idea of the artist: independent, intransigent, always an outsider. His wife, Florence, had been a friend of Edna's at N. Y. U. Roszak was originally a constructivist, with a strong sense of design, and the first cover of Partisan Review was designed by him. Later his style shifted, and he went in for bizarre and draconian subjects.

The abstract expressionists came from nowhere (many started on the WPA art project in the thirties), flared into the limelight, became rich and famous, conquered the international world of art, then went off in different directions and no longer occupy the center of the art scene. Most of them are dead, and their place has been taken by the flashy, new pop figures. The story is an old one, and very American. Their fate seems to me to be illustrated by an incident in the late forties. Clem Greenberg had advised a wealthy couple he knew to buy a large Pollock. But since they had no room, they said, for so large a painting and, I presume, did not like it much, Clem suggested that it be kept in my apartment, where it took up one high, narrow wall, vertically. Some years later, the couple separated and the husband, a businessman, moved into a large Park Avenue apartment with his new wife. An interior decorator whom they hired had trouble figuring out what to do with one large wall near the fireplace, when they recalled they owned a large painting by someone whose name they had forgotten. When the decorator found out it was a Pollock, she could not contain her excitement, I was told, and insisted they get it immediately. The innocent collectors were to come to my house to see the painting, and to arrange for moving it. They came one evening when I had a few people over, including Will Barrett and his wife, Julie, Delmore Schwartz, Clem and Susie. But the owner did not come alone. He came with two men who looked like bodyguards; why, I did not know, except that I had heard he never went anywhere without them.

They stared at the painting but did not dare let on that they could not see what all the fuss was about. Nevertheless, they measured it and noted its colors. Then they settled into what they thought was the spirit of the party. They told banal and off-key stories which they must have felt were appropriate in a Village atmosphere, but, obviously, the only connection between them and the other people was that everyone took the evening to be an eccentric one and was curious about characters they had seen only in the movies and associated with money and power. The two guards, who seemed to feel at home, got drunk and began to sing wild Irish songs.

A few weeks later a mover came and took the painting. It was about eight feet high and four feet wide, a dazzling free association of colors and forms, which I heard was worth forty thousand dollars fifteen years ago. At the time it was in my house, before the interior decorator said it was chic to hang it, I could have bought it for five hundred dollars. But we did not have five hundred dollars, and, besides, it never occurred to us to think of it as a great investment because Pollock and the other abstract expressionists might make it on the art market.

9

THE FORTIES

THOUGH the literary scene changed rapidly, it was not signaled at any time by spectacular events. But as one looks back, the shifts stand out more clearly. This, of course, is the way history converts an invisible process into stages and reduces a network of interacting influences to a few lines of force.

As I have suggested, the forties saw the beginning of the slow shift that was to change everything: values, aims, forms, relation to money, audience, the media, commercial publications, the very idea of what is serious and what is art. One could sum it up by saying it was the beginning of a new romanticism, but this would be too sweeping a generalization unless this process and the terms themselves were defined and documented.

To begin with, new faces appeared on the literary scene, with new visions and aims, and they were more naturally adaptive to—or part of—the changing cultural and political situation. They had only a historical, not a personal, tie to the experience of an earlier period. (In the United States, which has converted the break with history and tradition into a dominant myth, new generations of writers, no matter how traditional some of them may have thought themselves to be, were usually conspicuously different from their predecessors.) Of course, one need not be a Marxist to recognize that modifications in the culture were responding to social transformations. The radicalism of the thirties was played out; even those who still thought of themselves as radicals or socialists were no longer bent on changing the system, but on reevaluating the doctrines and organizational forms of the left—particularly those that led to the tightening of intellectual life where the revolution had succeeded and to its loosening where it had failed. This made not only for a turn in thinking about social change but for a shift from the styles of militancy to those of inquiry and speculation. It was a shift from global and visionary thinking to more skeptical attitudes and more specialized and disciplined studies. And it was bound to be reflected in the changing literary atmosphere of the forties.

In criticism, the center of gravity moved from social criticism to the New Criticism, from a study of the historical context to an analysis of the text. In fiction and poetry, the changes were even more far-reaching. Poetry became more controlled, more ironic, more academic. Fiction introduced more open structures, usually in the form of more straightforward narrative. But probably because I was, myself, so steeped in the attitudes of modernism, I was not aware of the extent to which the modernist idea was being left behind. I certainly did not realize that the age of Joyce and Eliot was coming to an end; and in the pages of the magazine we kept insisting on our commitment to modernism and experiment in literature. What made it hard to understand what was happening was that in painting the shift was concealed by the rise of abstract expressionism, which, as we now can see, represented a delayed reaction of the medium.

Yet we, too, were changing. Not that we succumbed to the popular pressures against "highbrow" art and criticism. But our own emphasis on historicity and rationality and, perhaps even more important, our own unconscious accommodations to the changing scene, led us toward fiction and essays—poetry was more entrenched in its own traditions—that were not popular but were more open and more public in form and language than one associates with the aesthetic of modernism. That we were in a new era should have been evident from the variety and strength as well as the distinction of the writers.

Among those we published were Saul Bellow, Bernard Malamud, Mary McCarthy, Elizabeth Hardwick, James T. Farrell, Jean Paul Sartre, Flannery O'Connor, Delmore Schwartz, Isaac Rosenfeld, Paul Bowles, Paul Goodman, Eleanor Clark, Ignazio Silone. It was indeed a new creative tide.

But they were not Joyce, or Beckett, or Kafka. In this sense, we, too, were contributing to the ethos of that era, whose dominant form in fiction was the social novel, the novel of manners, and which represented at least a partial return to earlier ideas of narrative continuity and social panorama. I am not suggesting that the new writing had anything to do with mass taste; on the contrary, it was distinguished by its treatment of ideas as natural components of fiction. But it did help to foster the conception—or the myth—that the gap between what was known as serious or "high" art and popular or "middle" art was being narrowed.

In fact, the whole tone of the magazine, and the loosely formed movement it represented, with its cultural and political concerns and its belief in rational and systematic analysis, was a departure from the avant-garde styles of the twenties and early thirties. One has only to think of magazines like *transition, Broom, Pagany,* and of the surrealists and dadaists, to realize that their irrationality, eccentricity, dedication to language and experiment and commitment to spontaneity had been supplanted by a broader, more sober perspective that attempted to reconcile the tradition of modernism with a sense of history, with an awareness of the entire culture, and with a feeling for the bizarre quality of individual lives. Obviously, anything like a celebration of the "revolution of the word," for example—one of the slogans of the group around *transition* and other little magazines of the twenties and early thirties—would seem outdated in such an intellectual atmosphere.

As I have suggested, we were occupying a kind of aesthetic and political middle ground—a position, to put it in its most favorable light, that seemed at the time to represent the only mode of continuing the traditions of modernism in the new intellectual climate. To have done anything else would have meant, I believe, to swing to either of two cultural extremes: that is, to an updated academicism that pretended the past was still alive, or to a concealed commercialization of the culture that rationalized and masked its true meaning in an aes-

thetic of democracy. One could not then conceive how far the drift to
a reconciliation with the culture of Madison Avenue would go, for all
these trends were still in their infancy. But some of the signs were
visible in the attacks on "elitism," "snobbery," "the cult of small
audiences," "esoteric writing," "incomprehensibility," "social irresponsibility," etc. One of the more dramatic turns was that of Van
Wyck Brooks, who certainly had not been a darling of the media, in
his high-minded disapproval of what he called "coterie" literature.
Partisan Review naturally responded, with all the righteousness and
aesthetic virtue at its command, running a number of pieces excoriat-
ing Brooks for the shallowness of his apostasy—by F. W. Dupee, Allen
Tate, William Carlos Williams, John Crowe Ransome, Henry Miller,
Louise Bogan, James T. Farrell, T. S. Eliot. Another salvo in the same
direction came from Russell Lynes, in a famous piece in *Harper's* in
which he argued that Clement Greenberg and I were the leaders of an
aesthetic movement to deny popular figures and currents a place in
the sacred domain of art. It is usually fruitless to answer such arguments because they rely on a distortion of the issues, but it might be
pointed out that no serious writer or critic has ever, to my knowledge,
advocated a sanctuary for art inhabited by purists and high art cultists,
and closed to fresh political or popular currents. It is a commonplace
of literary history that all art is fed by popular and vulgar strains, but it
does not become them any more than one who eats pizzas becomes a
pizza. Nor is there any question that serious art may reach large as
well as small audiences, especially when it becomes a classic, which
means it has been transformed into a cultural staple, though the
instances of large, authentic audiences have been exaggerated, with
the examples of Dostoevski, Dickens, and Shakespeare being vastly
overworked and used to bolster a false issue. In any event, what is
usually overlooked is the question of money in the expansion of the
literary market, which is played down by those who claim they are
interested only in broadening the cultural base.

Though one could not recognize it at the time, the change in the face
of the culture was foreshadowed in the literary atmosphere following
World War I. The period saw not only the boom in modernism and
experiment of all kinds; it also marked the appearance of serious
writing with a popular touch. Hemingway and Fitzgerald, for
instance, both coming out of a narrower tradition, helped channel

fiction into the larger arena in which writing and publishing flourish today. Fitzgerald, who absorbed the spirit of the new age when he was still at Princeton, was impatient for recognition, money, love, popularity, and headed directly for the big time. And though this is not meant to devalue his achievement, the truth is that Fitzgerald helped bring serious fiction into the middle range of audience appeal. Similarly, Hemingway, despite the fact that he went to school to Gertrude Stein mostly to pare down his prose, though other influences worked to lower the pitch of his rhetoric, brought the novel back to those commonplaces of man's fate that sustained the popular myths about courage, manhood, and honor. Hemingway's neurotic frontiersman, who had to look for women and war to test himself, was a far cry from the Gertrude Stein who tested reality and tradition by reasserting and questioning everything. This is not to deny Hemingway's accomplishments, but to emphasize the cultural forces that even the best writers represent.

Perhaps the strongest elements of *Partisan Review* had been its literary and cultural criticism, with an emphasis, particularly in the forties, on the relation of social questions to matters of text. A small core, which included Rahv and myself, were interested in pursuing whatever seemed of value in the methods and insights that Marxism brought to the arts and incorporating them into the more established traditions of criticism. This meant, of course, abandoning the dogmatic and narrow versions of Marxism in the thirties. It also meant that a historical approach had to take account of the complex and subtle, though narrower, critical work of the conservative modernists, such as Eliot and Richards, and of the New Critics. For what the Marxists had done in fiction to destroy the modernist tradition had its counterpart in their almost total ignoring—or ignorance—of modern achievements in philosophy, criticism, sociology, which were conveniently relegated to bourgeois ideology. I myself had always had trouble reconciling these highly advanced and sophisticated studies with what passed for Marxism in the thirties. I had even spent a summer at the time trying to write a Marxist aesthetic and criticism that would go beyond the standard versions of Marxism popular in that era. But I had to abandon it, and I still have one hundred pages of concocted theory in my files along with other overambitious efforts of my youth, like an unsuccessful play and some unfinished stories. In fact, I do not know of any Marxist work that has incorporated the textual awareness and analytic subtlety of non-Marxist criticism—not even Walter Benjamin, who was the best and most imaginative of the Marxist critics, nor the better of the more orthodox theorists, like Georg Lukacs and Ernst Fischer. Nor has Frederick Jameson, in my opinion, succeeded in bringing Marx and modern criticism together. I think the only viable means of relating radical doctrines to criticism is to add a historical sense to its traditional range of insight and analytic possibilities. And this is precisely the dimension that such critics as Trilling, Schapiro, Howe, Rosenberg, Rahv, and Kazin have brought to criticism. As I have said, the pages of *PR* were open to the best of the New Criticism—a policy that was not simply an expression of open-mindedness and flexibility, but also a belief that criticism moves in many directions and that no one method has a monopoly in the literary market. My own reservations about the value of New Criticism were strong, as were those of other social-minded critics. As the short life of the New Criticism would indicate, it arose out of certain very special literary and social needs of the period. This is not to deny the value—or the brilliance—of many specific studies by critics like Blackmur, Warren, Ransome, and Tate, or the usefulness of their general emphasis on the primacy of the text. But it was clear from the beginning that the theories had their origin in a more classical and anti-impressionist aesthetic, with one foot in the academy, and in a reaction against the social approach that tended to play down the text. Of course, the southern wing of the New Critics had its roots in the ideology of the Old South, but like most conservative ideologies, it could be concealed behind an apparent dismissal of all ideologies— particularly in the de-emphasis of history. Only occasionally did the ideology show clearly, as in some of Allen Tate's writing and in Cleanth Brooks's essay on Hemingway. Thus what we were open to were not the theoretical assumptions of the New Critics, with which we disagreed, but to their careful reading, mostly of poetry, and to the idea that criticism, like fiction and poetry, was a collective effort, evolving through unpredictable combinations of its more speculative and imaginative forms. There are no formulas for creative or critical effort, but it is clearly out of a blend of bias and centrality, of novelty and tradition, that new talent emerges. It is largely a question of balance—a question that becomes problematic in periods when either tradition or originality is overemphasized. And though there are no preventive measures nor any cures in creative matters, one does note that the talents that survive the artificial stimulation of fashion and publicity are those that are both original and traditional.

Some critics, like Hilton Kramer, for example, have charged that the literary achievements of the forties and fifties have been played down by those who argue that this was a conservative period and by those who complain about the quality of the culture. Kramer is right. There is no necessary connection between the political complexion of a period and its creative output, and it is true that there was a dazzling display of virtuosity at that time.

Obviously, a period that produced such writers of fiction as Malamud, Bellow, Warren, Ellison, Baldwin, Mailer, Doris Lessing, Camus, McCarthy, Roth, Schwartz, Orwell, Faulkner, Welty, Flannery O'Connor; such poets as Lowell, Ashbery, Ginsberg, Agee, Hollander; social and literary critics like Arendt, Jarrell, Fiedler, Trilling, Blackmur, Howe, Kazin, Harrington, Greenberg, Goodman, Podhoretz, Marcus, Sartre, Lichtheim, Hardwick—a time that produced such figures, to mention only some of the outstanding talents, could scarcely be said to be lacking in fertility. Indeed the distinctive character of the period lay in its multiplicity of talent, and although my colleagues and I on *Partisan Review* continued to act as if we were adapting old attitudes to new circumstances, the fact is that it was the beginning of a new pluralistic era. For what the thirties buried was not only the earlier concept of art as bohemian, anti-bourgeois, experimental, playful, committed to the medium, limited in audience appeal, and certainly not tuned in to the market; what it put an end to, also, was the idea of a monolithic tradition and accepted standards, even though the official burial did not take place until the sixties. Although an idea like Leavis's version of the "great tradition of the novel," which was limited to Jane Austen, George Eliot, Henry James, Joseph Conrad, and D. H. Lawrence, was considered to be too parochial by those of us who had been brought up on the great European novel and looked to Joyce, Mann, Proust, Kafka, and Dostoevski as the towering figures of modern fiction, still the idea itself, of a dominant tradition, had not been thought to be absurd. And T. S. Eliot's conception of the relation of tradition to individual talent actually defined the prevailing assumption about the relation between the two; for while original work, according to Eliot, modified tradition, it did not destroy it. In fact, by changing the past, it was possible to preserve it. It was assumed by most writers and critics that, as Eliot said, one had the art of the past in one's bones, which meant that definitions of quality, form, and meaning are derived from the history of art. This does not close the door on new art, as some of the extreme advocates of novelty claim, but it does suggest that unless there is some way of judging the new art, any innovation can demand immunity from criticism.

But beginning with the forties, there has been a steady decentralization of art and an erosion of the very idea of tradition itself. In addition, a number of liberation movements have sprung up, with competing claims but with the common assumption that they represent a break with the traditions and criteria of the past and are not to be judged by them. Who could have predicted a black or a feminine or a gay aesthetic—or the general proliferation of causes and currents, with so wide a variety of style and substance that the very concept of tradition has been seen as an academic category and no longer an active principle of creative work? And criticism, which is at its best when it is rooted in actual art being produced, has tended to become largely theoretical and frequently irrelevant to the art of the time. Earlier, even the seemingly academic New Critics were connected with a certain kind of poetry, a poetry that cloaked its sense of order and impersonality in a reaction against romanticism and an affinity with the English poets of the seventeenth century. On the other hand, the work of critics today like Harold Bloom, Geoffrey Hartman, Northrop Frye, or the deconstructionists has more to do with the study than the production of literature and is connected with the literary scene only in the sense that Bloom and Hartman reflect— quite indirectly—the new romantic revival, while Frye is an expression of the scientism of the social sciences that has infected some critical thought. The new structuralists and deconstructionists are even more remote from the immediate concerns of writing.

Perhaps the most interesting aspect of the shifts from the thirties to the present, and one of the most difficult to sort out and assess, is the enormous variety of artistic personalities that have emerged since the forties. Perhaps the past spreads a cloak of homogeneity, or apparent homogeneity, over its artists; in looking back, we see affinities, correspondences, and influences. But the present certainly does look much more diversified and more chaotic than earlier periods. Perhaps we are not distant enough from our own experience, so that, by comparison, earlier figures seem like lonely, giant statues, dominating their time. Perhaps because contemporary writers lack the aura of classics, they seem so much more familiar and accessible; and because we see them close up, we are as much aware of their blemishes as of the enormous variety of styles and imagination. There are those, of course, who put a premium on this kind of diversity and give it a theoretical halo by calling it the new pluralism—a term, by the way, that has honorific connotations in a country that plays up the idea, if not always the substance, of democracy.

In a sense, the forties may have been the most productive and most serious of recent decades. There was a feeling around *Partisan Review* of a fresh beginning, of a kind of minor renascence, as new American writers were brought together with European writers who also seemed to be part of a new ethos. Existentialism (later in the decade), neo-Marxism, anti-Stalinism, the flight from ideology here and abroad, were mingled and transcended in a spirit of exploration and discovery that went beyond doctrinal origins and allegiances. As in all fertile periods, writing exploded its ideological bonds. Yet, despite the spirit of change in the air, many of us still believed in the idea of a literary community (buoyed by purely intellectual ambitions) free from commercialism, the manufacture of celebrities, and the inflation of reputations. Occasionally a new talent would leapfrog into the mass magazines, but usually he would have to begin, at least, in a noncommercial literary review. Thus it was a time when such writers as Bellow, Malamud, Lowell, Berryman would find their natural habitat and audience in publications like *Partisan Review*. Similarly, serious novelists and literary and social critics abroad like Sartre, Camus, Orwell, Koestler, Spender, Connolly, Aron published much of their early work in this country in the pages of *Partisan Review*.

10

A CHARMED CIRCLE

I did not meet the Europeans until after the war when the first contingent came here and when I went to Europe in 1949. But two Americans, H. J. Kaplan and Nicola Chiaromonte, served as links to Europe. H. J. Kaplan or Kappy, as he was called, was one of the most congenial, good-natured writers I have known, with a quick wit and without the usual acidity or malevolence. His early work was impressive, and I think it was unfortunate that he permitted his psychological and economic needs to take him away from writing into the more immediately gratifying career of a successful State Department middle-rank officer. His talents seemed to have been overpowered by his more worldly abilities and his Francophilia. He was also indirectly and innocently involved in one of the most bizarre incidents in my life, a momentary encounter with the CIA.

In the winter of 1949 I went to Paris with Edna for several months. As I recall, we were guests at a luncheon given by the American Embassy. The lunch went on for hours, but it did not take long for everybody's tongue to be loosened by the flow of whiskey and wine. One of the embassy people told Edna at lunch, and me afterward, that he was the head of the CIA for all of Europe and that he would like to talk to me about something. I thought this very odd and certainly an example of very weak security, but who knows what a combination of whiskey and vanity can lead to. Characteristically, I forgot about it for a week, then phoned him, and he asked me to come over to see him as soon as possible. Unfortunately I have forgotten his name, but I cannot forget the very American, long, lean look, slightly on the academic side—I had heard he had been a professor at some eastern college, perhaps Williams.

I arrived at the embassy at the Place de la Concorde where the CIA had an office on the ground floor. Before getting down to business, he complained about the lack of security at the embassy, pointing out that the Russian embassy was shuttered and tightly guarded. "Anybody can see that you came here," he said, forgetting that I had no reason to conceal my movements. After a few minutes of small talk, he suddenly said to me, "How would you like to work for us?"

What, I thought, could he possibly have in mind for me? The idea that I might look like a spy, or was furtive in any way, or seemed to be cut out for the CIA, scared me. But to sound cool I asked matter-of-factly, "Doing what?" They needed somebody, he told me, to pass money to friendly Europeans and he thought I was in a good position to do this, with a ready-made cover as writer and editor who could legitimately be coming to Paris frequently. Without thinking, and with no discussion, I turned down the best—and easiest—job I had ever been offered; surely the work was minimal, in fact it could be done in one's spare time. "Why not?" he asked. All I could think of saying, though I now realize it was all I had to say, was that it was not my line of work.

But, it suddenly occurred to me, I knew somebody who might jump at this golden job offer. I told him about Kappy, who had been so capable that he kept advancing to executive positions that took more of his time and left him less time to write. I agreed to ask Kappy whether he would want to change his job. Again, I forgot about it for a week, when I received an urgent call to see the CIA again. I was given the same recitation about security, but this time he told me that there was a security scare because there had been too many leaks, and he asked me whether I had spoken to Kappy or anyone else. I told him I had forgotten, and he said to drop the whole business, which I was quite glad to do, since, after my curiosity and excitement had subsided, my feeling of discomfort and of being compromised by anything having to do with secret agencies had come back.

Perhaps the least circumscribed, the least predictable, the most difficult figure to define, was Hannah Arendt. I first met her sometime in the forties, I think at a party given by Schocken Books, where she was working as an editor. She had recently arrived in this country from France, where she had gone from her native Germany, keeping one step ahead of the Nazis. She had difficulties with the language; in fact, for a number of years her understanding of English and her ability to use it were much less than she—or others—seemed to realize. This was most evident when she submitted something she had written and one tried to untangle the meaning from her awkward prose, which had the look of precision one associates with philosophic jargon, particularly with a German flavor, but was actually vague. Perhaps this is the special gift of German thought and writing; I recall the difficulty I once had trying to help "English" some lectures by Max Horkheimer, a leading figure in the Frankfurt school, which he delivered at Columbia University in 1944. I could not tell whether the trouble lay in the German language, the German philosophic tradition, the ambiguity and vagueness inherent in Horkheimer's attempt to reconcile Marx and Freud, or in the quality of Horkheimer's mind and in the usual difficulty of translation, or in my own shortcomings. All I know is that I was constantly struggling not only to find an English equivalent but to figure out what Horkheimer really meant. Hannah Arendt charmingly summed up the difficulties of language when I asked her where she would go if the U.S. were to become fascist. "I would stay right here," she said. "I do not want to learn another language."

Hannah Arendt was also seemingly trying to make sense out of America and its literary intellectuals—something that even native thinkers were not always able to do. But one was immediately struck by her intense alertness, as though she were actually trying to penetrate ideas or people simply by looking through them, which one associated later with the power and the originality, as well as the eccentricity, of her mind. I also remember being impressed by the unusual combination of gentleness and force which, perhaps, was her

105

most distinguishing trait to the end of her life. It was a very strange and seductive combination: firmness of tone and strength of conviction with a soft, almost caressing manner. Even at her most insistent, when she was rejecting an idea or a person and talking louder and more impatiently, her eyes seemed to be smiling benignly. But there was never any doubt where she stood; and anyone who took her on in debate knew he had taken on a heavyweight and usually found out that he was overmatched. She would begin in a low-keyed, pedagogic tone, and in a gravelly voice, "Now listen here," and then go on to demolish her opponent in a mesmerizing combination of persuasion, wit, intellectual authority, and a logic that I can characterize only as a kind of insistent rhetoric.

Hannah Arendt had the quality one thinks of as originality, the ability, that is, to put ideas in a fresh form. Occasionally, this led to quirkiness or one-sidedness, as those with positivist or Marxist leanings, on the one side, and conservatives, on the other, have been quick to point out. But this might be the price one has to pay for originality. And perhaps it is ungenerous to emphasize her shortcomings at a time when so few figures come near the range and depth she strove for in her thinking.

In her personal habits, Hannah could be described as old-fashioned, almost like one's parents, without any of those affectations of style or tastes for luxury cultivated these days by successful intellectuals. Even her apartments looked quaintly European, like the apartment of someone who had not acquired the new American ways of living. (They reminded me of the immigrant look of my parent's house.) Her living rooms were small, and there was no attempt to create any decor beyond coziness and comfort. She lived quietly and modestly and did not go in for flashy or fashionable forms of experience or amusement. Nor did she make a show of gourmet cooking and serving. The last time I had dinner at her house—for about ten or twelve people—the meal was catered, but very simply, and the main course was a filet. She believed in such outdated values as friendship and loyalty, loyalty to a community as well as to people. Not long before she died, I saw Hannah at Lionel Trilling's funeral services. She did not say much, but her hurt and resigned look was a comment on the sadness of the occasion. She was not a close friend of the Trillings; in fact, they had many sharp disagreements. But I assume she felt she should be there out of respect for Lionel and a sense of belonging to the same little world.

Her thinking, however, was a coalition of opposites. She had an uncanny sense of contemporary issues and moods, but she reflected her early philosophical training by going back to traditional subjects and categories. In her basic social outlook, she was anti-Marxist and generally conservative, which led Marxists and pseudo-Marxists to be critical of her political theories. On the other hand, her radical stands on current political questions brought her into conflict with conservatives. And her skeptical attitude to Israel, with whose destiny she did not identify herself as a Jew, offended both professional and amateur partisans of Israel.

So far as I know, there is no balanced analysis of Hannah Arendt's work. My own feeling is that the value of her writing lies not so much in any of her theories as in the texture of her thinking and in the unexpected insights with which she handled those areas in which philosophy, history, and politics cross. Thus I am not sure that Hannah Arendt's theory of totalitarianism will stand up, particularly in its failure to distinguish sufficiently between the differing origins of fascism and Stalinism. But her book on totalitarianism is a very striking illumination of the organized irrationality of the Nazi years in Germany. Her idea of the banality of evil in the study of Eichmann could be questioned, though I think the main issue is a verbal one, involving the use of the term banality in relation to evil. But the description of little men wielding large destructive forces has an enormous suggestive power, particularly for nontotalitarian countries like the United States, where corruption has become almost a way of life and is spread by little people who do not otherwise qualify as monsters. More questionable, in my opinion, are Hannah Arendt's views on revolution and her philosophy of history, which are, in effect, a rejection of Marx's philosophy of history. To be sure, to be a Marxist today is largely an act of faith—often mindless faith, in the more orthodox disciples of Marx—but Hannah Arendt sometimes swung to the other extreme, to a view of history without causality and without any mechanism for social advance beyond human intelligence and moral will.

My own relation with Hannah was warm and friendly if not intimate, except for one interlude of several years, when each of us acted out the role of the hurt and misunderstood victim. It began in 1963 when her book on Eichmann appeared. Lionel Abel called me one day to say he wanted to review the book for *Partisan Review*. He said he liked it and indicated a general sympathy with what Hannah Arendt was doing. So sympathetic did he seem that I said we did not want a puff and that I hoped he would be critical, too. He said yes, of course, and I forgot about it until the piece came in. It turned out to be an essay, not a review, and an assault, not a puff. The gist of Abel's piece was that she was too hard on the Jews for collaborating in their own destruction, and not hard enough on the middle rung of fascist executioners whose guilt was softened by reducing their crimes to the level of banality.

My own feeling was that there was, aside from intellectual differences and animosities, a semantic misunderstanding, perhaps a semantic confusion on Hannah Arendt's part, for it seemed to me what she meant was not that evil was banal, but that people like Eichmann, of whom there are millions all over the world, are little, banal people who, in extreme situations, where their behavior has wide social approval, are drawn into the most barbaric acts. I also thought she exaggerated the possibilities of resistance to the Nazis by the Jews in Germany and Eastern Europe. In any case, the issue was what to do about Abel's piece. I felt it was in many ways a put-down, though some of the things he said were true and certainly fell into the area of legitimate criticism. And there were also personal considerations since both Arendt and Abel were friends. In situations like this, there are no satisfactory solutions. All one can do is to look for some nonexistent middle course that preserves friendship, intellectual integrity, editorial ethics, and some undefined ideal of fairness, and then muddle through the situation while wishing that it had never happened, or that one had been more astute in foreseeing the mess that was bound to follow.

I showed the piece to Hannah, who was upset by it and clearly felt it should not be published. I asked Dwight Macdonald's opinion and he, too, thought *PR* should not print it. This surprised me for Dwight had always stood for free and open controversy, though I should add that Dwight was a friend of Hannah's and no great admirer of Lionel. I tried to get Abel to make the piece more balanced and less strident. But all this time I was under enormous pressure from Philip Rahv, who was still an editor of the magazine though not very active. Rahv did not like Arendt or what he called her conservatism and anti-Jewish bias. And he had on his side, as did Abel, the fact that respectable editorial practice dictated the printing of a commissioned piece unless it was libelous, or personally offensive, or intellectually below the level, or generally beyond the pale.

Admittedly, we were in the middle of a dilemma that had no clear resolution, certainly not to everyone's satisfaction. What was finally done—which was my decision—was to run Abel's piece and then open up the question in a wider discussion. In the next issue Daniel Bell tried to act as a peacemaker by judiciously weighing Abel's arguments against Arendt's thesis and lifting the whole issue to the contradiction between the ideals of justice and humanity and the more immediate questions of guilt and retribution involving the Jewish people.

In the following issue, we published comments by Mary McCarthy, Dwight Macdonald, Marie Syrkin, Irving Howe, Robert Lowell, Harold Weisberg, and myself, with a reply by Abel to his critics. Most of the comments, as I said in my piece, which was cast in the form of a letter to Mary McCarthy who had expressed some doubt about whether I would take a position on the controversy, were clever, some brilliant, but they were too polemical, too busy tripping each other up, to add much to the argument. Syrkin and Weisberg were snarling and sneering, Lowell Olympian and touching in his affection for Hannah, McCarthy brilliant, especially in the writing, and honest in stating her bias, though her division of the protagonists into Jewish and Gentile only fueled the polarization, and Macdonald journalistically sharp and agile, but going along with Mary's arguments. In my piece, I tried to be fair and judicious, but that is a thankless job, especially when extreme positions are fashionable, and it makes one look as though he is avoiding taking a strong stand. (Elizabeth Young-Bruehl's account of this incident in her biography of Arendt is neither full nor correct.)

The only tangible result of the whole controversy was that Hannah and I did not speak to each other for a few years. Hannah felt betrayed by me. And though I tried to explain that my conduct was the only proper one for an editor of a magazine that prided itself on being open to any serious view, and that you could not just kill things that had been commissioned, I could understand her reaction. Indeed, I now feel, as I have said, that our little world was deficient in friendship and loyalty and that objectivity often has been a mask for competitiveness, malice, and polemical zeal—for banal evils. As I recall, we made up when I suggested that we meet and talk about the whole business. We both stuck to our views, but we agreed that there should be a statute of limitations on feuds of this kind, particularly one that arose out of a single incident. We both seemed to feel we were taking the more difficult course in making up, for it was easier to fight than to be friends.

I had known Lionel Abel, the other protagonist in this collision of ideas and personalities, since the early thirties when I was breaking with the Communists and Lionel had already become an oppositionist. I had always thought Lionel was very intelligent and clever and charming in argument and conversation. In fact, he was a great talker, like Harold Rosenberg and Paul Goodman, both of whom would have been much admired in the verbal culture of ancient Greece where they would have been more than a match for Socrates. Lionel also had a bit of perversity in his thinking, sharpening his wit by challenging what other people were thinking and saying, though this adversary quality also often led him to be original in his ideas and his formulations. (Recently, Lionel Abel has become excessively conservative in a way I find hard to understand.) Some memoirs by Abel that have appeared in a few magazines are charming and rich in detail, but they do not always coincide with my own recollections.

Of the writers who came into the sphere of *Partisan Review* at that time, the most enigmatic and, at least on the surface, the most contradictory was James Agee. Jim, as he was called, seemed at the same time the most tortured and the most contented, the most far out and the most conventional, the wildest and the most sensible. Like Delmore Schwartz, for example, he looked and behaved like the accepted prototype of the mythical genius, particularly in the intensity of his writing and talking—indeed, of his entire life. He drank heavily; everyone drank, but Agee was in the top ten; perhaps he was an alcoholic. He had a lanky body, a shaggy head, and a wild, possessed look. The picture of Agee that sticks in my head has him sitting on the floor, surrounded by mesmerized women, talking in a slow, insistent, and prophetic manner—all night if necessary—giving the impression that for him, time and space had been reduced to now and here. He had an enormous physical and intellectual charm, particularly of the kind that is directed toward women by literary men who prefer admirers to disciples.

One incident, I think, suggests the schizoid stability he achieved, a state that enabled him to inhabit with ease the two worlds of American culture, the serious and the chic, which at the time were more distinct than they are now. I was having a drink one afternoon with Agee at a bar on Forty-eighth Street near the offices of *Time*, where he was a senior editor. There was the usual gossip and small talk about big things, and I guess we both felt relaxed, for I asked Agee at one point what he would do if he had plenty of money. He talked about various projects and dreams, some having to do with films, but I noticed that none involved his leaving *Time*, which I had always assumed was, for a writer of Agee's talent, a job, not a profession. "You sound as though you would stay at *Time*; wouldn't you quit?" I asked. "No, of course not," he said. "Why continue to do something you don't have to do?" I asked. "I like writing for *Time*," he said.

Today this identification with *Time* would not seem strange. But then one still thought of the large commercial magazines as off limits. I myself for a short time had written unsigned reviews for *Time*. But I thought of it as a job for money, good money, I should say, and not as another place to write. When I was asked how one wrote in *Time* style, I used to say one stood on one's head. And I was finally fired when I did not welcome the suggestion that Auden's homosexuality, which was then not a public affair, should be brought into a review of his poems I was asked to do. *Time* was then also considering a new book review policy with a house critic who would sign his name, and Lionel Trilling was offered the job. I never could understand why Trilling would even entertain the idea, but it all turned out to be academic, for he did turn it down, and several reviews that he had written for *Time* while negotiating were found unsuitable and were never published.

How good a writer was James Agee? I do not know. The reason, I think, for my uncertainty is that his life had the style but not the accomplishment of genius and it is difficult to disentangle the two. *Let Us Now Praise Famous Men*, the stark Southern documentary, was an arresting work, exotic and offbeat. Agee's verbal and imaginative range was large, and it was augmented by an originality of perception. But it was all dispersed into poetry, reportage, fiction, film, film criticism, and talk, and there was not enough energy or mind to build these into a large body of work. In addition, his energies and concentration were divided between his purely personal output and the more public and commercial demands of the media, and in this sense he might be seen as a forerunner of the writing and the dilemmas of a later period. In some respects, he appears as a smaller and quieter version of Mailer, not only in his divided cultural allegiances, but in his oblique, personalized vision. On a less grand scale he had some of the outrageousness of Mailer, too, as when he wrote a negative review of a play he had not seen. *The New Yorker,* that guardian of intellectual responsibility, slapped him down for his avant-garde disregard for the rules of evidence, and Agee answered with a logic that underlies many large cultural judgments: a logic that says one knows that all kinds of things one has not seen or read are bad.

Two of the most able women who came into our circle at that time were Elizabeth Hardwick and Eleanor Clark: Eleanor in the late thirties, Elizabeth later. I knew Eleanor Clark better. She was temperamentally not disposed to consider herself part of a group and thought of herself primarily as a writer of fiction. Though she had literary and political opinions and wrote occasional reviews, she usually presented herself as someone whose main dialogue was with her own experience. She also felt herself outside the intense verbal and intellectual atmosphere of New York and had a distaste for the malicious gossip and infighting that was often associated with the overheated air of intellectual life in New York. Although Eleanor sometimes overemphasized the creative side of her personality, she had the grace and style of a natural writer—the surest sign being that the craft is never visible. Her fiction, as well as her nonfiction writing, is distinguished by a lack of pretension and the complete mastery of the subject and the medium.

Eleanor Clark's person was almost the opposite of her writing. She was tall, athletic (a good tennis player), extraordinarily handsome, with an outdoor complexion, Nordic blond hair, a hearty, good humor, and an air of robust, country health.

Elizabeth Hardwick was a writer of fiction, too, but perhaps because she came from the oral culture of the South she found herself at home in the verbal, cosmopolitan culture of New York. Articulate, witty, very clever, freewheeling, she became a master of the slashing critical style of the politicized literary intellectuals, though lately her writing has become more discursive and allusive. She was one of our more cutting minds, and she made us aware of our faults as well as our virtues.

Our faults? The truth is that the sophisticated, sharp-eyed, and skeptical intelligence that contributed to the high level of critical thinking was accompanied by a super-rationalism, a competitiveness, an intellectual hardness, and an indifference to loyalty that was humanly destructive. This intellectual style also tended to feed on itself and to exclude other forms of thinking and sensibility. I suppose that all of us who accepted the rules of the game bear some responsibility even though many of us did not like them. No doubt there were gradations of responsibility, which are not easy to measure and which we can all hide behind.

Elizabeth Hardwick was, from the beginning, an excellent critic, acute, wide-ranging, alert both to texture and to meaning, politically sophisticated, and aware of the social dimensions of literature. Recently, in turning her critical sense to the overworked, overheated, and oversimplified question of women in literature, she has produced in *Seduction and Betrayal* what is in my opinion, one of the best works on the subject.

Elizabeth appears never to have changed. She has always been thin, wiry, and flexible as a Calder mobile, quick and nervous in all her movements. A marvelous talker, she has usually managed—like the English—to be charming even when most devastating or malicious.

Irving Howe first appeared in the magazine in 1946 with a review of Sholem Aleichem's *The Old Country*. But I recall him more distinctly shortly after, when he wrote a piece on Sherwood Anderson.

113

He came to the office, which was then on Broadway, and we sat for a couple of hours going over his piece. He was still a Trotskyite but was at the beginning of his dual career as literary critic and political writer. At that time, Howe had the drive and sense of purpose that became even more marked later, but unlike the young authors who worked on their egos as much as their writing, he also seemed modest, flexible, and reasonable. He had a quick and responsive intelligence, but it was distinguished from that of many other writers by the fact that it was not morose or brooding. Both his thinking and his personality were those of a supreme rationalist, which, I believe, has been the outstanding quality of his political and critical writing, giving all his work— and his political stands, too—an air of sanity. And though he has veered politically a number of times, from left to right and back— who has not?—he has rarely gone to extremes, nor has he taken wild or eccentric stands.

We have, of course, often disagreed, usually when he has zigged while I zagged. In the fifties, for example, we published a piece by him questioning what he thought was our accommodation to the conservative atmosphere of the time, his criticism coming mostly from the viewpoint of an earlier radicalism. Howe was not entirely wrong in noting a shift, but I naturally was made uneasy by his invoking the moral spirit of our common radical heritage. Of course, I justified my position—or was it a rationalization—by thinking that we were in a new era and that the old solutions did not fit the new problems. In the sixties, however, Howe had swung right and I had swung left. This time it seemed to me that Howe was too critical of the counterculture. Granted that it exceeded the normal quota of radical foolishness and fashionability, it was not all of a piece, though I might have overrated its idealist spirit and some of its individual talents. Still, minor differences aside, Irving Howe is certainly a first-rate critic and intellectual historian, among the two or three best, and one of the few political observers who have retained a sense of proportion at a time when most of us have had trouble keeping our footing. He has been a leading figure in that dwindling group with common assumptions.

Another important critic in our shrinking literary world has been Alfred Kazin, whose learning and freewheeling, almost lyrical prose one must envy. Kazin first appeared in the magazine in 1940 with a piece on Van Wyck Brooks. I met him a few years later, as I remember, over a drink in the Village, and our first meeting turned into our first disagreement. Alfred said he had just heard a work of Beethoven, opus 132 or 133, he said, as I recall, and it was so great it made his belly turn to water, which, I suppose, was his way of rejecting pompous aesthetic theories, and indicating that he was responding to Beethoven, not repeating the encomiums of academic critics. I assume the abrasive and difficult side of myself did not make things easier when I said, "If your belly turns to water, you are not listening properly to the music." Besides, I was in my stern, antiromantic, modernist phase, under the influence of T. S. Eliot and T. E. Hulme, and looking for system and objectivity in thinking about everything, including the arts. My temperament is at the opposite pole from Alfred's, and my stubbornness and prejudices have been at least as strong as his. But I have always regarded Kazin as one of our leading critics and literary historians. Tough-minded critics sometimes have found his work too lush, too romantic, and occasionally too willful, but his highly personal approach is also his strength, for he relies more on literary values than method, on insight more than generalization, and thus he has managed to avoid both the parochialism and the one-sidedness of the textualists and the self-indulgent speculations of the critics who ride a theory or ideology. Like Wilson, Trilling, and Howe, Kazin has to be defined as a social critic of literature. But more than any of them, he often has been an enthusiastic critic, which enlarges and makes very attractive the figures of writers he likes.

I first met Ralph Ellison in Catherine Carver's apartment in the forties. It was before he had published *The Invisible Man,* but it was clear he had the mind of a gifted writer. Catherine Carver was the managing editor of *Partisan Review,* which meant, at the time, that she was responsible for everything from editing to business operations. She was a superb worker, quick, bright, energetic, and endowed with literary taste. If she had one fault, it was that like the English who had contempt for trade, she did not like to devote herself to things having to do with money. (She once threw out some manuscripts by famous writers—presumably because their value lay not in the paper but in the text.) She lived in a cold-water flat on the top floor of a walk-up on Bedford Street. That evening, there was just Katie, as we called her, Ralph, Edna, and I. After some preliminary small talk, we soon got to the question of black life and experience as though we were drawn irresistibly to a subject we had decided to avoid. Edna kept kicking me and giving me eye signals to change the delicate subject, but we were like missiles that had been programmed for their target. And, I must say, Ralph talked as though the subject were on the top of his mind, making no effort to switch to anything else. Ralph was in the position—a difficult but honest and intelligent one—of maintaining the primacy of literary quality over ethnic politics, but, at the same time, he believed and kept insisting that black experience is always distinct from white experience, and always shapes black thinking.

Perhaps I was in a polemical mood, for I immediately asked him how his looking at a baseball game differed from mine. I had in mind, obviously, our common sports—and human—experience. He replied just as quickly that the question of black players, like Jackie Robinson, affected his view of baseball. But how, I asked, about the game itself on the field, isn't that separate from the color of the players. No, he said, color was always present. And though I did not agree, I could not further question the authenticity of his experience, but I did add that I did not think being Jewish entered one's mind at a ball game.

This was long before the idea of a black aesthetic was advanced by black writers, but it is a difficult and serious question that has haunted black and white criticism concerned with black writing. It is, of course, an old problem in a new form, and essentially a political one. It has been posed since the thirties by those Marxists who insist that art expresses class interests and experience and, more recently, has appeared in the claims of the women's movement that female experience is different from male experience and that the art of our civilization is dominated by masculine values.

It seems to me that all these movements—radical, black, and women's—have reduced experience to—and equated it with—its class, ethnic, and sexual origins and have denied the existence of a more general human experience that transcends or transmutes its origins. They have also assumed that the experience, say, of a bourgeois, or a black, or a woman is clear, defined, and recognizable and, furthermore, is not transformed in art or life. If all art and thought were not seen as a complex and mysterious combination, encompassing what is specific in a writer's experience with his view of a larger world, it would be difficult to explain how art travels from one social or intellectual locale to another, or to maintain any criteria for judging works from different countries, periods, experiences, or traditions— which to be sure, is actually denied by the extreme exponents of minority aesthetics.

In 1963, a section of Ellison's new, so far unfinished, novel appeared in *Partisan Review*, one of the few places where any of it was published—and it was very good. He was delighted at the manner of acceptance: he read the piece over the phone to me and I told him I liked it. But in 1964 we were unable to print a part of his book of essays, *Shadow and Act*, because we could not time it before the book came out, and when later on we asked Joseph Frank, who reviewed the book, to make some changes to include a critical discussion of the questions raised by Ellison, our request was misunderstood and the review never appeared.

It seems silly that there should have been a few petty misunderstandings with Ellison, for when he was relaxed, especially over a few drinks or in some congenial situation, Ralph had that great raucous charm, as he told grotesque stories about other writers or about his own youth. And Fanny, his wife, is a marvelously sensitive and observant woman.

It was a charmed circle. But perhaps the most charmed was Saul Bellow, the only one who got as far as a Nobel Prize. He always thought of himself as a maverick, a loner, not a New Yorker; whether this self-image was literary or personal I cannot say, perhaps a bit of both. But we did think of him as part of the new alignment of writers, and there was a good deal of affection and respect for him. As with Trilling, my differences with Bellow tended to be dissolved in the feeling of community and friendship that bound us for many years. Unfortunately, in the sixties two critical comments about him appeared in *Partisan Review*, one by Richard Poirier, the other by Morris Dickstein. At the time I felt such criticism need not be unfriendly, but as I look back there appears to be a conflict between literary sympathy and adverse criticism. I now feel the claims of community and loyalty to the history of the magazine may be more important than an abstract principle of objectivity.

We met about the time his first story, "The Mexican General," appeared in *Partisan Review* in 1942. Here was a fresh talent, exhibiting a remarkable control of tone and subject. The early work of a critic is usually more revealing than that of a fiction writer or poet, for judgment and sophistication in handling ideas are not hard to spot. But if a writer's destiny can be seen at all in his early work, I can say only that Bellow's first stories appeared to be masterly rather than spectacular—which, of course, was to his credit. They had a sure touch and an easy complexity.

On the whole, however, I felt that the writers coming up in the forties and associated with *Partisan Review* had a marginal quality. I still thought of America as having two cultures, and we were the other culture. The dominant culture of the country was staffed by the Salingers and the Wouks and supported by the media, the popular and the middle-minded magazines, and the book clubs. I never thought that the rebel and maverick writers of the time would become the mainstream of culture, at least the serious part of the mainstream. In fact, I—and the group around *Partisan Review*— probably underestimated the stature of the writers we grew up with, partly because one tends to underrate the members of one's family, partly because they did not have the mythic aura of earlier generations. Thus it never occurred to me to think of my contemporaries as being on the same plane as our predecessors.

However, Bellow must have had early on a strong sense of being set apart. I recall once when he was visiting us for a weekend at our summer place in New Jersey, we were sitting outside, talking, and our landlord who lived next door began to mow the lawn. The noise of the mower interfered with our conversation each time it came close to us, as it moved in a narrowing circle. Saul became irritated and said quite matter-of-factly to me that we should tell my landlord to stop mowing: it simply did not occur to him that we might move. I also have frequently felt that the existence of other people interferes with my existence, but have been reminded of the elite assumption behind such a feeling so that I usually try to divert it by expressing it ironically. However, I can only admire and envy the assertion of one's being—when it is justified.

118

A Charmed Circle

Two other incidents illustrate Bellow's sense of himself. At the end of 1948, just before I left for Europe for a few months, Bellow sent in a story, "A Sermon by Dr. Pep." I had read it and liked it, but in the confusion and anxiety of my first trip abroad I had forgotten that I had read it. Bellow was living in Paris at the time, and shortly after I arrived he asked me what I thought of the story. I told him I had not had a chance to read it but would do so as soon as I could. When I picked up the story again, I realized I had read it, and told Bellow I had seen it and liked it. He was surprised—perhaps properly—that I had forgotten.

The other incident was more complex. I was having lunch with Bellow in a dairy restaurant on Fourth Avenue and Fifteenth Street, near the *Partisan Review* office. Bellow was complaining about a review of *The Adventures of Augie March* by Norman Podhoretz in *Commentary,* in which Podhoretz said, among other things, that Bellow was not as good as Balzac or Dickens. Bellow was disturbed by what he thought was a put-down, and nothing I could say could convince him that to say he, a young writer, was not yet as good as the classics was high praise.

Saul's reserve sometimes seemed self-protective, as though he were not sure of one's regard for him and was set to ward off any unfavorable opinion. At the same time, he was cocky and self-assured, almost relaxed, which might have been the other side of his person. But except for occasional episodes of suspicion, when he questioned someone's loyalty or attitude toward his work, Saul was extremely sweet and gentle, and, when he felt at home, extraordinarily charming. Even his egocentricity added to his charms. Unlike the egocentricity of someone like Delmore Schwartz, for example, Bellow's self-absorption did not ordinarily take a cranky or ugly form. He was also extremely handsome, with soft, large eyes and long lashes, giving focus to a soft, quizzical look that was not entirely lost on women.

As for Bellow's fiction, one might prefer the earlier to the later fiction, but he is a writer of major stature. Even in his first stories it was apparent that Bellow was one of the few novelists who could fictionalize ideas and who could steer a course between experiment and narrative tradition. Earlier works like *Dangling Man* and *Seize the Day* and *The Adventures of Augie March* had a natural combination of a unique, against-the-grain mode of perception and a command of

119

the medium that found its distinctive tone, a tone that transcends problems of form and substance and is usually the mark of a superior writer. There was also a sense of having let the story take the author wherever it led. However, in *Mr. Sammler's Planet*, a more recent work, one feels that Bellow's beliefs occasionally act as a brake on his fictional instincts. Even though I myself agree with many of Bellow's views, I feel our time is too complex for ideological certainties, particularly in fiction. In any case, Bellow at his best has been marvelously sensitive to the ironies of existence, as in, for example, his masterful portraits and scenes in *The Adventures of Augie March*, with their intriguing combination of comic exaggeration and faithful observation.

11

EUROPEAN CONNECTIONS

THE forties, as I have suggested, marked a turning point for both politics and literature. It was a time of conversion, deconversion, apostasy, enormous shifting of belief, and, particularly for those who had been associated with *Partisan Review*, a time of intellectual and personal crisis.

World War II was the force that catalyzed many of the incipient tendencies of the period. The reaction against the Soviet Union, and, later, against all forms of communism, was accelerated by the nationalist impulses aroused by the war. To be a Leninist one had to cultivate an indifference to the fate of one's own country, if not an actual desire for its defeat in a war, as Lenin did in World War I, and only the most Moscow-bound or totally disoriented radicals could be untroubled by such a prospect. (The Communists, it will be recalled, were anti-American and anti-war at the time of the Nazi-Soviet pact, and pro-war before and after.) But those of us who had a radical heritage and were both anti-Communist and anti-fascist had a difficult time adjusting to the new situation. We were still under the influence of Marxist doctrine, which held that wars of the West were fought for economic not moral reasons, and we were suspicious of American motives for waging war against Japan, Germany, and Italy. At the same time, though information about Nazi extermination camps was meager and cloudy, it was becoming clear that World War II was not a rerun of World War I, for fascism posed political threats to human freedom that gave another dimension to the war beyond the ordinary rivalry between capitalist countries. At the same time, the issue was even further complicated by the fact that our ally, the Soviet Union, was also totalitarian, which made the official propaganda that the war was being fought for democracy as suspect as that of the other war, World War I, which also had been fought to make the world safe for democracy. It was one of those muddy situations where clear-cut support of the war or clear-cut opposition was not completely viable theoretically. As in all predicaments where it was necessary to compromise or adopt a lesser-evil policy, one had to act before resolving all the tangled political problems.

To demonstrate that we were still the captives of theory, we published a debate on the subject between Clement Greenberg and Dwight Macdonald on the one side and Philip Rahv on the other. Greenberg and Macdonald maintained, in general, the traditional revolutionary anti-war position, while Rahv argued that Hitler had to be defeated. I still do not know whether it was to my credit or discredit that I stayed out of the controversy, at least publicly, for I was torn and could not resolve the issue satisfactorily in my own mind. My sympathies were with the anti-fascist, pro-war view, if only on a human, practical basis, but I was also conscious of the pitfalls of out-and-out support of the war and it seemed obvious that after the downfall of Hitler all the old social problems would remain, plus the new ones posed by the Soviet Union. As I look back, I realize that in the abstract terms in which the issue was posed both views were right, and that the answer was some kind of critical support of the war to destroy Hitler, which would have satisfied both sides of the political dilemma. The trouble is that the formula of critical support is an idle gesture, designed only to soothe one's political conscience, unless there is a large movement to enforce the criticism as well as the support.

The fact is that our hatred of Hitler and our concern for civil liberties and for the fate of the Jews made most of us passive if not

122

active supporters of the war. We were indecisive because we did not take in the full meaning of the Holocaust. Irving Howe, who has recently reminded me of the meager attention we paid to the Holocaust, regards this lapse as a serious instance of moral failure on our part. This may be. As I recall, the information we had about the Jews was spotty and not always clear. But the main reason for our inadequate response lay in our politics. It is not that we did not react but that our feelings lay outside the boundaries of our political thinking, and we could not easily fit them in. Though we were no longer orthodox Marxists, we tended to understand events in terms of the historic categories we had inherited from Marxism. Genocide and the totalitarianism of the right, however, were new phenomena. We understood the totalitarianism of the left in the Soviet Union, but, we still tended to think of fascism as a desperate and extreme form of capitalism. In any event, the Holocaust was too overwhelming in its horror to be written about in the old political terms. It was a colossal disaster, a monstrous human act, not another symptom of reaction. At least at the beginning, it was primarily something we had to know more about and learn how to digest.

The fact is we did not oppose the war. And this political act, for it was a decisive political act, had far-reaching consequences. It meant the end of traditional radicalism, particularly of the Marxist or Trotskyist variety, which was predicated on the pure idea of internationalism. And it opened the door to the legitimization of nationalist feelings and doctrines, both in the advanced and the "retarded" countries, and to the sanctification of ethnic feelings and aspirations. Old-fashioned Marxism no longer worked, but the new profusion of political creeds was no better: it has brought us to our present state of ideological confusion in which any notion, conventional or crackpot, can find some justification and rationalization.

The new nationalism was worldwide and took different forms: for example, in Asia and Africa it became dictatorial and violent; in France the resistance to fascism reinforced traditional French patriotism. In the United States the new sense of belonging to one's country, which was fed by a combination of anti-fascism and anti-Communism, was accompanied by the removal of traditional barriers and distinctions. It was as though the abandonment of radical positions left all cultural and political questions wide open. As Dostoevski had

Ivan Karamazov say, "If God does not exist, then anything is possible."

But this is all history, all in retrospect. At the time, we were conscious mostly of opening new horizons. One of the first and most important infusions was a new awareness of Europe, literary and intellectual Europe, which had been closed off by the war. The revival of a literary internationalism was also probably a compensation for the destruction of political internationalism. We had been hearing things about the new philosophy of existentialism abroad, about the writers involved in the resistance movement, particularly in France, about such new literary figures as Sartre and Camus, and a number of lesser but interesting poets, novelists, and critics. It was not until a few years later that I met these writers. But in the spring of 1946 *Partisan Review* put out a special issue devoted to new French writing. H. J. Kaplan, who was already in Paris, was responsible for collecting and selecting much of the material in the issue. The opening piece was a long essay on "French Literature since 1940," by Claude-Edmund Magny, the noted French critic and literary historian, and there were representative contributions by Sartre, Malraux, Genet, Camus, Paulhan, Gracq, Queneau, Char, Leiris, Michaux, and others. This was a gala presentation of what looked to us like a French renascence in letters. But it also marked the beginning of a continuing friction and irritation on the part of Sartre, Simone de Beauvoir, and their followers. For in this issue William Barrett, in an examination of Sartre's philosophy, fiction, politics, and literary criticism, found flaws in all of them, though he acknowledged the scale of Sartre's talent and achievement. Barrett was particularly critical of Sartre's naive assessment of the role of the Soviet Union and the Communist party of France.

Simone de Beauvoir came to New York in the spring of 1946. Despite political differences, we were excited by the prospect of seeing writers from abroad as though they were lost relatives rescued from the war. However, I had not anticipated the naiveté of de Beauvoir's pro-Soviet and anti-American attitudes. I had expected Sartre and de Beauvoir to be less critical of the Communists because they had collaborated with them in the resistance and because the Communists were a mass party the French had to take seriously. But I had thought the disagreements would be on some sophisticated and informed level, and I certainly did not expect Simone de Beauvoir to sound like the most simple-minded fellow-traveler. An intimate friend and confidant of Sartre, the guru of French thought, herself a trained philosopher, fiction writer, essayist, advanced feminist—how could this cultivated and renowned figure not know what any knowledgeable American intellectual knew? After the first flush of greetings and questions about France, we got down to basics. She delivered herself, without any of the shyness or reserve of a stranger in a foreign land, of her opinions on America and American literature. She was an admirer of John Steinbeck, pronounced Jean Steinbéck, with an accent over the "beck," who, she thought, gave a true picture and was properly critical of the miserable state of the American working class. She also admired a book called, *They Shot Horses, Don't They*, by Horace McCoy (an almost unknown book made into a movie years later), for reasons I have not been able to fathom, unless she thought it, too, gave a true, critical picture of life in America. And, of course, she respected Upton Sinclair, who also, in books like *The Jungle*, exposed the exploitation of workers and minorities, and Sinclair Lewis, another realistic critic of American mores. Some famous writers, like Faulkner, she was aware of but did not really know their works; others, like Robert Frost, Wallace Stevens, W. C. Williams, Robert Penn Warren, she had never heard of; and Trilling, McCarthy, Lowell, Schwartz might just as well have been Eskimos for all she knew about them. To some extent her ignorance of American writing reflected the chauvinism and parochialism of the French, who regarded the rest of the world as an intellectual colony of France. But one expected more of presumably internationally minded people, who were existentialists and were influenced by Marxism, and who talked about the problems of the world not in the national but in the international terms one finds in radical circles.

Simone de Beauvoir knew, as any educated Marxist knew, that America was an imperialist country in the death throes of the class struggle and that Russia and the eastern Communist countries represented the forces and hopes of man's liberation. She also knew all about American education, especially that it was class education; and even in this area, where generalities gleaned from fashionable Communist notions in Europe were not enough, she knew that students at Vassar came only from wealthy and privileged families and that ordinary or poor young women could not get in. And she could not be swayed by either arguments or facts.

One of her first questions when I met her was how to get to Canarsie. I said I had never been there and had only the vaguest idea of what subways to take; but why, I asked, did she want to go to Canarsie. To see how the workers live, the workers' quarters, she said. And when I said that there are no workers in Canarsie, that unlike France, there are no workers' quarters in the United States, and that, generally, workers could not be distinguished from the middle class, it was clear that nothing I could say would lead her to abandon the theoretical baggage she had brought with her, which served to prevent her from seeing or hearing anything that did not fit in with it. The only thing that puzzled me was why she picked on Canarsie, not some industrial center like Detroit, for example, and the only explanation I could come up with was that she had read about Canarsie in one of John Dos Passos' early novels. Of course, she wanted to see Harlem, Wall Street, the slums, and where, she asked, did the workers eat. Then she got to the fundamental questions: how fast was reaction growing in this country, could imperialism be controlled, when was the next depression due. Naturally, there were arguments, many of which I stayed out of. Most people were restrained, partly because she was a woman (this was before the women's movement made women equally liable to intellectual abuse), partly because she was a guest, and a distinguished one—but mostly, I think, because people did not believe their ears. As de Beauvoir admitted in a book she wrote later about her American experience, *America Day by Day*, her English was not good and she missed much of what was said. But this did not prevent her from being dogmatic, even truculent, in asserting her opinions and preconceptions. When anyone disagreed with her and tried to explain American writing or politics, she dismissed him as a chauvinist or malcontent, using these words indiscriminately, often as though they were synonymous. Once I went so far as to suggest politely that instead of dispensing her opinions about American culture so freely, she should try first to grasp what American writers had to say about it. If I were to come to France, I said, I would not immediately begin to set French writers straight about French literature, for I would assume that they, too, knew something about it. She looked at me as though I had said something too shocking even to discuss. Another time, on a less lofty plane, I told her she could learn a lot about this country by going to a baseball game. Again she responded with a disdain that put me in my proper place among the unenlightened.

It is hard to say whether her literary or political opinions were more arrogant. Her political attitudes were at least clearer. I could not understand how she could say that American literature was vulgar and shallow and escapist at the same time that she was so enthusiastic about our most hardboiled, "realistic" writing. In the field of politics, however, her assumptions were unmistakable. She talked passionately about the workers, the revolution, capitalism, and Russia. When anyone disagreed with her on politics, she quickly characterized him as a reactionary, imperialist, or a Trotskyite—again, terms she seemed to use interchangeably.

Her remarks on most subjects were couched in a strange mixture of Marxist and existentialist terminology, which sounded like a somewhat simplified version of the fusion of the two strains by her mentor, Jean-Paul Sartre. I also heard her talk a few times about purely philosophical questions, and, while her existentialist leanings represented a profound philosophical tradition, that did not justify the contempt she showed for all analytic and empirical thinking, which she seemed to regard as Anglo-Saxon aberrations. In general, her formulations were quick, facile, almost ready-made, and she often sounded more like a spokesman than the groping, questioning mind one expects of a renowned European thinker. You were forced to suspect the authenticity of her existentialism because she was so glib about it. I once asked her, half-jokingly, what kind of angst she felt most, and she replied, with the heartiness of an athletic woman, that she felt none at all, she was happy and well adjusted, never even missing an hour of sleep. I said nothing, but wondered about the anxiety the Parisian existentialists talked about and what connection it had with the anguish of someone like Kierkegaard.

This was before she left for the grand tour of the country. I assumed—or hoped—that she would slow down in her generalizations about life and letters in America, and that she was enough of a writer to yield somewhat to the testimony of her eyes and ears and to discover that the picture was a little more complex than the stereotype she brought with her. But when she came back to New York it was with the same vested opinions, which she was now able to support with the argument that she had seen it all for herself and that her views were corroborated by people she talked to. Except for one or two she mentions in *America Day by Day* I do not know who these people were, but I have no doubt it was possible to find some for whom reality was a branch of ideology. In her book, she described them as "friends whom I always seemed to have known. I knew they loved jazz, and hated American capitalism, racialism, puritan moralizing, and indeed everything I most detest in America." Some of her friends, she said, told her "We need a depression, then things would change." Others, less optimistic—or, as she puts it, "more thoughtful"— disagreed. "A depression," they said, "would only render the situation worse without rousing the political conscience of the masses. We have had depressions before, and nothing resulted from them. If a new one were threatened, it would only be averted, and once averted it would be forgotten immediately: we are not even ready to learn our lessons." One is reminded that Lenin, who did not play at revolution, once said, in response to someone who asked whether he advocated famine because famine promoted revolution, that Communists did not advocate misery however good it might be for the revolution.

Naturally, her visit went sour, mostly because, I guess, people like myself took her—and maybe ourselves—too seriously. After all, Simone de Beauvoir was charming, and certainly attractive, and even if you do not agree about slave labor camps, that is not all there is to life. Hannah Arendt once chided me for treating de Beauvoir as a thinker instead of a woman. One occasionally flirts with women, she reminded me; one does not only discuss deep questions. I still do not know whether this was a comment on de Beauvoir or me, or on both of us.

I think the whole notion of the responsibility of intellectuals has been worked to death on all sides of the political spectrum. It should be clear by now that the very nature of intellectuals demands that they be erratic, irrational, personal, biased, and, in some respects, irresponsible. And one of the virtues of a democracy is that everyone is free to write nonsense and take the consequences. But since de Beauvoir's book *America Day by Day* was basically a piece of reporting, it asked to be judged on its accuracy and perceptiveness. Her basic thesis was that America is both a spiritual wasteland and a sanctuary of reaction. And it was heading toward fascism, though nobody seemed to care—not the intellectuals, nor the teachers, nor the youth, who were either scared or apathetic.

Some of her observations are worth noting.

Too many people die of heart disease in New York.

Traffic circles are confusing, and fast and drunken driving is a menace (all cars, she thought, go fifty miles an hour on the East River Drive).

The girls' colleges are only for the rich and elite.

Roxbury is an artists' colony.

Blacks are not admitted to Princeton University.

There are signs telling people to grin.

Congress is busy passing antilabor laws, which begin with a purge of black workers.

Fifth Avenue has shops for the "elite" and "democratic shops" for the masses.

She referred to "Jewish beaches" in Connecticut, as distinct from gentile and black beaches. And she noticed that "A good American is never ill, and it is not polite for a stranger to catch cold in New York."

Here are some of her generalizations:

Scotch is the key to America.

Women live in solitude and rarely talk to each other.

American girls pet without being aware of the consequences.

American women are frigid and the men do not know how to make love.

American women are not independent because they do not go on trips alone.

Blacks are free and relaxed, and it is "this relaxation that gives vent to dreaming, emotion, drifting, laughter, things that are ignored by the majority of Americans."

University faculties are dead because they are not opposed to the Marshall Plan.

Women's clothes are uncomfortable and servile.

The country is overrun by psychoanalysts whose sole object is to get people to accommodate themselves to society, especially soldiers returning from war.

Perhaps the high point of the book is in the remark that rare steak, "red and underdone," which she was served in California, "usually scares American puritanism."

This is not to say that there were not a number of accurate observations and criticisms of American life. But the impression of the book as a whole was of some kind of literal-minded fantasy, with just enough semblance of reality to make America seem like a lost planet, recently discovered, a little like the earth, but with its own strange ways.

I have cited de Beauvoir's views at length, not because she was so important to me or the magazine, or to literary life either here or abroad, but because she illustrated so dramatically the intellectual breakdown and polarization that took place in the forties and fifties. I need hardly add that my disagreements with her have not been motivated by any chauvinist desire to defend my country to the bitter end against foreign assaults. It is true, as I have said, that the disaffection with the Soviet Union and the Communist parties, particularly in the United States, was accompanied by a swing to the right. On the other hand, many writers, especially abroad, were frozen into a left stance, not really revolutionary, but compounded of many elements taken mindlessly from the Marxist and liberal traditions, and strongly influenced by Russian theoretical and tactical considerations. In this respect, Europe has been decades behind America, and one can still see vestiges of this mentality.

Many French intellectuals, even those who do not think of themselves as Communist, have certain pat attitudes about America, the revolution, the working class, the Third World, Marxism, the "dialectic," the Soviet Union, the Communist parties. Furthermore, the French have a special problem in reconciling the essentially hardheaded and practical approach of the Marxist heritage with the fanciful ideology and the tortured rhetoric of such fashionable modes of thinking as popular existentialism, structuralism, deconstruction, and the more recent linguistic theories. The French do manage, however, if only on paper, to put all these things together; and one marvels that it seems never to have occurred to them that the old stereotypes and the new concoctions make a bizarre intellectual mixture. But then the French thrive on a verbal culture in which words take the place of ideas, and rhetorical solutions are mistaken for literary, political, or philosophical ones. One has only to hear French thinkers use the word "dialectic," which they have picked up from the Communists though they prefer to think they have inherited it from Hegel, to realize that they regard it as a magic formula that fills in all the gaps in their thinking. (The classic expose of the meaningless way vulgar Marxists use the concept of the dialectic was made by Sidney Hook in the thirties.)

More recently, in addition to the victory of the Socialists, there has been an anti-Communist swing as well as one to the right among many writers in France. There has also been a weaning away from left postures and simplifications, and the general intellectual atmosphere seems to have been transformed.

I met Sartre in Paris in 1949. His English was no better than my French, and by then he seemed to be irritated by the criticism of him in *Partisan Review* and by what he regarded as our reactionary politics, so the exchange was not very open or extensive. We met the first time in the underground bar of the Hotel Royale, which was where Sartre hung out while all the tourists were looking for him at the Flore or the Deux Magots. Simone de Beauvoir, whose English at the time was still only slightly better than my French, acted as interpreter. Sartre was guarded, his remarks to the point but not expansive, like someone being interviewed. But I suppose genius cannot be hidden, for he did not babble or talk nonsense, nor did he go off into foolish theories as he sometimes did in his writing. His talk was meager but always on a high level. I had the feeling, as I often have had while reading him, that unfortunately this extraordinary mind was unduly pressured by the political and intellectual ideas around him, and that, like so many other contemporary figures, he was in the impossible position of trying to go with the revolutionary tide and still maintain his independence and critical sense.

This requires a superhuman juggling act.

After the war, Albert Camus and Arthur Koestler also arrived in New York and, like Simone de Beauvoir, each wanted to meet some American writers. But unlike de Beauvoir and Sartre, neither Camus nor Koestler reflected the fashionable European political and intellectual currents. Camus was very French in his intellectual personality, despite his Algerian and working class origins, but he was too stubborn in his sense of himself and too little of an ideologist to become the kind of spokesman for prevailing currents that Simone de Beauvoir, in her innocence, and Sartre, despite his sophistication, permitted themselves to become. Camus was said to be an existentialist, but he denied this, and there is no reason to read any of his novels or essays as exercises in existentialism, though, obviously, wisps of contemporary thought can be found in his writing. He was naturally influenced by Marxist ideas, but the influence took the form of a radical spirit rather than the popular Communist catch phrases. He collaborated with Sartre during the resistance and for a time after the war, but he broke with him in 1952 over the issue of Soviet concentration camps. There was a strong exchange between Camus and Sartre in Sartre's influential magazine, *Les Temps Modernes*, in which Sartre exhibited his polemical agility but it was evident that Camus' position was clearer and more principled.

In his person, Camus was almost the opposite of Sartre. He was reserved, and though he wrote and talked with a certain controlled facility, he had none of the rhetorical flashiness or the theoretical sweep of Sartre. Sartre was short, odd-looking, one eye out of focus, tense, nervous—a prototype of the intellectual who carries his precocity into middle age. Camus was one of the most charming and impressive men I have met, inordinately handsome, with a combination of sensitiveness and ruggedness, and a suggestion of boldness and adventurousness that must have been most attractive to many women. He was not an ideological talker, and our conversations with him were not notable as an exchange of ideas or theories about Europe or America, or about literature or philosophy. He talked about people and events in a rather personal and casual way, and though he indicated his disagreements, he was not nasty or malicious or self-promoting. One had the feeling that his vanity, which appeared to be enormous, was in his work and in his idea of himself— that is, at the core of his being, not in any aggressive behavior.

Arthur Koestler was something else. When he came here, in the spring of 1948, he was one of those middle-Europeans who had been through it all. He had lived with fascism and Communism, and was an active anti-Communist and anti-fascist. He acted as though he had experienced every political and literary movement of the time—all-knowing, slightly jaded, skeptical. He had the sophisticated air of a cosmopolitan who was not bound by his roots; he was tough, quick, with an uncanny sense of the zeitgeist. He was vain, touchy, and obviously liked to think of himself as attractive.

Koestler had written to us, saying he was coming and wanted to meet us. Rahv and I met him as soon as he arrived, took him to lunch, and spent most of the day with him. His reaction to us was both flattering and depressing, because it revealed again, but from an opposite view, how misinformed the Europeans were about the United States. We were the first people he wanted to see because he thought *Partisan Review* and the writers associated with it were at the center of American culture. He was, of course, projecting from the experience of Europe, where equivalent magazines, like *Les Temps Modernes* for example, were central to the main literary and intellectual currents and an important part of the life of the intelligentsia. And there was not in Europe, as there was in the United States, a fashionable counterculture to create reputations, rewards, and influence for writers who flourished in the commercial world and in the mass media. Hence Koestler overestimated the power of the serious culture here. We were pleased by this elevation of our role but embarrassed, as one naturally is when one's social or literary position is inflated. Nevertheless, we got along well, though we disagreed with many of his views and did not like some of his glib formulations. Despite our differences, we seemed to have a common history and a common language, and it was reassuring to find, as we had always assumed, that we were part of a world outlook and that what separated us from some European writers, particularly among the French, was not our provinciality but theirs.

A few days later we invited some of the people Koestler wanted to meet to a dinner party at my house. It was a small group, including Mary McCarthy, Hannah Arendt, Sidney Hook, Elizabeth Hardwick, Dwight Macdonald, Delmore Schwartz, and William Barrett. As one can imagine, it was a spontaneous piece of theater: everyone was a rhetorical prima donna, a great talker, proud of his wit and eager to display his or her charms. Mary McCarthy was glowing, and I have never seen her so handsome and youthful. She has always had a miraculous ability to rise to an occasion and this time she was alive to all the possibilities of the situation. I do not think she was excited so much by the idea of meeting Koestler, who was not one of her heroes, as she was by the social requirements and expectations of meeting a famous European writer. In fact, one side of Mary, in addition to her strong critical sense, has been her sensitiveness to social propriety, and it is the interplay of these two qualities that usually determines her behavior in social and intellectual situations.

Everyone performed at the top of his or her personality, and the result was a strange combination of confrontations and connections. Koestler, with his flair for drama, particularly for sexual drama, almost immediately made a play for Mary McCarthy. But he had too many bridges to cross. For one thing, he was a tough anti-Communist, and in most matters a confirmed rationalist, while Mary's opposition to Stalinism did not dominate her thinking, and, recently, she had become interested in some aspects of anarchism and in an emphasis on morality in politics. In addition, I had always thought she did not like the brashness and intellectual aggression that in Koestler gave him both his abrasiveness and the kind of charm that assaults one. Koestler, however, either knew or was shrewd enough to discern where Mary's interests lay, and he proceeded to talk about Eastern philosophies, passive resistance, and personal morality as a political force, which was a strain in his thinking, but a minor one. The only trouble was that this brought him into conflict with Sidney Hook, the super-rationalist and hard anti-Communist, who never let social considerations stand in the way of his intellectual principles. They got into a sharp argument—whose ostensible subject was philosophical and political, but whose real subject was Mary McCarthy—which ended unpleasantly when Koestler said to Hook, "I didn't come three thousand miles to hear this nonsense."

For reasons I have never been able to understand, Mary McCarthy and, later, Elizabeth Hardwick, continued to be fascinated by Koestler—unless it was because one had a sense of some perverse, perhaps evil, energy in him, beneath his outrageous and aggressive behavior. His coming to New York was arranged by the International Rescue Committee, for whose benefit he was to give a lecture in Carnegie Hall. There was endless talk about the occasion, as though it were the social triumph of the year—some women discussed constantly what to wear. But Koestler himself treated the whole thing lightly, saying he was not going to prepare anything, in fact he was not even thinking about it. The result reflected his cavalier, almost contemptuous, attitude toward the audience and the occasion. It was a disaster. Koestler stood fidgeting at the center of the stage, pinned down by inescapable floodlights, floundering, not knowing what to say, barely audible. He tried several different tacks, relying mostly on his implacable charm, but it was soon clear that one could not get by so easily, as the tiny figure seemed lost and helpless on the large stage in the vast, terraced hall. The three thousand people who came to hear the message from the author of *Darkness at Noon* felt sorry and embarrassed, but also cheated and angry, that Koestler did not think it necessary to prepare the lecture. For Koestler, it might be said he probably had no idea of the immensity of Carnegie Hall and had never had any trouble talking to smaller groups.

The last time I saw Koestler was in 1949 when Edna and I spent a weekend at his country house, an hour's drive from Paris. It was the weirdest and most disconcerting weekend I have ever spent, and weekends can, at best, be very trying. Weekends, like long plane trips, create their own kind of jet lag between one's normal existence and the intense, claustrophobic feeling of being locked up in something like a continuous cocktail party for three days. To the normal difficulties of a weekend, however, Koestler added a few innovations. There were four other guests besides us: a wealthy industrialist and his wife and a young couple Koestler picked up somewhere. Koestler's wife, Mamaine, was away in a dry climate, for this house, which was on a river, was too damp for her asthma. The first morning, before breakfast, Koestler gathered everyone in the living room and insisted we all have champagne. Now I do not like champagne at any time, but I find its connotations as well as its taste particularly offensive in the morning. So a tug of will began almost immediately. Then we had a buffet breakfast of delicatessen and exotic fish, which I do not care for. After breakfast we played games, the most intellectual one being for each person to tell which painting he would want most with him if he were stuck on an island—a game that permitted each one to exhibit quite effortlessly his bad taste and ignorance of painting. And so on. But what contributed most to the feeling of being cooped up, of having to do everything together, like a group at a middle-class resort led by the social director, was that to move from one room to another one had to be careful to avoid two large boxer dogs who growled and tried to get a piece of your clothing. By the time we left on Sunday evening I was fed up, and Koestler and I were snarling at each other like two dogs. I remember particularly one remark of his, evidently made to explain why he was so polite a host: he said he took advantage of his reputation in only one way, he permitted himself to be rude to people he did not like.

I am not suggesting any specific connection between Koestler's person and his work; obviously, I did not know him well enough for that. All I can say is that I do not like his later ventures into science and psychology as much as his earlier writing. Perhaps his novels will not stand up in the history of fiction, but at the time they seemed superb examples of political and journalistic fiction, very deft and swift, and extraordinarily tuned in to the moods and issues of the times. In this respect, *Darkness at Noon* was especially impressive as a realistic fable about the reasons the old Bolsheviks confessed, though it now appears that the confessions were forced by torture more than by the logic of bolshevism. However, Rubashov's dilemma still has a suggestive, symbolic meaning. Koestler has also been a superb journalist and a forceful essayist. But I think his contribution was mainly in his political influence on the intellectual climate of the thirties and forties, in making people think more sharply about the nature of the Communist movement. In this sense, he was the kind of figure whose meaning comes directly out of the time; and I wonder whether his abandoning the concerns of his early writing and going off into new and more popular subjects is not a tacit recognition on Koestler's part that his earlier career would not have the same impact or meaning today. I suppose there is a perverse lesson in this relation of a writer to his time: namely, that engaged writers, which would include political writers, are less likely to survive changes in the social climate. There are, of course, notable exceptions, like *Uncle Tom's Cabin*, which survived for other than aesthetic reasons, and some of Brecht's work, the literary quality of which, in my opinion, came from energies in Brecht that were in opposition to his professed opinions. Solzhenitsyn is another writer who deals with contemporary political subjects but whose powers as a novelist are so great that they are not reducible to their political content.

136

12

THE BIG TIME

SOME changes in the magazine in the forties were mostly organizational, though they had wider literary and political effects. But the facts have been so distorted by gossip and inaccurate reporting that it seems necessary to tell what happened.

In the summer of 1943, disagreements that Dwight Macdonald had had for some years with Philip Rahv and me came to a head. Dwight was becoming more political and less interested in purely literary matters. He also had been moving toward an anarchist position, one that places morality rather than power at the center of politics, and though Rahv and I were disillusioned with the Communist versions of Marxism and no longer believed in the possibility of socialism in any foreseeable future, still we leaned toward the more rational and systematic analysis of society found in Marx. We had no faith—and, frankly, little patience with—the new interest in left circles in anarchist and moral panaceas as a solution to the problems both of capitalism and of Communist dictatorship. It was understandable that many radicals—like Paul Goodman, Nicola Chiaromonte, Mary McCarthy—who opposed Stalinism but remained on the left would focus on the moral abuses of systems in which power was centralized and wielded arbitrarily by ruling bureaucracies. This was all very nice, and it was intellectually more attractive to talk about purity and decency and community controls than about the difficult questions involved in changing the structure of society. But however appealing the new moral rhetoric may have been, it seemed to me a reversion to the kind of Utopianism that Marx had taught us did not work. If I had learned nothing else, one lesson that I had had drilled into me was that governments or social systems do not feel threatened by moralists who dream of a society without a government. But it is worth noting that Macdonald and McCarthy anticipated the later concerns with political morality when social solutions no longer seemed to work.

In addition, Macdonald seemed to be chafing at the three-editor system, which permitted one to be outvoted. I had the impression that he wanted to run his own magazine. I could not blame him, but his ambitions conflicted with those of Rahv and myself. To resolve the problem, Macdonald proposed one day that we split, and that the magazine should be taken over either by him or by us, depending on who could put up the money to get out the next issue. This suggestion gave Macdonald the advantage as both he and his wife had private incomes, while neither Rahv nor I had any money. We had no choice, however, but to go along with Macdonald's practical solution. So I set out to raise the money. I spoke to Joan Simon, who was working for the magazine at the time, and she offered to contribute five hundred dollars, the sum needed to cover the cost of the next issue. (At the time, Joan did not want it known.) Macdonald seemed surprised when he was told we would be able to take over the magazine, but he accepted his loss graciously.

Macdonald's letter of resignation appeared in the July-August 1943 issue, with a reply by Rahv and myself, and I think it valuable to quote both in full, for the divergences indicated in them represented some of the political divergences that had developed at the time.

Dear Colleagues:
Please accept my resignation from *Partisan Review* effective next issue. Naturally, I regret severing connections with a magazine to which I have given much time and effort. I feel, however, that the

divergence between my conception of the magazine and your own has become too great to be bridged any longer. This divergence is partly cultural: I feel *Partisan Review* has become rather academic, and favor a more informal, disrespectable and chance-taking magazine, with a broader and less exclusively "literary" approach. But the divergence is mainly political.

When we revived *Partisan Review* in 1937, it was as a Marxian socialist cultural magazine. This was what distinguished it from other literary organs like *Southern Review* and *Kenyon Review*, and this orientation, in my opinion, was responsible for much of the magazine's intellectual success. The war, however, has generated sharp political disagreements. Not only has the Marxist position been reduced to a minority of one—myself—but since Pearl Harbor there has been a tendency on the part of some editors to eliminate political discussion entirely. For my part, I have opposed this retreat and I have insisted that precisely because of the urgency of the crisis, social questions should bulk even larger in the magazine. The conflict has reached the point where there remains little of the *esprit de corps* necessary to put out a "little" magazine. I should have liked to carry my viewpoint. This being impossible, I am withdrawing. From now on *Partisan Review* will devote itself to cultural issues, leaving the thorny field of politics to others.

What interests me, however, is a magazine which shall serve as a forum and a rallying-point for such intellectuals as are still concerned with social and political issues. A magazine which, while not ignoring cultural matters, will integrate them with—and, yes, subordinate them to the analysis of those deeper historical trends of which they are an expression. The degeneration of the liberal magazines seems to render this kind of publication important today. I hope it will be possible to launch such a venture this fall.

Finally, I should add that Nancy Macdonald, who has functioned in the demanding capacity of business manager of *Partisan Review* for the greater part of the past five years, is also severing connections with the magazine. Her reasons are about the same as those indicated above, and she will work with me on the new project. Both of us wish the new *Partisan Review* the best of luck.

Sincerely,
DWIGHT MACDONALD

A Partisan View

A Reply:

We naturally regret Macdonald's resignation. We regret even more, though, that Macdonald allowed himself to be carried away by his political passions. What he wanted was to abandon the cultural policy of *PR* and to transform it into a political magazine with literary trimmings. The use of literature as bait is a familiar strategy of left-wing politicians. Having failed, however, to convert the magazine to his special political uses, Macdonald had no alternative but to sever his connections with it.

There is this much to be said, too, that the politics Macdonald stood for were basically Trotskyite—plus a few personal variations, or heresies, if you will. Only in this sense can we take his word for it that he was the sole "Marxist" left on the editorial board. Hence it is rather disingenuous of him to suggest that the issue dividing us is the issue of aestheticism versus a Marxist grasp of "historical trends." No such issue was ever debated. The truth is that Macdonald tended more and more to think of the magazine as an organ of political propaganda; and the more evident it became that the old revolutionary movement is in a state of decline, the more he wanted *PR* to take over its functions. We, on the other hand, have always maintained that no magazine—least of all *PR*, which from its very inception has been edited mainly by literary men—can put itself forward as a substitute for a movement.

We could never agree to "subordinate" art and literature to political interests. It is precisely this sort of disagreement which led, in 1937, to our break with the Stalinists. For it is one thing to introduce the Marxist point of view into the analysis of culture, and something else again to impose it on culture in a total fashion. We all should be impatient these days with those attempting to set up an ideological or any other type of monopoly. Macdonald speaks of the magazine's "intellectual success"; but he shows his bias in ascribing it largely to the Marxist slant rather than to the specific modulation achieved in combining socialist ideas with a varied literary and critical content. This will continue to be the policy of the magazine.

The kind of liveliness ("disrespectable, chance-taking," etc.) that Macdonald appreciates is equally appreciated by all of us. There is no connection, however, between this longed-for liveliness and a sectarian political line, which invariably results in self-righteousness, academic revolutionism, and the incessant repetition of a few choice though all-too-elementary notions. Macdonald's preoccupations made it increasingly difficult for him to find value in writing that offered no excitement to his political sense. True enough, the fate of all of us may depend on political events, but this in no way makes literature less attractive or less meaningful to those of us who respond to it.

We hope Macdonald's new venture will turn out exactly as he wants it. We wish him luck.—The Editors.

Soon after Macdonald's resignation, Delmore Schwartz and William Barrett joined the board as associate editors. Macdonald's new magazine, *Politics*, was lively and informal, very much like Macdonald's own writing, and both its strengths and weaknesses came from its political biases and from Macdonald's large journalistic abilities and instincts. *Partisan Review* continued as a literary and cultural quarterly, which we always conceived of as its primary purpose, but with a political dimension and a concern with social questions.

One day, however, in September, 1947, a letter arrived at the office of the magazine, signed by Allan Dowling, a wealthy man who wrote poetry, asking us whether we would be interested in enlarging the scope and making it a monthly. Dowling said *Partisan Review* was the only magazine that could continue the great tradition of *The Dial*, and he would help out financially to make this possible. We were, of course, elated, but we were not sure it was not a hoax, and we also had all the anxieties aroused by the prospect of unknown changes. For whatever else it meant, such a move suggested that the magazine might leave the territory of the "little, littles," in which poverty was assumed to be a guarantee of purity and where literary magazines were sustained by a community outside the cultural marketplace. We would be entering a world, we feared, dominated by considerations of circulation, publicity, the size of authors' fees, budgets, salaries—all the things taken for granted in commercial publishing. And everything would be speeded up because Dowling wanted *Partisan Review* to become a monthly.

But you do not say no to progress, expansion, financial stability, and the opportunity to pay higher fees. Part of the problem of noncommercial literary magazines—as of most nonprofit cultural activities—

is that in our society they constitute a form of mixed economy. Half a magazine is purely literary, having to do only with questions of quality and cultural importance, and is thus utterly impractical and Utopian; the other half, however, is submerged in business, a losing and not very dynamic business, to be sure. Thus all the machinery of a profitable business is applied to an unprofitable one. In commercial magazines, the confusion of the two realms is normal, for the need for sales and advertising naturally affects the editorial side. In fact, the so-called editorial side is a packaging enterprise in which considerations of quality and those of sales are merged, though editors often maintain, partly out of habit, partly to keep their self-respect, that they publish things only because they are good.

But the drive for quantity is infectious, and little, literary, noncommercial magazines are often bitten by the commercial bug, getting involved in unworkable and costly promotion and distribution schemes that distance them from their literary purposes. Even if some editors are aware of this, still they are under pressure from foundations and individual donors to increase circulation and to erase the deficit. Indeed, the American ethos demands that enterprises worthy of respect must act as though their aim was to make a profit—even when that is palpably impossible.

Some years ago, a large foundation invited several writers and editors to discuss with the directors the problem of financing literary magazines. At one point, one of the directors asked us why we could not make a profit or at least break even. I thought of the character in Dostoevski's *The Possessed,* who, during an argument about the existence of God, said "There must be a God, otherwise how could I be a captain." I was about to say that if noncommercial enterprises, like literary magazines, could make a profit, there would be no job for the directors of the foundation. But I did not feel such a remark would be appreciated. The obvious solution would be for foundations and the government to support completely the leading noncommercial ventures in all fields: the leading operas, theaters, dance groups, museums, literary magazines, etc., instead of the present hit-or-miss policy. This is the practice in many European countries, including the Communist ones. I know there are many arguments against such complete financing, but they all seem spurious—all come down to the

American myth that nonprofit ventures can somehow become self-supporting.

Anyway, being human and children of our time, we jumped at the chance to put out a magazine without constantly worrying about money. For the magazine to come out monthly, we needed a larger office, a bigger staff, and a much faster pace. We figured out how much we needed in our own amateurish fashion—this always led to underestimating expenses and overestimating income—and Dowling agreed to meet the deficit, which came to about forty thousand dollars a year. We moved uptown to Forty-fifth Street and Broadway into a building that Dowling owned. The office was comfortable enough and not too posh, but the neighborhood seemed grotesquely wrong for us, as though to remind us daily that this was not where we belonged. Most incongruous was to see Delmore Schwartz sitting half-dazed and uncoordinated in his own office, like some comic version of a midtown executive, or looking distractedly out of the window at a world as foreign to him as Disneyland. But we did learn to have lunch at Lindy's, with its famous cherry cheesecake, or at some of the sumptuous dairy cafeterias that were still going at that time. We hired a managing editor, an assistant editor for production, a business manager, a secretary, and we were in business. The production editor was Bowden Broadwater, Mary McCarthy's husband at that time. He had a sharp tongue but was very competent and efficient. I have never been very astute in hiring people, but Bowden was by far the best of the staff we chose. The secretary was unusually advanced. One day I discovered that her letters had no capitals, all lowercase, including the addresses on the envelopes. When I told her this was not the usual practice, she said she was using avant-garde punctuation, which she thought appropriate to an avant-garde magazine.

Putting out a monthly, compared to a quarterly, was almost full-time work. We came to the office every day, thought about the magazine constantly, and, as a consequence, had less time to do our own writing.

How good was *Partisan Review* as a monthly? I think it kept its standards while broadening its content. In addition to the writers already associated with the magazine, we published in this period a

A Partisan View

number of new figures who have since become well known, which would seem to indicate that as a monthly the magazine continued its earlier momentum. Because it was possible to pay more for contributions—the munificent sum of two cents a word—and because of the general acceleration, the contents probably had greater variety. We also tried to maintain the earlier polemical spirit, which was one way of relating to and affecting the cultural atmosphere of the time. Clement Greenberg's strong art comments appeared regularly; there were pieces about atonal music by René Leibowitz and Kurt List; and the shifts in the cultural scene were examined in lengthy symposia on "The State of American Writing" and "Religion and the Intellectuals." But the change from a quarterly to a monthly was more than a change of frequency. It is difficult to define the change, but the stepping up of the tempo produced a greater emphasis on topicality, on journalistic interest, and something called readership, which involves both the size and the nature of the audience. A monthly is also usually closer to the world of the commercial publications, not only in content but in a concern with circulation, distribution, promotion, and advertising. The slower pace of a quarterly permits it to be content with publishing things that may not be popular, and to rely on a smaller, devoted audience of writers, teachers, and sophisticated professionals who identify with the aims of the magazine. In this respect, and quite unconsciously and without design, we were moving into another era, one in which both writers and readers were slowly being homogenized into a more general culture, while writers were being divided into those with academic and scholarly interests and those who were adapting to a larger market. This is largely why, in my opinion, so large a gap has developed between the literary magazines, particularly the quarterlies and those devoted mainly to criticism, on the one hand, and the more popular publications like *Esquire, The New Yorker, Harper's,* and *The Atlantic,* on the other. It is also why, today, students of a subject become specialists, leaving the intellectually exciting but risky task of generalizing and polemicizing to the cultural journalists.

There are, of course, other compelling reasons why this has become an age of specialization—not the least of which are the complexity of knowledge and the feeling of helplessness in the face of the overwhelming problems confronting us—but in addition, the academic climate has become conducive to intense work within narrow limits.

144

The Big Time

Partisan Review's life as a monthly lasted three years. It was pleasant, relatively carefree—an intellectual cruise in which you left behind familiar routines and worries and got a glimpse of other worlds. We learned something about Madison Avenue techniques, particularly advertising, promotion, and distribution. And we also learned something about the relation of a literary magazine to its potential audience. We reached a peak of about thirteen or fourteen thousand buyers—readers are calculated differently, for us we figure about ten readers per copy—which probably represented as large a circulation as was possible then without radically changing the contents of the magazine or spending hundreds of thousands of dollars on promotion.

There has been considerable speculation about the maximum readership size for a serious literary and cultural magazine. It seems to me, however, that the question, posed in a simple, abstract form, is a non-question, a belief in size and numbers transformed into a question. For the answer depends largely on the amount of promotion. If we could have spent hundreds of thousands of dollars I do not know how many copies we would have sold, but certainly circulation would have jumped. On the other hand, it would have been thoroughly wasteful and irresponsible, financially justified only by a false analogy with commercial magazines. The economy of commercial magazines is based on the simple principle of buying circulation, which then pays off in increased advertising, which, in turn, depends on the size and exploitability of the circulation.

In 1951, Allan Dowling told us he had to retrench because of his own financial troubles. He was getting out of an expensive marriage and into a divorce from a Bulgarian opera singer. We cut back the magazine to a bimonthly and Dowling scaled down his contribution to twelve thousand dollars for a year. After that he said he could no longer afford even this much, and *Partisan Review* became a quarterly again, moved back downtown, and resumed its old pure and marginal existence. We took a little dark office on the ground floor on West Twelfth Street, reduced our staff to one business and production manager and one secretary, plus occasional volunteers on work-study intermissions from women's colleges. The office was most notable as the place where Saul Bellow met his second wife Sandra, who had come down from Bennington.

13

CULTURAL FREEDOM ABROAD

IN 1949, the American Committee for Cultural Freedom, and in 1950, the Congress for Cultural Freedom (in Europe), were founded. Both organizations have haunted Communists and anti-Communists, and the latter has been revealed to have had CIA connections. I was a member of the American Committee from the beginning, later became a member of the executive board, but had nothing to do organizationally with the Congress, though as one of its critics I was engaged in some controversies with it.

It all started with the staging of a peace conference of writers and some people from the other arts at the Waldorf in April 1949. The auspices and most of the participants were pro-Communist, with official delegates and speakers from the Soviet Union. A few anti-Communist writers—Robert Lowell, Mary McCarthy, Dwight Macdonald, and Jean Malaquais—went to the meeting and tried to talk from the floor, but they did not get very far. As Irving Howe pointed out, in the May 1949 issue of *Partisan Review*, the main speakers included Fadeyev, the Russian literary bureaucrat who headed the Writers' Union, Shostakovich, the composer, who was a cautious and enigmatic figure, and such illustrious Americans as Lillian Hellman; Howard Fast, the novelist who later broke but at that time was one of the faithful; F. O. Matthiessen, whose allegiance to the party baffled everyone; and fellow-travelers like Harlow Shapley, O. John Rogge, and T. O. Thackrey, then editor of *The New York Post*. As Howe observed, the conference had its quota of innocents, fools, and congenital sympathizers. There were some mild, almost ritualistic remarks at the conference about the lack of perfect democracy in Russia, but they were lost in the torrent of praise for the Soviet system, criticism of the United States, and incantations to "peace," which meant nothing more than a recital of the peaceful aims of the Russians and the warlike aims of the Americans.

There were three thousand delegates, but the meeting was totally controlled by the Communists, a feat that is not very difficult.

Anyone who has been involved with Communist organizations, especially from the inside, has seen how the mechanism of control works. To begin with, the participants are carefully chosen to include only those known to be faithful or sympathetic, plus a neutral contingent who create a cover for the inner core and give the impression of a non-stacked meeting but whose history would indicate that they are not likely to challenge the leadership or join an opposition. The inner core that ensures absolute control is, of course, the party faction and people very close to the party.

To counter this big circus for peace and Communist propaganda, a number of writers, including myself, hastily organized another group, called Americans for Intellectual Freedom, which operated from a suite at the Waldorf, to expose the true character and false claims of the Peace Conference. It was my impression that David Dubinsky, who was then the president of the ILGWU, contributed five thousand dollars to cover the cost of the hotel and other expenses. The leading figure, non-elected but by common consent, was Sidney Hook. But the actual on-the-spot activities were conducted by Arnold Beichman, then the public-relations director of an electrical workers' union and later a professor of political science at the University of Massachusetts at Boston, and Merlyn S. Pitzele, the labor editor of *Business Week* at the time. As I recall, Beichman was brought in by others, but I recommended Pitzele who, I thought, was very smart and very competent. I liked Pitzele though he was tough, single-minded, and occasionally ruthless. He was politically sophisticated, but less interested in theory than in practical politics. The campaign, conducted from the little anti-Communist suite at the Waldorf, was fairly effective, although I suspect this was due more to the shabby positions and evasions of the Peace Conference and to the declining intellectual support of the Communist line than to the brilliance of the counteroffensive. The truth is that the operation of the Americans for Intellectual Freedom employed questionable tactics, such as intercepting mail and messages and issuing misleading statements in the name of the conference—tactics that upset all but the most hardened veterans of Communist and anti-Communist organizational fights. Even Sidney Hook, himself not a political virgin, was annoyed at the things done in his name when he became aware of them. Others, like myself, who usually did not know all that was going on, protested strongly but saw no way out of the situation other than to repudiate the entire activity or to recognize the unpalatable political reality that the ones who do the work control the organization. (The Communists used to say that those who ran the mimeograph machine had the power.) I could understand that purists would have nothing to do with this kind of politics, whatever the cause, for it simply reintroduced, on a smaller scale, the Communist principle we all opposed in theory, of the end justifying the means (which, of course, led ultimately to the perversion of the ends). But the alternative appeared at the time to be a complete withdrawal from politics, which, in practice, meant leaving the field open to those who did not abdicate. Today surrendering to the activists appears less Utopian, and since intellectuals often make fools of themselves when they get involved with political organizations it might be presumed that they are more qualified to deal with theoretical and long-term questions.

In the forties, however, I had not gotten the notion of activism out of my system, and I moved, skeptically and critically to be sure, from one organization to the next. The Americans for Intellectual Freedom served as the nucleus for the American Committee for Cultural Freedom, which was formed shortly after, and I soon found myself on the executive board, which, I confess, I did not resist strongly. Organizations, like everything else, tend to fade into the past and in retrospect appear more monolithic and sinister than they really were. Thus the American Committee, because its name sounded like the Congress for Cultural Freedom, and because it did have some connections with the European outfit, has been mistakenly associated with the CIA and has been accused of all kinds of nefarious and reactionary activities. The truth of the matter is that the American Committee, to my knowledge, had no connections with the CIA, had ambiguous and often antagonistic relations with the Congress, and was itself full of internal disagreements. This is not to confer a certificate of purity on the organization, for as I look back it had many questionable aspects. Its aim was to protest all violations of freedom, but it did put more emphasis on the transgressions of the Communists, particularly in Russia and the satellite countries, though that could be justified by the fact that there were many groups defending civil rights and freedoms in the United States and other democratic countries while there were very few concerned with intellectual freedom in the Communist world. It was also true that intellectuals were particularly vulnerable to the kind of apologetics that used the dream of socialism to play down the persecution of dissidents.

Despite the steady barrage of criticism by the anti-anti-Communist left, which finds all forms of anti-Communism reactionary, the American Committee helped liberate American intellectuals from illusions about the Soviet Union. Nor was it a sect, as its left opponents made it appear; among the members were most of the leading non-Communist liberal figures in this country. But unfortunately the Committee could not escape the polarization that separated the conservative from the liberal anti-Communists and led some of its members to support conservative positions that were not necessarily anti-Communist. In any case, I suppose it can be said that the hard-liners dominated the American Committee, but not without some opposition. To understand the character of the organization, one must take account of other considerations and issues that cut across the main divisions.

The composition of the board changed, though not much, until the organization was dissolved in 1969. But the core was relatively constant. Generally on the "right" were Sidney Hook, James Burnham, Elliot Cohen, Hans Kohn, Irving Kristol, Bertram D. Wolfe, Arnold Beichman, Irwin Ross, George Schuyler, Norbert Muhlen, and Sol Stein, the executive director from 1953 to 1956, who wanted to keep the organization as broad as possible. Somewhere in the "middle" were Diana Trilling and Merlyn S. Pitzele, who was on the "right" at the beginning but gradually moved to the "left." On the "left" most of the time were Norman Thomas, James T. Farrell, Daniel Bell, who preferred to think of himself as a man of the "middle," and myself. These terms are used relatively, and are intended to designate only the different positions within the organization. By "right" I mean mostly the subordination of other issues to that of anti-Communism, the general support of the status quo, and a hostility to most radical movements. By "left" I mean a sympathy with the values and aims of liberalism (or socialism), as well as anti-Communism, and a critical attitude to all existing governments and institutions. Perhaps the most dramatic example of these differences were the stands on McCarthy and on the CIA, which involved the relation to the Congress. On the issue of McCarthy, despite the various charges that have been made by people who have not been disinterested, the Committee was critical of the Senator. In fact, the Committee sponsored an anti-McCarthy book, written by James Rorty and Moshe Decter. The shadings of opinion on the subject came out in a melodramatic, soul-searching meeting of the membership at which each person, in turn, spoke his piece about McCarthy, the Communists, and civil liberties. As expected, what was revealed was that some members on the "right," though critical of the Senator's crude methods, were more concerned with exposing the Communists than with muzzling McCarthy, while on the "left," more of the fire was directed against McCarthy than at the Communists, and in between there were all kinds of variations and qualifications of the two main positions. I was in the middle. Perhaps I was too anti-Communist and not strongly enough anti-McCarthy, though I was both. I knew, of course, that McCarthy was thoroughly unscrupulous and a liar, and that his lumping of liberals, ex-Communists, and innocents along with Communists was a dangerous political game. But unlike those liberals and radicals who felt that McCarthy was the only enemy, I believed that McCarthy's lies did not make Communist lies more palatable. I thought, too, that McCarthy's fake anti-Communism made all anti-Communism suspect and served only to create sympathy for the Communists. In fact, anti-Communism was becoming an adjunct of patriotism as the credo of the land, although, like patriotism, it was a staple of political rhetoric, often having nothing to do with the real meaning of Communism. I also felt at the time that McCarthy, for all his ugliness and virulence, was a passing phenomenon, while Stalinism was here to stay. I recall that in 1953, on a train returning from a teaching stint at the University of Minnesota, I was reading a newspaper whose front page was covered by a streamer about McCarthy, and a woman across the aisle asked whether she could borrow the paper when I was finished, since she wanted to read the story about McCarthy. I said she could have it right away as I was bored with McCarthy. The woman, who turned out to be Rosalyn Turek, the distinguished Bach specialist, said she would like to know the person who was bored with McCarthy.

The other large issue that agitated the American Committee and almost divided it was its relation to the Congress, which had been rumored to be an arm of the CIA. There were always official denials, but the rumors persisted. Highly placed people in the State Department, particularly abroad where the CIA was known to operate through State, were often either evasive on the subject or made knowing but inconclusive references to CIA funding of the Congress. Secret funding, it is necessary to point out, was seemingly a common practice and, therefore, taken for granted in those circles. I remember walking in on an official of the embassy in Paris, and seeing him give a large sum of money to a leading French political figure. "It's all right, come in. I was just changing some money for him," he said, without thinking it queer, or that I might think it queer, that money should be changed at the embassy. I also heard stories about American subsidies to anti-Communist organizations and figures, many of whom were left wing. And one got the impression that the CIA, unlike the rest of the government, was savvy enough to have discovered that liberals and radicals were often more effective opponents of the Communists than were reactionaries, who were ignored by most workers and intellectuals.

One was also made suspicious by the fact that most decisions of the Congress that counted were arbitrary and made at the very top. Who, for example, chose the director and the officers of the Congress? Who chose the editors of the Congress magazines? Who picked Mike Josselson, who had been in OSS, to be the power behind the executive board? I recall when the first director, Nicholas Nabokov, was chosen, nobody I knew was consulted or listened to. When I asked about Nabokov's qualifications, I was told by Hook he spoke four languages. I replied that my mother knew seven. I also recall a meeting on March 16, 1953, of the executive board of the American Committee, when it was announced that there would be a new Congress magazine in India. I argued that the last thing we needed was a magazine in India, but several leading members of the board justified it on the grounds that it would be a magazine for the entire English-speaking world in Europe and Asia. So why base it in India? The rationalizations were so patently sophistical that one was made to wonder what it was all about. Then, shortly after, the signals were changed, and we were told that the magazine would be published in London. Who made all these decisions and why? Another dramatic instance was the time the Congress flew the Boston Symphony for a performance in Paris at a cost, I heard, of five hundred thousand dollars. Aside from the value, in general, of such splurges—presumably to sell America to Europe, an operation that sounded like a contribution of Madison Avenue to American foreign policy—the effectiveness of this event could be gauged by the fact that it became known as the most fashionable couturier's ball of the year. The Congress should have known better; after all, it had such sophisticated political figures as Raymond Aron and Manès Sperber on its board. So the explanation had to be found elsewhere. When, some years later, I asked Sperber, with whom I had become intimate enough to ask such questions, how they could have gone in for such foolishness, he said he was told the money was earmarked for the concert and had to be used for that purpose or not at all. Then why have it at all? He just shrugged.

This was long before the story about the CIA, the Congress, *Encounter,* and the other publications of the Congress broke in *The New York Times.* But the suspicions and rumors were troubling. At a meeting of the executive board of the American Committee in December 1955, after a long and agitated discussion it was decided to disaffiliate from, but to maintain a loose association with, the Congress. Not that, to my knowledge, we had ever received any money from the CIA. If we were funded by the CIA, why were we always broke? The American Committee had a two-room office midtown, two employees, one part time, at modest salaries, and very few other costs besides such basics as telephone, stationery, etc. To my knowledge, no personal expenses were paid. The source of our funds, so far as I knew, was membership dues and small grants from individuals and foundations. If the CIA had supported us, it would have been a variation on Marx's law of wages, according to which the working class was kept at a subsistence level. The only disturbing incident is one reported by Diana Trilling in her book *We Must March My Darlings,* where she says that at a meeting of the American Committee in 1954 or 1955, after a report that the organization was so broke it could not pay the rent, Norman Thomas said he could call his friend Allen and ask for a thousand dollars. Diana concluded that Allen probably meant Allen Dulles, and that since there was no eviction the money was received and may have come from the CIA. I do not recall the details of this meeting, but I suppose Diana's deduction is a possible one. However, Daniel Bell, who was a member of the executive committee, has told me since that he doubts the money came from the CIA. (Bell pointed out that it was not uncommon for someone like Allen Dulles to persuade a wealthy donor to make a contribution.) In any case, a thousand dollars was no big deal, and I know of no other instance of clandestine support of the American Committee, although I should add that I had nothing to do with its finances.

As for my relation with the Congress or its magazines, it was often quite hostile on both sides. At best I was treated as an outsider, and *Partisan Review* as a competitor. From the very beginning I was kept out of its councils and meetings—an exclusion I have often wondered about. The Congress was founded at a meeting in Berlin, in 1950, to which neither Rahv nor I was invited; nor were we aware of it until the formation of the Congress was announced. So far as I know, Sidney Hook, James Burnham, Mike Josselson, Arthur Koestler, Raymond Aron, Elliot Cohen, and Irving Brown, the representative of the American Federation of Labor in charge of anti-Communist activity abroad, were at this founding meeting. Obviously, neither Rahv nor I was considered personally or politically reliable enough to participate in the formation of an organization which at some point acquired a secret connection to the CIA.

The only public or private meeting I was ever asked to was in Berlin, in 1960, the invitation to which, I assumed, was extended because I had been complaining publicly about the Congress being run by a clique who excluded people critical of it politically or

154

organizationally. The meeting was one of those mob scenes that big conferences usually turn into, with several hundred delegates from all over the world, many from the African countries. The subject, which had something vaguely to do with the cultural and political situation, was quickly lost in the intellectual commotion that such a large and heterogeneous group is bound to produce. There were no common assumptions, and a conference without common assumptions is like a football game without rules. Yet the conference was shrewdly organized, for, despite the variety of views clogging up the discussions, there were very few disciplined and independent thinkers who might generate any kind of opposition or clear line of thinking. By my count, there were five such people, Mary McCarthy, Robert Oppenheimer, who had his own brand of fuzziness, Richard Hoggart, Stephen Spender, and I, if I may include myself—too few to counter the organized bedlam. The leaders of the Congress, veterans of organizational strategy and infighting, were clever enough to let the meeting take its own course, stepping in only when some dissidence that threatened their position seemed to be developing. Apparently, I was not tractable enough, for I soon found myself in a collision with Edward Shils, one of the architects of the meeting. Perhaps I should also admit that I have a tendency to get into confrontations at meetings, as I have rarely been able to relax into the cynical attitude that conferences are not primarily for intellectual purposes and that one should regard them as a nice change of scene, an opportunity to meet one's friends and to enjoy the food and the local entertainment. We were divided into groups and group leaders. At the first session, Edward Shils, who chaired the discussion, made an opening speech, repeating his known views about the beneficient advances of mass culture in the United States, thus setting the line for the meeting. After a few other speakers, I got up to question the beneficence of mass culture, but Shils kept interrupting me to point out my errors, until finally I asked whether he was going to let me talk, to which he said no. I pompously announced I was walking out of the meeting and would call a press conference to publicize my not being permitted to speak. Several other delegates, including Mary McCarthy and Robert Oppenheimer, walked out too, in support of my protest. The rebellion did not last very long. Several people called me at my hotel room to assure me I would be permitted to speak at the next session. And

155

Mary was glad to get back to the proceedings, which provided an occasion where her flair for drama and her rhetorical powers could shine. Oppenheimer was a curious combination of moral principle— according to his lights—and a way of looking at things so personally and egocentrically that it verged on the visionary. For example, in a talk at one of the sessions calling for greater understanding of China, he spoke of getting signals from afar that illuminated the political situation there and our relation to it. I assumed that Oppenheimer supported my stand, without knowing or even being interested in my views, because he saw it as a question of the right to dissent.

The best part of my stay in Berlin was an evening at a nightclub, with Ursula Brumm as my guide. She was a native Berliner, a sophisticated critic, who had written for *Partisan Review*. Berlin had become known as a center of transvestism, and Ursula offered to take me to a transvestite nightclub. We spent the evening guessing who was a man and who a woman, somewhat frustrated at the difficulty of identifying the transvestites. The next day she told me she had found out we had gone to the wrong club.

But my quarrel with the Congress over the source and use of its funds went beyond the question of its meetings and continued until the exposé by *The New York Times* in 1967. The matter of the CIA is actually more complex than it is made out to be by those who support its activities on national security grounds or those on the other side of the fence who oppose its secret operations from a democratic point of view. My own objections to the CIA support of the Congress and its publications were mainly that it was wasteful and ineffective and led to secret control. I recognize that certain governmental activities have to be conducted surreptitiously, and not to be aware that all governments have their secret intelligence arms—and secret political manipulations—is a species of innocence, a political luxury, that only liberals can afford.

But when it comes to intellectual matters, the problem is not the same, for the essence of work in culture and the arts is that it must be open and freewheeling. Hidden financing means hidden control, despite any denials about pressure or censorship. A literary and cultural magazine, particularly, must be responsive to new currents and ideas and hospitable to dissidence and experiments of all kinds. The defenders of the Congress for Cultural Freedom were able to argue that the organizations and publications were not intellectually controlled because generally conservative liberals rather than out-and-out conservatives were used to promote anti-Communist aims, and some latitude was permitted in the selection of pieces printed in the Congress publications. But if one examines their record carefully, the systematic bias is clear, and the deviations not only few but marginal—just enough to give some credibility to the argument that they were not official propaganda organs. One obvious example—perhaps it should not be inflated—was the refusal of *Encounter* to publish a piece by Dwight Macdonald critical of America.

Also, one was disposed to wonder how the editors of *Encounter* and *Preuves* were chosen—a process never made public or explained, and obviously conducted in secret councils. True, some independent spirits were chosen, like Dwight Macdonald and Stephen Spender at *Encounter* and Ignazio Silone and Nicola Chiaromonte at *Tempo Presente* in Italy. Also, Daniel Bell was the director of seminars at the Congress for one year. (And many good things were printed in these publications.) But Macdonald was a visiting editor for only one year; Spender resigned when the news of the CIA connection broke. And it was my impression that *Tempo Presente* was under less surveillance because it was not in English. However, writers like Silone and Chiaromonte probably agreed with the general line of the Congress, a point often cited to prove there was no coercion. But this argument cuts both ways, for usually only those who agreed with the Congress were put in charge of magazines or conferences.

Even if one were to grant the validity of its aims, such a propaganda operation as the Congress and its publications seemed to be to some extent a waste of money. It was directed at artists and intellectuals (the circulation of *Preuves*, for example, I understand hovered around three thousand), yet had very little influence on them because it was based on assumptions that grossly oversimplified the way politics entered the intellectual life of a country. The politics of intellectuals, particularly abroad, comes partly from their national situation, partly from their exposure to ideas in other countries. In any case, intellectuals are not swayed by external organizations and publications known to be instruments of the American government, but organically, through exchange with each other, within their own country, and with fellow intellectuals in other countries. It is important, too, that this exchange take place in working or social situations that are natural and professional. When Communists, for example, made some headway among intellectuals, it was not because of their persuasive powers at conferences or in literary publications; it was because the whole political and cultural climate had made intellectuals ready to accept the Communists and their doctrines. The recent anti-Communist turn of French intellectuals is due to a general change in the political climate and to Solzhenitsyn's revelations about gulag. As for the Congress and its magazines, it was no secret in Europe that they were fostered by the American government with only one purpose: to offset the influence of the Communists on European thought. Though there was no proof of CIA connections, it is not clear why the Communists did not make the charge anyway; they have never been fussy about supplying evidence for their accusations. The only plausible explanation I have ever heard, though so ingenious as to seem far-fetched, is that the Communists, who secretly finance all kinds of organizations and publications, take for granted that the Americans do the same thing and that nobody would be surprised by such revelations.

One question remains: I have been asked many times whether I would have accepted CIA support for *Partisan Review*, and it has been suggested that I would. All I can say is that I am now glad it was never offered; if it had been, who knows, I might have accepted it, for to be free financially was sometimes tempting.

At present, it is easier to be critical of CIA support because of the opprobrium attached to the CIA—an opprobrium nourished as much by revelations of its activities as by the assaults on it by liberal and left groups. However, there is as much confusion on this as on other political questions, for it is not at all certain that even a nice clean CIA would be acceptable to the critics of the CIA. In general, there is a blurring of the questions of national security and the national interest of the United States, though it is taken for granted that other countries, including the Soviet Union, have national concerns. There is also a tendency, especially after Vietnam, to label all Western political and military intervention abroad as reactionary and imperialist—except the war against Hitler.

I have presented the arguments rather strongly against CIA support of cultural enterprises. But in all fairness, I should give the counterarguments advanced by people of intelligence and integrity. For one, they maintain that despite everything that can be said against them, CIA subsidies are justified because the Soviet menace is so great. Furthermore, propaganda from the East is heavily subsidized, and though private and open funding would be preferable, it could not be had on a proper scale and consistency except from a government agency. It is also felt by many writers associated with the Congress that its publications and conferences did much to counter Communist intellectual influence. Perhaps there is no true measure of effectiveness. And perhaps the question is really how a democracy with opposing interests and ideas can cope with a political monolith.

The question of national interest has been strangely resistant to analysis. But this exemption has not prevented anyone from taking a position. Thus, while the right has usually defended what was presumed to be the national interest, and the left has mostly opposed actions taken in its name—while both ends of the political spectrum have had strong views about the national interest, it has never been clearly defined. Traditionally, prevailing opinion—the core of which is conservative and patriotic, but in crises has included most liberals and many radicals—has tended to assume that the nation is an entity with self-evident interests. Radicals, on the other hand, have frequently argued that there is no national interest, and that what we have are class and group interests masquerading as national interests. Both views, however, are too narrow, and do not allow for conflicting factors and for practical considerations that vary in different situations. A class approach, I believe, is too one-sided, unless one accepts Lenin's idea that for the workers and their allies the main enemy is at home. In that case, none but the wealthy would have a stake in defending the United States, say, in the event of an invasion even by a totalitarian power. Nor, on the other hand, is it only in the interest of American capitalism to protect Western Europe from military conquest.

Most situations that raise the question of American interests abroad involve a variety of such interests, often difficult to sort out. For example, the entrance of the United States into World War II was certainly not purely anti-fascist; on the other hand, it cannot be said it simply represented the interests of the American economy. Nor can Vietnam be reduced to business—or imperialist—interests in Asia, though these pressures do have an effect on political thinking and policy. Clearly, the American government believed it was in the national interest to halt the spread of Communism in Asia. Whether it was mistaken is another question: the issue is one of motive. Similarly, our official policies in the Mideast are compounded of many considerations and contradictions, such as the desire to defend Israel from annihilation along with wanting to appease the Arab countries, mostly because of their oil. Perhaps an even clearer illustration of the opposing aims and forces in determining the national interest is the question of Communism and anti-Communism. Obviously, not only ideologists of capitalism but also liberals and radicals who value human rights are opposed to Communist regimes. In some situations these very different positions might emerge to constitute a national interest—particularly in a time of political crisis or confrontation.

14

CULTURAL FREEDOM AT HOME

IN the American Committee, in addition to the concern about the funding of the Congress by the CIA, there were disagreements about the politics of the Congress, some of which took a bizarre form. For example, a few of the tougher anti-Communists thought the Congress was too soft on Communism—which meant, in effect, that the line of the CIA, normally conceived of as a monster of anti-Communism, was considered to have been infected by either liberal illusions or false tactical considerations. There was the Bertrand Russell affair, which split the American Committee. Russell, honorary chairman of the Congress, had supported some of the "peace" proposals of the Communists. Several members of the American Committee, led by Diana Trilling and James T. Farrell who were most disturbed by the tolerance of Russell's views by the Congress, argued that the Congress should disassociate itself from Russell, and that the American Committee should indicate its disapproval of both Russell and the Congress. I remember arguing with Diana and with Jim Farrell that what was wrong with the Congress was not its politics but its bureaucratic organization. I thought it silly to accuse the Congress of being soft on Communism when its only reason for existence was to put the Communists out of business, and I felt we would get lost in hairsplitting arguments about tactics that obscured the real issue—the control of the Congress by a hand-picked, self-perpetuating leadership. It was one of the anomalies of bureaucratized anti-Communism that an undemocratic organization could speak in the name of democracy. It would seem that for the Congress the idea of complete cultural freedom was mainly for export to the Soviet Union, which should have told us something about the nature of the Congress since governments usually do not apply their criticism of other countries to themselves.

The Congress was doomed by its funding by the CIA: as soon as this came out in the open, its credibility was gone. The American Committee continued until 1963, partly out of inertia and the reluctance to dissolve an organization that had been thought to be useful, for it is difficult to determine, as in human beings, just when senility sets in. For one thing, at the meeting to dissolve the Committee it was said that it did not seem necessary to maintain an organization devoted to the pursuit of anti-Communism when much of the country and most of the media had taken the line of hard, if uninformed, anti-Communism. In addition, differences within the organization were widening to the point where the anti-Communism of the right had little to do with that of the left. Political marriages are notoriously unstable, and in the case of the Committee, those for whom anti-Communism had become the center of their politics, and those for whom it was part of a larger, and generally liberal, perspective, found it hard to live with each other. The recently formed Committee for a Free World is more homogeneous and was apparently created in the belief that American anti-Communism had become soft and unreliable.

One of the most obsessive of the anti-Communists was Elliot Cohen, a very intelligent and witty man and a very enterprising and forceful editor of *Commentary*, though he narrowed its political focus and shaped its contents to fit his bias. It is hard to determine the connections between politics and psychology, but it did seem that Cohen's neuroses were channeled into his extreme and sometimes perverse politics. One had the feeling—no doubt exaggerated—that Cohen inhaled Communism and exhaled anti-Communism, that it was mostly what he thought about, and that many of his likes and hates were attached to this issue. No one seemed to be anti-Communist enough for him, and he was forever fulminating against the fuzzy-minded liberals and radicals. We had a quarrel once over some minor question in the Committee and did not speak to each other for a couple of years. Though the issue had to do with something else, with Cohen's blaming me for something he failed to do, I had the feeling that if I were sufficiently anti-Communist he would not have been so belligerent or he would have quickly tried to make up. His political purity was most vividly displayed one evening when he got into an argument with the late Judge Hays, one of the staunchest anti-Communists I have met, and accused Hays of being soft on Communism. Cohen radiated a political suspicion of everyone around him, and one was bound to wonder who would measure up to his ideal picture of the anti-Communist. There was, of course, something sad in such a shrinking of the mind to the dimensions of a single question. At the services for Elliot Cohen, who committed suicide on May 28, 1959, Lionel Trilling spoke of Cohen's editorial genius. This was probably true when Cohen started *Commentary*. But, perhaps for personal and political reasons, his mind had tightened and lost some of its flexibility and intelligence. I recall that when Cohen was trying to get me to write an article on the state of the novel, he kept telling me that I should explain the decline of the novel, which he assumed, by the death of "individualism." Aside from the fact that I had no such idea of the fate of the novel or of whatever it is that is called "individualism," that stereotype of popular thought, I was shocked to hear him talk about literary questions in such overpoliticized and unprofessional terms.

Elliot Cohen was the prototype of the extremist position, but there were others who shared his basic views though they were less aggressive and more modulated in their thinking. I am not sure that Bertram Wolfe disagreed much with Cohen's politics, but he had the quiet manner of an anti-Communist sage and an expert on Russian affairs. Sidney Hook was also not far from Cohen on essential questions, but he was much subtler and suaver, more diplomatic, and generally played the part of a strategist and elder statesman. He was also a trained philosopher with a very sharp mind; hence his methods were usually those of reason and logical persuasion, which made him most effective in debate or in steering a meeting to a desired course of action. He was usually right, but his preoccupation with the evils of Communism led to a distortion, in my opinion, of his political perspective, and to an underemphasis of the faults of our own society. It also led to a lessening of his earlier enthusiasm, at least in practice, for the free play of the mind—which was particularly disturbing to see in someone who had had one of the most agile and disciplined minds I had ever encountered. Hook's earlier works on Marxism were masterpieces of understanding and explanation. He was also a truly great teacher, that is, one who stimulated students by the example of a fine mind at work. And in his personal relations he was very scrupulous and warm, almost paternal. But I suppose no one was free of the intellectual ravages of the period. History had disfigured the thinking of an entire generation that set out to make history, and those of us who feel we have escaped are bound to wonder how much we, too, have been touched by the great reversals of political ideology in our time.

In 1959 *Partisan Review* needed a compatible tax-exempt organization as a publisher. We talked with several organizations, including Freedom House, but they raised so many questions about our politics, implying we were too liberal, that it became evident that such an association would never work. Clearly some organizations dedicated to "freedom" had their own inflexible line, and the term was often a strategic weapon against totalitarian regimes, mostly Communist ones. The American Committee also had its own political outlook, but it did have on its board people with cultural and literary sophistication who had a high regard for *Partisan Review* and for intellectual quality in general, despite their disagreements with some of its political contents. They also appeared to understand that a literary and cultural publication like *Partisan Review* had to be open to a variety of opinions—naturally within certain boundaries—and that an experimental approach was just as necessary to politics as to literature.

After some discussions with the leading members of the board, the American Committee became the publisher and legal owner of *Partisan Review*. It was clearly understood that the Committee was not to provide financial support, nor to have any control over editorial matters. The editorial autonomy granted the magazine, as I saw it, was partly a gesture of respect for the traditions and the importance of *Partisan Review*, partly a recognition that such editorial freedom was a common practice, rooted in the history of literary publications. For a time, the marriage worked, probably as well as most such marriages, despite the political disagreements and the rumblings of discontent.

Then the storm broke in 1967 with our publication of a polemical piece by Norman Birnbaum criticizing the Congress for Cultural Freedom. From the fuss that was raised, one would have thought we had printed a Communist tract. There were endless phone calls telling me how distressed and puzzled the members of the board were at our publication of such an unspeakable piece. Of course, we were free to publish anything we chose, but this went too far. We argued for months about what the piece actually said, about its political meaning, about the significance of our printing it, about editorial freedom and responsibility. All these issues became entangled with each other to the point where I began to feel nobody knew what he was talking about, that, in fact, there were no issues, only a barrage of accusations and insinuations.

Diana Trilling was critical of our political tendencies, but she told me she wanted the matter kept on an intellectual plane. Arnold Beichman, however, in his persistent, aggrieved tone of complaint about our politics and about all the other troubles he had to cope with because of our connection with the Committee, kept the fires burning. I never learned what happened in the inner councils, but Diana Trilling told me she brought the matter up for formal consideration in a direct and forthright way. She said she felt she was no longer welcome to write for *Partisan Review*, which I assured her was not so. But rather than have the Committee take action, she felt she should resign from the board. The others tried to dissuade her and seemed to be hesitant to take any specific, immediate steps, probably waiting for some break, while maintaining the atmosphere of a state of crisis.

In any event, it was clear that the association of the magazine with the Committee had lived out its natural life, but the board could not see a decent way of ending it without seeming to be vindictive and destructive.

In the meantime, I was constantly on the phone with Beichman, as was Steven Marcus, who was then an associate editor. Beichman found something new to worry about each day: if it was not a piece we printed or failed to print, it had to do with our bookkeeping, or tax reports, or our finances. The pot was kept boiling by Beichman's always acting the part of someone afraid of terrible consequences— over small and big things. It was hard to believe that he could be so concerned over routine matters. Beichman's manner was outwardly aggrieved, but he kept insisting that his intentions were friendly.

One concrete result of these daily questions and arguments, mostly by phone—which I wish I had taped, for they must have sounded like a Kafkaesque version of an interrogation—was that I lost my voice for several months. The medical diagnosis was a nodule on my vocal chords, produced by strain; the cure was not to talk until it cleared up, and exercises to retrain the use of my voice were prescribed by a doctor who had treated John Kennedy for a similar problem. It was at this time, while I was speechless, that J. D. Salinger, who was in town, wrote to say he would like to see me. It was my only concrete experience of what I assume the French critics mean by *silence*, though I am not sure it is more than a rhetorical concept for them. Salinger came to my house in the morning. To facilitate a voiceless conversation, I asked Caroline Herron, my assistant, to mediate, although it is not clear what mediating meant beyond reading my mind and rendering a very free interpretation of it. However, there was not much else to do. Salinger, a lanky, waspy, shy, untalkative, attractive New Englander, said very little, and mostly in short, hesitant spurts. I wrote my part of the exchange on pieces of paper, slowly and illegibly. At the end, we both acted as though we had had a calm but satisfying conversation.

My voice shaky but functioning, I was ready for a meeting with the board of the American Committee to discuss the possibilities of divorce. There were several freer spirits at the meeting but the general tone was disturbing in its organizational rigidity and its insensitiveness to those literary considerations that require flexibility, tolerance, and a feeling for waywardness. It was a sad reminder that principled anti-Communists who had no immediate connection with the arts could harden and act like commissars—commissars without power except over me. It seemed as though an iron law of bureaucratization dictated the course of anti-Communist as well as Communist organizations. I felt very uneasy about all my past commitments. Outwardly, everyone was properly sympathetic to the problems of the magazine and expressed a willingness to be patient and cooperative, but it was clear that a decision had been reached to cut *Partisan Review* loose. The composition of the meeting was politically significant and indicative of the development of the organization and its role in American intellectual life. The members ranged from Arnold Beichman, a hardliner, and Sidney Hook, a highly sophisticated and political man, to Daniel Bell, who was humanly and intellectually sympathetic, and Merlyn Pitzele, who was torn between his politics and his regard for *Partisan Review*. Aside from Norman Podhoretz, who had not yet made his move to the right, in between were people whose politics and organizational ties led them to side with Beichman and Hook. Daniel Bell's strong loyalties often put him in the role of mediator. He was, he used to say, a born centrist. At the meeting he did try to find a satisfactory solution, and was cordial and helpful. Though Bell had been associated with the neoconservatives, he is a more complex and flexible thinker.

Bell is a man of great learning and zealous observation, and when he has stuck to areas where he was not tempted to overplay his hand his work has been solid and sharp. His contributions to sociology have been large and in ways that have transcended the academic definitions of the subject. But aside from his professional achievements, Bell has always exhibited great personal warmth. He is a man of enormous energy and human enthusiasms, with an endless fund of Jewish jokes and stories. I must acknowledge, too, that over the years he has tried to assist *Partisan Review* in many ways. He has been a frequent contributor, and besides helping to arrange both the union and the separation of the magazine and the Committee, he was instrumental earlier in getting us a grant of five thousand dollars from the Luce Foundation. He always made one feel he could be called on when the magazine had a problem. For years he was a leading figure on *The Public Interest,* but in the eighties he joined the board of *Partisan Review.*

Norman Podhoretz, who was too young to have much power

among such high-powered people, was on our side. The historian, Hans Kohn, seemed to be in a fog. Bertram Wolfe was calm and deliberative, a veteran of such meetings. Irwin Ross was a journalist, a successful and popular one, who was not overtly hostile, but gave the impression that he did not care very much, and therefore was bound to go along with what sounded like shrewd organizational strategy as presented by Hook, Wolfe, and Beichman. Pitzele had been moving away from the anti-Communist line of the Committee. We had had our disagreements, but Pitzele valued the literary side of the magazine and had a surprising feeling for the byways and perversities of modern writing. In fact, he was instrumental in arranging a meeting in 1962 with Richard Poirier, who had been his son's tutor at Harvard, which eventually led to our move to Rutgers. But that is a later story.

I suppose Pitzele and Bell helped work out a flexible solution and one as favorable as possible to us. For the leading members of the board shrewdly found a way out that served their purposes, preserved their honor, and was not too summary in separating from *Partisan Review*. Instead of insisting that the magazine be detached from the Committee because of its suspect politics and cultural irresponsibility, they proposed to dissolve the Committee, on the grounds that it had outlived its usefulness—which was hard to argue against because it was true. We needed time, however, to make other arrangements. The Committee could now afford to be gracious, and to give us a few months—longer if necessary—to settle our affairs.

15

VICTIMS
AND CRITICS

THE fifties began with McCarthy and ended with the counterculture—an incredible turnaround. What happened to turn the decade upside down? There are many versions, as contradictory and confusing as was the period itself. Clearly, however, it was an incubating time for the anarchic and highly personalized forms of revolt that flourished in the sixties, and as such is difficult to sort out. But the problem of writing the history of the era, in fact the problem of writing contemporary history, is that there are no central lines or traditions, or, at least, they are difficult to find. The main characteristic of our time is its kaleidoscopic quality, its shattering into literally dozens of currents, its rapid changes, its endless contradictions, its amnesia, its cultisms—on the whole, its appearance of dispersion, like a galaxy of stars moving in all directions. Many factors, in my opinion, have produced this state of controlled chaos. For one thing, we are in an era of failed revolutions, which normally produces social tightening and regression, but now the failed revolutions have produced repressive regimes in the East and societies without a sense of purpose and direction in the West.

In the Communist countries, the channels of dissidence, political idealism, revolt, even the normal channels of reform as well as of disaffection have been bottled up. In the West, the traditional forms of protest and change have been distorted. We are clearly in an age of transition, but because of all the contortions and diversions of history, not only is the future uncertain, but because our idea of the future has a bearing on both the past and the present we have no clearer sense of where we have been than where we are going. On top of this, in the United States, where there has been less restraint than in Europe by tradition or government, the anarchy and the insatiable appetites of the market have dominated the culture and the politics of the country. Hence the incessant demand for novelty, the lack of interest in the past, and the confusion of quantity with quality. This explains such things as the coopting of experiment by the needs of the media, the retreat of art into regionalism, and the general substitution of the idea of pluralism for tradition. It has been a field day for all kinds of psychological, cultural, and political cults. Official politics has become celebrity politics, and the idea of continuity has given way to the idea of change, while, of course, the old corruption and incompetence persist, covered up by the rhetoric of innovation and popular participation. Unofficial dissident politics is given mostly to gestures of revolt, to liberation movements—women, black, gay, youth, etc.—with competing interests and programs, and to offbeat trends that combine politics with sex panaceas, health theories, and trendy therapies. I am not, in this quick summary, condemning an era; on the contrary, I am suggesting a peculiar combination of energy, idealism, and talent expressing itself in commercial enterprise, at one end of the spectrum, and undisciplined experiments on the other—the result, palpably, of diversion and frustration. And this strange and disorderly mix, which has tended to break down the very notion of intellectual authority, makes it difficult to chart the era's history. When there are so many competing views of what happened and what should happen, one almost has to take an authoritarian stand to insist that one's own view is the correct or the more plausible one.

How, then, do we assess the McCarthy period? How, indeed, do we understand any part of the past? For the question is nothing less than the general question of history applied to the last few decades. It goes without saying that the facts come first. But in addition to the facts one's version of the past has much to do with one's outlook and assumptions and one's idea of the future. And it is evident that different views of the McCarthy years and of the fifties, in general, reflect different cultural and political attitudes. Thus, on the subject of McCarthy, the Neanderthal anti-Communists stomached his wild and dishonest charges until they felt he was embarrassing even the government and the army; the sophisticated but extreme anti-Communists deplored his excesses but were not too displeased by his attacks on the Communists; the liberals disliked the whole business but were divided. Some managed to forget that McCarthy's lies did not confer sainthood on the Communists; others condemned both sides. The Communists and fellow-travelers used the obscene politics of McCarthy to promote their own cause by presenting themselves as the innocent victims of a campaign against all the liberal values of society. As I have said, my own view, which to me seems so sane and right I am surprised it is not the standard one, has been that our condemnation of international Communism should not blind us to the evils of McCarthyism any more than the evils of McCarthyism should distract us from recognizing the nature of the Soviet Union and its allies. Unfortunately, political thinking of the last few decades has not been noted for its balance. And it is this imbalance, this failure to maintain an opposition both to the forces of the right and to those parts of the Communist movement dominated by the Russians, that has warped our political ideas and paralyzed the possibilities of action. It is this selective myopia that has made disguised patriots and defenders of the status quo out of some of us and guilt-ridden liberals out of others, liberals who have imbibed enough of Marx to be critical of the vices of capitalism and to celebrate every movement and every nation, however authoritarian and demagogic, that appropriates the slogans of liberation, socialism, and peace.

There have been many dismal eras in American history, but the McCarthy period was one of the most stupid and shameful; and though its lessons have been the subject of countless books and articles, its political meaning is still apparently not clear, as it continues to be the subject of interminable debate. In Lillian Hellman's book *Scoundrel Time,* for example, which relates her confrontation with the House Un-American Activities Committee and the experience of other prominent writers, mostly from Hollywood, she talked about the role of *Partisan Review* and a few of its contributors. Miss Hellman, though a gifted woman, lacks the gift of political judgment. Some of the facts and political conclusions in her book need to be corrected, not only for what is pompously referred to as the historic record, but to place the events in a perspective that might make sense for the future. Otherwise, the antics of McCarthy, or the broader phenomenon of McCarthyism, become the occasion for a display of martyrdom and left ideology. And we are likely to repeat the same mistakes.

As we know, Miss Hellman was a victim of HUAC's investigation of Communists, fellow-travelers, and a number of innocent people who were either caught in the crossfire or were falsely accused. In her book, Miss Hellman asked bitterly why high-minded anti-Communists did not come to her or to Dashiell Hammett's defense when they were being persecuted by the Un-American Committee, and consequently lost their lucrative Hollywood jobs. She went on to suggest that such anti-Communists bear some responsibility for Nixon, Watergate, and Vietnam. "There were many thoughtful and distinguished men and women on both magazines," she said, referring to *Partisan Review* and *Commentary*. "None of them, so far as I know, has yet found it a part of conscience to admit that their cold war anti-Communism was perverted, possibly against their wishes, into the Vietnam War and then into the reign of Nixon, their unwanted but inevitable leader." And of *Partisan Review* Miss Hellman also said: "Although through the years it has published many pieces protesting the punishment of dissidence in Eastern Europe, it made no protest when people in this country were jailed or ruined. In fact, it took no editorial position against McCarthy himself although it did publish the results of anti-McCarthy symposiums and at least one distinguished piece by Irving Howe."

Now these statements contain a number of questionable facts, selective observations, loaded questions, and political biases, all lumped together. First, as to the facts. *Partisan Review* may not have been in the forefront of the resistance to McCarthy, but, though it printed only two editorials during this period, one was a reply to James Burnham's letter of resignation from the advisory board because of the magazine's anti-McCarthy position. Burnham claimed to be neutral on the question of McCarthy, to which the editors replied that neutrality was not possible.

Also, in addition to the essay by Irving Howe, "The Age of Conformity," cited by Miss Hellman, which was mostly against the intellectual drift to the right, there were anti-McCarthy statements by Richard Rovere, Arthur Schlesinger, Dwight Macdonald, and Philip Rahv. Besides, I wrote several pieces critical of the new conservatism. And in an article about Simone de Beauvoir, in the July 1953 issue of *Commentary*, I wrote, "In the face of such ominous things as Senator McCarthy and the new wave of 'Americanism' and anti-intellectualism, a serious and radical criticism of American society is more necessary than ever. . . ." The view implicit in this statement, which was representative of our position, unlike the one-sided attitude of the Communists and of many liberals, was that our opposition to McCarthy was part of a larger political perspective, which included opposition to all authoritarian trends as well as an exploratory attitude to the possibilities of a socialist movement not dominated by the Communists. The anti-McCarthy part of the equation was questioned by conservatives, while the fact that it was accompanied by an unabated criticism of the Soviet Union and the Communist parties associated with it was objected to by the fellow-traveling left.

Furthermore, although I have not put in any claims to martyrdom or heroism, I, too, was harassed by the FBI and grilled before a grand jury to give names. Nor did I get any publicity for the nobility of my stand, since I was not a Hollywood celebrity. Miss Hellman spoke of the loss of lucrative jobs and contracts by the Hollywood Ten and others. Again, though it was not front-page news, I and other writers who had broken with the Communists were kept from not-so-lucrative writing for various journals and prevented from getting not-so-lucrative university jobs by the pressures and machinations of the Communists. These acts were not public and were often difficult to prove, but it was clear that there was some kind of blacklist of people on the left, like me, who had broken with the Communist movement, in those fields where the Communists and their liberal sympathizers had most influence: in the publishing houses, universities, and liberal magazines. Let me cite three instances from my own experience. I had talked with the dean about teaching at a college not far from New York, but on my way back to the city a friend who had been with me spotted someone he knew to be a Communist looking at us and said that would end it—as it did. Another time, I was cut off from writing for a large metropolitan publication, to which I had been contributing frequently, and was told that the decision was political and was made at the top. And in the late thirties Rahv and I had been doing reviews for *The Nation* until one day Margaret Marshall, the literary editor, told us that she had been given orders not to print any Trotskyites—a designation used by the Communists to cover any left or liberal anti-Communists. This was particularly shocking because Margaret Marshall had been a friend—and a non-Communist, at least. For years I did not publicize this incident, which was more a betrayal of Margaret Marshall's principles than it was of me, because I assumed she was protecting her job, and I had learned in the rough school of Communist politics that one cannot demand, or even expect, people to be heroes at the expense of job, family, or status.

Obviously, there would be no history without heroes. Yet I have never understood the psychic and intellectual makeup of heroes and martyrs, such as, for example, the dissidents in the Soviet Union who face torture and years in brutal labor camps. Perhaps they do not have the fear of pain and death that, because of my own vulnerabilities, I assume to be the normal condition. In this country, where heroism involves loss of friends and financial sacrifice but has few physical consequences, one would expect more people to stick to their principles. But, unfortunately, among people of superior intelligence characters are usually not as strong as minds. In any case, I said nothing about Margaret Marshall's political behavior until 1965, when *Partisan Review* published a piece by Bernard Haggin in which he wrote that Miss Marshall ran the literary section—known as "the back" —of *The Nation* independently of the Stalinist politics of "the front" part of the magazine. To keep the record straight, I felt I had to append an editorial note indicating that in one instance, at least, this was not true. I should add that Margaret Marshall denied taking orders from above or telling Rahv and me that as Trotskyites we were not welcome at *The Nation*, but we know that memory is often at the service of one's guilt.

Lillian Hellman's question as to why we did not come to the defense of those who had been attacked by McCarthy is not so simple as it appears. First of all, some were Communists, and what one was asked to defend was their right to lie about it. My own code was to tell the truth about my own politics, but not to get innocent people or dupes into trouble; still, I suppose this was easier for me than for card-carrying Communists since I had never been a member of the Communist party and had nothing to tell. Another consideration was the feeling, which I am sure was shared by others, that Communists did not have a divine right to a key job in the government or a glamorous one in Hollywood—anymore than anyone else was owed a job in any institution one believed had to be destroyed. I do not recall, for example, any instance of Lenin's, or Trotsky's, or Rosa Luxemburg's demanding that they be employed by the institutions of the enemy. Frankly, too, it was hard to take seriously those Communist and fellow-traveling celebrities who were playing with revolution without realizing that such politics might have consequences. The political game created by the special needs of the Soviet Union produced a new type of radical, unknown before in the history of revolutionary movements, a political figurehead, a celebrity who may not engage in direct Communist activity but who helps the party in secret ways and promotes its line publicly on various domestic and foreign issues. To call this new political creature a parlor pink does not convey his full role, for while it suggests his political frivolity, it leaves out his commitments to the cause of the Soviet Union and its affiliated parties.

Furthermore, the question of defending Communists went beyond liberal or left fraternalism. It was not just a case of defending people with whom we disagreed but who had similar aims. The Communists, we felt, had betrayed the principles socialists, liberals, and humanists of any kind had originally shared. They had branded us as the enemy. They were under orders not to speak to us. Their press called us every name in and out of the political lexicon. And they were the apologists for the arrest and torture of countless intellectuals in the Soviet Union and in other Communist countries.

I suppose if we had been selfless libertarians, without a political history and principles, we might have transcended all these considerations and come to the defense of people who were being persecuted, even though we thought them to be the instruments, conscious or not, of a new barbarism. What has confused the issue is that the new barbarism often has an innocent face. As Hannah Arendt pointed out, fascists often had the look of banality. In the case of Communists, their politics frequently have been obscured, particularly in people aglow with idealism and filled with more than the normal quota of naiveté, who do not think of themselves as having any connection with oppression in Russia or with the shady activities of the party. Unfortunately, no method has been devised for separating their innocence from their guilt, to enable us to defend one while condemning the other.

In any event, one wonders how Miss Hellman could not know about such things as slave labor camps and the torture of writers and dissident intellectuals. And just as she asks how we could not come to the defense of McCarthy's victims, one could ask her how she could not come to the defense of all those who had been killed or defamed by the Communists. How could she be silent so long about the persecution of writers in Russia? Why has she not spoken up against Russian anti-Semitism or the lies about Israel? Or, to bring things closer to home, why was she silent about the campaign of lies and abuse against Rahv and myself and the magazine in the Communist press in the thirties and forties?

One explanation of Lillian Hellman's attitude is that she does not distinguish sufficiently between the anti-Communism of the far right and the anti-Communism of liberals and the left. I myself do not believe that even the conservative intellectuals were responsible for Watergate.

That is too simple a reading of the forces behind these macabre phenomena; and it is one of the canards of the left that all anti-Communist conservatives support corruption and the abuse of power of the kind revealed by Watergate. Indeed, some of the current political confusion comes from the fact that neither the conservatives nor the liberals have any monopoly on foolishness or on bad faith. Anyway, those liberal anti-Communists who have been critical of our own society as well as of Russia have had no more to do with Nixon than with McCarthy. And one would have expected Miss Hellman to make these discriminations and to identify herself with those writers who have not selectively protested against oppression and injustice.

Miss Hellman spoke at one point of writers who have not "stepped forward to admit a mistake, even now," and she says of herself that she "took too long to see what was going on in the Soviet Union." This is a wholesome confession, even if somewhat understated. But it is easier to admit other people's mistakes; and admitting a mistake is sometimes a substitute for correcting it. The fact is that it has been very difficult to maintain one's political balance in these chaotic times that constantly wipe out traditional standards of behavior. And it is only just that if I point out what I think to be Lillian Hellman's errors I confess a few of my own.

As I look back to the thirties, when many of us were born politically, it seems clear that my own swings, though they seemed to correspond to the needs of the time, tended to go too far. At first I was taken in, if only for a short period, by the Communists. Then my anti-Communist recoil carried me too far in the other direction, despite the fact that I maintained a critical attitude to our own society. In the sixties, though I disagreed with the new left and the counterculture, I could be said to be too tolerant of their childish politics and amateur culture, because it seemed to me that however misplaced was the idealism and energy we had always expected from the young, it was not permanently dissolved in smugness and careerism.

Perhaps we cannot avoid such excesses; in a period of rapid change, constant stability and moderation are reserved for those who take no chances, and they become pseudonyms too often for rear-guard actions. But if we are to be saved from the blind extremes that have seduced so many intellectuals, it can be only by preserving a critical attitude toward all ideologies and power structures, and all organized rhetorics of salvation. What went wrong—for the dupes of McCarthy and the apologists for the Soviet Union—was to permit one lie to be substituted for another.

The true meaning of the McCarthy episode, in my opinion, lay not in the injustices perpetrated by the Senator, but in the bad faith exhibited on both sides. To put the question of persecution in its proper perspective: it was not so much a purge as the creation of an atmosphere of fear and suspicion and the whipping up of an old-fashioned chauvinism to combat the "Communist menace." McCarthy did not have any of the appurtenances of a genuine fascist movement, and he was lazy, careless, and unsystematic. It was a one-man show, and, without an organization, the mood it stimulated could not last. Unlike the situation in Germany in the thirties, the Communist "enemy," if not concocted, was at least inflated, and the different kinds and effects of Communist activity were all mindlessly jumbled together. The truth is that McCarthy had to invent an internal Communist danger. There were Communist espionage agents and some filtered into government agencies, but that was a normal condition for any country, and presumably it was a problem to be handled by counterintelligence organizations like the FBI or the CIA, and not a project for public accusations. Then there was the Communist party, which was tiny and impotent. What excited McCarthy and other home-grown conservatives was the influence of the Communists on liberal opinion—an influence that did not harden into a set position but consisted mostly of a general sympathy with the Soviet Union, a mouthing of Communist aims and slogans, and a critical attitude toward the United States that was vaguely Marxist on domestic questions and reflected the policies of the Soviet Union in foreign affairs. But McCarthyites were confused by the fact that non-Communist liberals shared many of these views, particularly on economic and political matters inside the country, so that, like most movements of the radical right, as Daniel Bell pointed out in an essay on "The National Style," published in a volume entitled *The Radical Right*, they went in for a populist form of patriotism that took all liberal and radical ideas to be "foreign" and, therefore, inherently suspect. In essence, McCarthyism lumped all criticism of American society and the American government with Communist propaganda. No doubt some liberal opinion drew on Communist doctrines to supplement traditional views, but it hardly needs to be said that McCarthyism was not the cure for an intellectual disease. On the contrary, the effect was to create a certain amount of sympathy and solidarity with the objects of McCarthy's attacks. Communist-inspired liberal views probably had some effect on government policy, but it was neither decisive nor lasting. What hard anti-Communists fail to see is that even American business is anti-Communist only when it suits its purposes; when selling to Russia is profitable, capitalists have no problems trading with their ostensible enemies. The notion of détente as a way of bypassing political realities, or the idea that Russia is above all dedicated to peace, or that the cold war was manufactured in the United States—all these views that would seem to serve the interests of the Communists undoubtedly made their way into government circles. But the failure to define a clear-cut policy, a policy that promoted a genuine national interest, not the

178

interest of foreign investments or conservative alliances that do not work, a policy that really supported democratic governments and movements as the alternatives to the Communist regimes—this failure has its roots not in Communist propaganda but in our own system and the ideologies it has engendered. Greed and the primacy as well as the chaos of the market usually override considerations that might lead to both a decent and a practical policy. In any event, they usually promote political confusion in government and the media. One need go no further than the case of Israel to observe the erosion of political sanity by the unsuccessful appeasement of the Arab nations.

I do not know how many casualties HUAC and McCarthy were responsible for. Aside from the well-known figures in the entertainment and publishing industries, a number of teachers who were admitted or known Communists were dismissed. As for the right of Communists to a job either in government or private institutions, I confess I do not have the legal answer. Sidney Hook, for example, argued that Communists do not have open minds and are therefore unfit to teach. Hook is right about their closed minds, although the Communists are no more incompetent and biased than some other teachers. But the larger question of Communist influence on public opinion is more complex, and involves the question of how certain progressive myths have become entangled with Russian interests.

And it is almost a commonplace of intellectual life that the battle of ideas has to be conducted not by legal or administrative measures but through persuasion and argument. In any case, McCarthy's scattershot methods further confused the right-to-work issue, for most Communists and fellow-travelers were not touched. The Communists continued to function as a movement, and many went on teaching and working for the various media. After all, McCarthy wanted only publicity, and a few victims suited his purposes better than a complete purge, which would have produced situations he could not handle.

My own experience during this time reflected the chaotic and contradictory character of the political scene. I had no direct confrontation with McCarthy or the Un-American Activities Committee. I did, however, protest the persecution of several writers who were not Communists but who had not taken any anti-Communist stands, and

179

whose past associations were being used against them. But the FBI, a number of times, and a grand jury once, tried to involve me in their fishing expeditions. Since I had never been a member of the Communist party, I had very little information of the kind they were seeking. But they did try to exploit my having been secretary of the John Reed Club.

I suppose it is an axiom of political life that governments and official agencies, like people and movements, expose their true nature in everything they do. The FBI and the grand jury were no exceptions, and my confrontations with them ranged from the unnerving to the absurd. Once an FBI agent came to see me about someone who had been a professor at N. Y. U. many years earlier, when I was a fledgling instructor and graduate student and knew very little about the more solid members of the academic establishment. All I knew was that the person he was investigating was reputed to be a homosexual, but I did not have any idea he had anything to do with the Communists, and I got into a somewhat irrelevant argument with the agent about homosexuality. I took the righteous stand that a man's private life or sex habits were of no concern to the FBI, while the agent took what I learned was a typical intelligence posture, one that was noncommittal but vaguely accusatory.

Another time, when I was teaching at the University of Minnesota, some agents phoned and said they wanted to talk with me. I said I was on my way to an early class and we could talk if they drove me to school. So in a steaming car, with twenty-eight below zero outside, they plied me with questions about a writer who, they said, had been a member of the John Reed Club and had had other left-wing associations, but who did not strike me as a great threat to American democracy. This time we had the kind of ideological confrontation one finds in the novels of Dostoevski and Conrad, a confrontation that goes to the heart of the issue, yet involves so great a disparity between the protagonists as to create a comic and grotesque scene.

I made a rather pompous speech, saying that the FBI did not seem to have any serious or responsible aims and was simply casting a net to see how many former radicals it could catch. Of course, it may have had some knowledge of espionage activities about which I knew nothing, but then it would be wasting its time on me. I added that even

180

if one felt as I did, that Communists represented an evil cause, the FBI and, for that matter, the American government subordinated their anti-Communism to narrow political interests and ideologies. It was, of course, an absurd exchange, for their very inability to understand what I was talking about underlined our different political ideas and concerns.

The highlight of my relations with investigative agencies during the reign of McCarthy came when I was summoned to a grand jury in Washington. One morning Philip Rahv called me to ask me whether I had gotten a subpoena to appear in Washington. My subpoena had been delivered just a few minutes earlier. Rahv was nervous, as he always was when he thought the government was breathing down his neck. "Can you come over immediately?" he asked. He paced up and down the room as I tried to assure him—and myself—that since we were not guilty of anything, we had nothing to worry about. We took the sleeper down to Washington to be ready for the grand jury early in the morning. My first surprise was on the train, for just before Rahv climbed into his bunk he took a sleeping pill and showed me how he crunched it so it would take effect more quickly. This I had never heard of, and it stunned me to see Rahv, who knew almost nothing about non-intellectual matters, so knowing about Seconal.

The grand jury, about which I had heard disturbing stories, turned out to be in its interrogation methods a modern version of the Inquisition. We were told nothing in advance about what we might be questioned on, nor were we permitted to have an attorney. I had no idea what we were there for. So far as I could make out, we had no rights. It seemed almost as though some evil genius had tried to pattern an investigation on Kafka's *Trial*.

Rahv went first. After a couple of hours he came out shaky and whispered to me, as I was being ushered in, that it had been rough.

It was a large square room, lined on one side by a jury of tight-lipped, righteous-looking, but puzzled citizens, the jury of my peers, as they say. There were two hyperactive prosecutors who took turns firing questions at me, their technique apparently being to fire them so fast I would have no time to figure out my answers. To counter this method of rattling me and catching me off guard, I immediately began to answer deliberately and tried generally to slow down the whole process. They started out by asking me about my personal history, and then zeroed in on my precise connections with the John Reed Club and the Communist party.

But it soon became clear that they had two objectives: one was to establish that Anna Rosenberg, a former Assistant Secretary of Defense, had been a member of the John Reed Club; the other was to pin something on as many other people as possible. I told them the truth about my own political associations, but I said I did not know about other people's affiliations with the Communist party as I had never been a member. It was clear from the beginning that my interrogators knew nothing about Communism or anti-Communism or about radical history of any kind; they were simply out to get anyone who might have had a Communist or fellow-traveling past.

I told them that I did not know Anna Rosenberg and did not recall her ever being a member of the John Reed Club. If she had been a member, it left no impression on me and I might have forgotten it. But this would have been unlikely. The denouement came when they began to press me for the membership lists of the club. By this time they had shed the suavity lawyers often use to pry facts from witnesses, and they had become pretty tough. Where were the lists of members, they shot at me. I did not know. What had been done with them? I could not remember—which was the truth. I could hear their teeth gnash and their anger clogging their voices.

Then they shifted. They threw questions at me, rapid fire, about my break with the Communist movement. I tried, slowly and patiently, to describe a process over a couple of years of gradual disillusionment, questioning, arguing, weighing the positives against the negatives, with diminishing returns. "How did the Communists act toward you when you broke?" one of the D.A.s shot at me, ignoring my tedious exposition of the process. "They were hardening and cooling toward me," I said, "though different people acted differently." "Who were *they*?" the D.A. snapped. "What were their names?" He thought he had me cornered.

I took my time before answering, then proceeded slowly and thoughtfully. "I don't know," I said, "whether you are familiar with the Freudian theory of projection. According to this theory, when one has an attitude or reaction to a group or a movement, one tends to project one's own feelings on to them and to give them a personal

182

existence like one's own. In that sense, the 'they' was a creation of my own psyche." Literally, there was no "they," in their sense of the word. There were well-known Communist leaders, but that is not what they wanted to know. I had stretched Freud a bit but did suggest the complexity of the situation. The rage and frustration of the D.A.s seemed to fill the room, and I wondered what they would do to take it out on me. But I guess they had had it, for they dismissed me with the warning to be ready to be called again.

When I got outside, there was Rahv waiting for me, scared and tense. "Did they ask you about the membership lists of the John Reed Club?" was the first thing he asked. I noticed one of the D.A.'s standing nearby and tried to get Rahv to shut up until we were outside, but he persisted. "What did you tell them?" he insisted. I said I could not remember. "Don't you remember?" he screamed at me. "You're stupid, they were thrown out." This was the last I heard of the Anna Rosenberg "case," which would indicate that it was just another example of random harassment and of the purely legal approach to the question of Communism.

I do not mean to make myself out to have been a model of virtue and sanity in the days when McCarthy rode high. But I am suggesting that I did not succumb to the hysteria that was whipped up at the time and is now coming back again, in a kind of retroactive indignation and an attempt once more to use the abuses of McCarthyism to suggest the innocence of the Communists. Recent examples have been Doctorow's and Coover's fictionalizing techniques for painting the history of the last few decades as a struggle between good and evil, with good standing for the left and evil for the right. (Even the Rosenbergs emerge as martyrs of the resistance to the vices of American capitalism.) More recently, Victor Navasky in *Naming Names* has revived the issue of McCarthyism. Garry Wills, in his introduction to *Scroundrel Time*, even went so far as to say that the cold war was created by Truman as a ploy to win the election.

Now there are certain ideas that are so palpably false that it is difficult to disprove them by the ordinary means of logic and the marshaling of facts. Two things are clear, however. Regardless of one's position or sympathies, the fact is that the East and the West have been locked in permanent conflict since the Russian Revolution,

183

and the cold war is simply the form the conflict takes so long as nuclear war is too destructive to both sides.

In my opinion, the lessons of the McCarthy period are not to be found in the rhetoric of those who are trying to play it down or those who are trying to blow it up. What McCarthyism demonstrated, perhaps more dramatically than ever before—though the Palmer raids and the assault on civil liberties of the World War I era were a good preview—was that reactionary forces and demagogic leaders are always lurking on the American scene. But they are not likely to attain genuine power so long as discontent does not get out of hand and sections of the middle and working classes are relatively prosperous. Ironically, too, the power of reactionary forces is limited by the absence of a threat from the left. One of the things that ultimately destroyed McCarthy was that the attempt to paint Communism as an internal danger was too patently absurd to too many people. The lack of a strong and independent radical movement in this country works both ways: it weakens the forces dedicated to reform and progressive legislation and, at the same time, makes it difficult and implausible to mobilize a countermovement to cope with a "red menace."

16

DISCOVERING EUROPE

IN the winter of 1949-1950, my first trip to Europe was the pilgrimage that every American writer and editor does at least once in his life. Unlike earlier generations, who went abroad either as a form of exile or to renew their creative energies, and later ones, who went back and forth with the mobility provided by the boom in the tourist industry and the new affluence for writers and academics—unlike those who came before and after our generation, most of us had been homebodies. We were literally a depression generation, which meant not only that we did not have the money to hop over to Paris or London but that our sights were limited to our own territorial limits, not too far from New York. (Nor did we get a trip to Europe as a graduation present.) It was also before the great academic migrations to universities across the country, which created the cultural equivalent of agoraphobia. There was a striking contrast between our preoccupation with nothing less than the most global problems and our actual intellectual provinciality. New York acquired the qualities of a nation: it was not only the homeland; it took the place of the rest of the world.

But the economic base of our immobility was poverty. Some years later, at a party of the harpsichordist, Sylvia Marlowe, a wealthy man who lived in the demimonde between chic and seriousness was talking about his European jaunts as a fulfillment of dual citizenship. When I confessed that I had not been to Europe until 1949, he said, with the patronizing air only official cosmopolitans put on, that he could not understand it. And when I said I could not afford to go before then, he sounded as though I simply did not belong in intellectual society.

Anyway, he had a point, at least for my personal life, even if it came out of a false sense of aristocracy. For my first trip, despite all my glib talk about European thought and politics, was full of anxiety about the terrors of an alien world. To some extent this was just a travel anxiety, added to a fear of the unknown, which had been cultivated in my childhood by my being uprooted from the age of one to four. But I had learned, as I grew up, to transform my fears into ironies of feeling and style and into intellectual values and ideas. So going to Europe became a form of Jamesian innocence exposed to the cultural traps of the old world. And the stormy crossing by ship—I was then too scared to fly—became a reenactment of all the rituals of death by water.

When I landed on the streets of Paris, I felt the way ghetto Jews from Europe must have felt when they arrived in New York. I could read Baudelaire and Valéry, but I could not tell the taxi driver where I was going. I stood at the Gare du Nord, numb and stiff as though I had been dropped by parachute, not in the most sophisticated city in the world, but somewhere in the African jungle. Somehow, Edna and I got to the small hotel, Le Beaujolais, on the north side of the Palais Royale, which had been picked for us by Kappy (H. J. Kaplan) because he thought it was the best introduction to Paris. It had the added recommendation that Cyril Connolly stayed there on his frequent jaunts to Paris, and among its assets were its dinginess, its discomforts, its inefficiency, its cheapness, and the fact that the *patron* and his wife spoke no English.

We stayed in Paris for about six weeks and I learned to convert my reading French into a negotiating French, though I never trusted myself to carry on serious conversations. I also got to know the city by walking for hours from one end to the other. But since I have neither the eyes nor the feet of a tourist, and have very little interest in sightseeing, I missed most of the monuments and spectacles though I got to know neighborhoods and shopping centers.

As my personal life has been tied up with the magazine and with writing, I spent most of my time with European writers and Americans living in Paris. We saw a good deal of Saul Bellow and his first wife, Anita; Kappy and Celia who were most gracious and helpful; Hannah Arendt; Herbert Gold and his lovely wife; Sheba and Mac Goodman, who was working for an economic branch of the American government. Among the Americans we met from time to time were also Norris Chipman, first secretary of the embassy, Nicholas Nabokov, secretary general of the Congress for Cultural Freedom, and Mike Josselson. I occasionally saw Richard Wright, whom I had known before he left America to live in Paris. Unlike his books, Wright was sweet and gentle. But he lived in his own limbo, for he was in his anti-American phase and therefore not part of the American contingent, nor could he become French.

We were a small American colony, but we had none of the bonds or stances of an émigré group, and our relations with the French were tenuous, since we had no aesthetic doctrines or fashionable anti-American attitudes that would link us to them. And the French were notoriously provincial and inhospitable to American writers who did not fit their picture of the exiled American apprenticing himself to French culture. The new wave of anti-Americanism served only to strengthen the traditional insularity of the French. I suppose we were all in some way anti-Communist; hence we found more in common with Europeans who were politically more sophisticated than the French—and freer of the cultural nationalism that was infected with superficial Marxist jargon and attitudes.

What held the Americans together was mostly congeniality and common assumptions about literature and politics that the French did not share. It was fun to wander around Paris with Saul Bellow and Kappy. Bellow was less expansive, but he was marvelously observant and sensitive to new situations. I remember particularly several excursions with him into an Arab quarter, his soft, questioning eyes alert to the irony and oddities of Americans in Paris. Kappy was open, extraordinarily good-natured, constantly in buoyant spirits, and seemingly always ready for any kind of experience, personal, political, and intellectual. The Goodmans were more political; they cultivated many of the European refugees from Germany and Russia, and it was at their house that I saw a good deal of Arthur Koestler and first met Czeslaw Milosz, the Polish essayist and poet, whose book, *The Captive Mind*, was impressive in its description of the control of totalitarian countries. Recent events, however, have shown that it did not allow sufficiently for the strains of dissidence buried in the heads of people under Stalinist rule. Milosz was one of the few European political figures I had met who were not monolithic in their thinking. Perhaps because he was a poet as well as a political person, he was flexible and was aware of the dimensions of doubt and of all the intellectual modulations in the area where literary and political questions cross.

Hannah Arendt, whom I think of as an American European, came to Paris briefly while we were there. One of the things she said she had to do was to visit the house where she had stayed briefly as a German refugee. She was very tense about it and asked us to go with her. When she came out after having seen the landlady, who was still there, she was shaken, but Hannah was a remarkably strong woman, and she acted as though the catharsis was necessary to permit her to go on with her life. I also got to see another side of Hannah, the side that housed her warmth and wit. One day I asked her why it was so much easier to walk in Paris than in New York. It was because the sidewalks are softer, she said. And in some surrealist way she was, of course, right. Another time I had asked her about French intellectual customs. I had been to see Jean Paulhan in his office at *La Nouvelle Revue Française*. He was impressive, very French in the combination he displayed of wit, rhetoric, and literary authority, even though the conversation was not memorable. In fact, what I remember most clearly is that the woman I assumed to be his secretary was there all the time, seated on the edge of his desk. She was handsome and charming and spoke English easily. Her name was Dominique Aury, a name that did not mean anything at the time, but later people in the know said it was she who had written *L'Histoire d'O*, for which Paulhan had done the introduction. When I told Hannah about Paulhan, I asked her whether it was customary in France for secretaries to remain in the room, seated on a desk, when one comes to see the boss. "Let me explain it to you," she said. "You see, in America we have a democracy, in France they have a secretariat."

Discovering Europe

Most of the French intellectuals in the arts—like Michel Leiris, Eric Kahnweiler, Georges Bataille, Francis Ponge, Edgar Morin, Eugene Ionesco, Raymond Queneau, Henri Michaux—were very French, which for me meant that they were rather inaccessible, not only because of the difficulties of the language but because they were insulated by French traditions and made little effort to get outside their national intellectual borders. Even Alberto Giacometti, who was Italian, and Eugene Ionesco, who was Rumanian, seemed Gallicized. But I saw much more of people like Raymond Aron, who was not only multilingual but spoke a witty and incisive international intellectual language; Manès Sperber, a very knowing, stubborn, but gemütlich novelist and essayist who had had to leave Vienna when Hitler took over; René Leibowitz, a very intelligent and cosmopolitan twelve-tone composer and conductor, born in Russia, who was living at that time with Ellen Adler, a lovely and vivacious woman, the daughter of Stella Adler; and some of the writers later associated with *Preuves* and the Congress for Cultural Freedom, like Jean Bloch-Michel, Francois Bondy, and John Hunt. I also saw Simone de Beauvoir and Jean-Paul Sartre occasionally, but relations were badly strained, and toward the end Sartre would turn away when we found ourselves in the same place. I met Merleau-Ponty several times, before he had broken with Sartre, but the relation was stiff and formal, though not unfriendly. I had seen him in New York, once at my house, where we both seemed more relaxed, but the first time we met was at lunch at Chez Hausmann. For some reason, we got into an argument about Stalinism, and though he spoke quietly, I noticed I was shouting. It suddenly occurred to me that he might be upset if people around us heard that he was open to arguments against the Communists. So I asked him whether he was embarrassed because my voice carried. No, he said, there is nothing to worry about, none of the people around understood English.

Aron struck me as the Sidney Hook of France. Quick-witted, intellectually agile, using all the resources of logic and reason to their fullest, Aron was a skilled polemicist, a master at punching holes in his opponents' arguments. Like Hook, too, his face was sharp and mobile, in keeping with his intellectual personality. And, also like Hook, his main concern was to expose the stupidity and corruption of the Stalinists and their array of fellow-travelers in France.

189

The people around the Congress and *Preuves* were, of course, primarily anti-Communist, and though some produced distinguished work they generated an atmosphere of ideological concentration. Not that one could blame them for their almost professional anti-Communism, for French intellectuals had just discovered the appeals of Marxism, and the entire cultural scene was filled with apologetics and confusion. I felt I was back in the thirties, as the French were reenacting the stale ideas and controversies of the earlier decade in America. Even the jargon of vulgar Marxism, with special emphasis on the magic of the dialectic, a term that was used honorifically to denote some vague idea of change and fluidity, dominated the writing of leading intellectuals. In such a retrograde political situation, it was only natural for those who understood the corrupt nature of Stalinism and its ideology to be driven by the need to expose it. But, as in the political battles of the thirties in America, a generation of anti-Communists wasted its talents on obsessive polemics. Many were dragged down to the level of their opponents, losing sight of their original aims; and a number turned to a conservatism as narrow as the leftism they were trying to counteract.

Figures like François Bondy, Jean Bloch-Michel, and Mike Josselson typified the careers of those who were on the right side. Bondy was a very good cosmopolitan Swiss journalist; Bloch-Michel was a serious novelist. Both were squeezed into the bureaucratic structure of *Preuves* and the Congress. Josselson, on the other hand, was the anti-Communist functionary. Before the war he was a buyer in Paris for a New York department store, but during the war his knowledge of languages led him to one of the psychological warfare units of the American army. After the war, he was in the Army of Occupation in Berlin. From there, according to his own admission, he went to the CIA, and he helped set up the Congress for Cultural Freedom. I have no way of knowing, but I assume that his connection with the CIA ensured the funding of the Congress and control of its activities and policies.

I found Josselson a man of considerable charm and personal honesty, capable of very shrewd and informed political judgment. Yet it was precisely his virtues that fit him for the role of cultural bureaucratic with concealed ties and powers. In fact, it is in a democracy, as against a totalitarian system, that such a role requires a man more responsive to a larger community and therefore more contradictory. What one questions is not the character of Josselson but the manner in which he acquired cultural power.

The writer I was closest to for years after my first visit to Paris was Manès Sperber, until politics once again interfered. There were things about Munyu, as he was called, that could put one off. I often found his petulance, his stubbornness, and his assertiveness hard to take. But these difficult traits, which I took to be the expressions of an expansive personality, were more than made up for by his quick mind and a quality I can describe only as a kind of old world wisdom, the wisdom of a Jewish patriarch, which was both soothing and exasperating. Like the head of a Jewish family, too, he had a warmth and a homely interest in anyone he regarded as a friend. One felt at home with the Sperbers. Munyu was short, bustling, like an intellectual bird, always shouting or laughing or making a speech; Jenka, his wife, was larger, motherly, very warm. They took you into the family if they decided they liked you. On literary and political matters I always had my differences with Munyu. Understandably, because he had known both fascism and Stalinism at first hand, in Austria and Germany, he was more preoccupied with opposing the Communists than I was. In aesthetic matters he was more inclined to the social side of the arts and less concerned with formal traditions and questions. He was also drawn to the conservative American anti-Communists, whose onesidedness he was unable to see. But our differences were dissolved in common assumptions about many things and in cosmopolitan small talk.

How can one summarize an accumulation of disagreements? In general, Sperber kept moving "right" slowly, by which I mean he became more and more impatient with liberal attitudes and less critical of conservative ones. The logic of his evolution was almost fatally determined, as it was for entire generations of anti-Communists for whom the politics of anti-Communism became ultimately the main criterion for judging any theory or action. Let me emphasize, however, that it was not his views about the Communists with which I disagreed; it was the extremes to which he was willing to go to justify these views. For example, at the beginning he was critical of the Congress for Cultural Freedom, even though he was a member of the executive board. But gradually he became an apologist not only for its policies but for its secret controls.

Things came to a head in 1967. Sperber had written me that he was going to be in New York and that he would like to discuss the whole question of the CIA and the Congress with me. It was just after the revelation in *The New York Times* about the support of the Congress by the CIA, which indicated that it had a man at *Encounter*. Subsequently, *Partisan Review* ran a statement, signed by a number of writers, opposing the secret subsidizing of literary magazines by the CIA. A few people did not sign on dubious grounds. But the most self-serving refusal was by George Steiner, who wrote me that since *Partisan Review* had never published him he saw no reason to protest the funding of *Encounter* and other Congress publications by the CIA. I suppose it was no great loss as Steiner's standing as a critic and scholar was not too high.

Munyu and Jenka came to my house for dinner with Norman Podhoretz, Midge Decter, and Lou and Polly Cowan, an intimate group. The evening began with the customary raucous exchange of gossip and display of wit, while we brought each other up to date on what had been happening on both sides of the Atlantic. But there was an undertow of uneasiness as if we were all waiting for the main act of the evening. Finally, the argument broke loose. Munyu asked me straight off why I objected to CIA backing. I began a long, slow, carefully formulated, slightly pompous recital of how I felt, which I had stated and written many times. Sperber argued that those who ran the magazines and the Congress believed in their aims and cited all the good things they did.

The exchange became more bitter and more personal as I characterized his arguments as the kind of apologetics that I had not expected of Sperber. Finally, he abandoned the defense of the Congress on the grounds that it was really free, which I assumed he could not really believe, and he shouted that, goddam it, he thought any means of achieving the anti-Communist ends of the Congress were justified. I shouted back that this was his real position, and I had been wondering why it took so long for him to come out with it. At this point, all pretense of a civilized exchange disappeared. He had been defending the new conservatives who were associated with the Congress, and he yelled at us that any one of them was worth more than any two people—or three, I forget which—in this room. I yelled that this was rude and beside the point, and that, besides, we did not need his estimates of anyone's worth, including his own.

The Cowans, who were not argumentative people, were shocked into silence. Norman and Midge obviously were not exhilarated by these comparisons, but they did not respond. In fact, throughout the evening, though they seemed to support my views, they did not say very much, which was unusual for people who had not been known to avoid intellectual arguments. I had the feeling that they were not eager to get into the middle of these issues because their own opinions were then changing. After this meeting I did not see the Sperbers for years—which I regret not only because political differences of this kind should not envelop one, but also because I still have a good deal of fondness and respect for Munyu and Jenka. Besides, I now wonder why I made so much fuss about the Congress. Was I right? Were my own motives pure? And I am glad to say that our personal differences are being patched up, and that Munyu will be writing for *Partisan Review*.

Next stop on the grand tour of Europe was Italy, which, I had been told by all those who put themselves in charge of my European education, meant at least Rome, Florence, Venice, and the history-laden towns between Rome and Florence. Rome, like Paris, was the unknown, full of exotic dangers.

But the Italians, unlike the Parisians, make you feel as though you were back in New York, in Little Italy, except that the food is better. There is also a warm, homely ring about the Italian language that lets you imagine you can speak and understand it, even when you do not know any Italian. In addition, my knowledge of Spanish did help when the Italians spoke slowly. However, as Mary McCarthy said when we saw her in Florence and I had asked her about my accent in Italian, the question of accent had no meaning when one did not know the language.

Like refugees, we immediately made for the Americans in Rome. Fortunately, there were several friends, the Malamuds and the Ellisons. Bernard Malamud was there on a fellowship from *Partisan Review*°. Ann Malamud, who came from an Italian family and, therefore, helped make everyone feel at home, was a gracious and lovely woman, nervously attentive to people and to all the little things that make living comfortable and civilized. Bern, as he was called, was like a writer from an earlier period: methodical, endlessly observant, always thinking about his craft, in control of his life, jealous of his time and the use to which he put it. He had sent in a marvelous story, "The Magic Barrel," which was published in 1950. At the time, it seemed to have an experimental quality in its originality of tone and atmosphere. But later, particularly after reading his subsequent work, I began to feel that his talent was of a more classical kind; it lay in the careful development of his narrative, in the setting of mood and the laying out of detail, like the painstaking methods of Flaubert and Stendhal. His fiction was like his life, or so it seemed, orderly, and creating the impression of constantly being constructed. This was the quality that made you feel, even in his earlier novels and stories, that he was a writer of major stature. It was also a quality that could sometimes make him remote. I have always loved Bern and Ann, but occasionally, when he talked about writing as he did with Ralph Ellison in Rome, one had the feeling that professionalism also increased personal distances.

Ralph Ellison was at the American Academy in Rome on a fellowship. We were all younger, less combative, less touchy, more carefree, and we had a good time eating, drinking, talking. Once Edna and I hired a car and arranged with the Ellisons to explore the countryside for the day, knowing that in Italy one could stop anywhere for a good and cheap lunch. Ralph said he would drive, as he knew his way around better than I did and could cope with crazy Italian drivers. All the way out of Rome Ralph was yelling at the "wops" who kept cutting in front of us and at the pedestrians who acted as though they

°The Rockefeller Foundation had given a grant for three years to *Kenyon Review*, *Sewanee Review*, *Hudson Review*, and *Partisan Review* for four thousand dollar fellowships by each magazine yearly, to permit young writers some time off. The other *Partisan Review* fellowships went to James Baldwin, Elizabeth Bishop (poetry), R. W. Flint (criticism), 1956; Augusta Walker, Sam Astrachan (fiction), John Berryman (poetry), Sonya Rudikoff (criticism), 1957.

owned the streets. At first I was taken aback, but soon Ralph's half-mocking, ironic cursing made me realize something I had not thought of before, that American blacks, like everyone else, thought of themselves as American, and whether they were angry or joking, had the same reflexes toward "foreigners." And why not?

Fanny Ellison was a remarkable woman, marvelously good-natured and sympathetic even when she was complaining about Italian men, who, she used to say, pinched your ass in the bus but were scared of sex. Ralph, as I recall, was working on *The Invisible Man*. He talked a lot about writing, but not about the book—and who suspected that this magical novel was in the making? Ralph roamed the city, told odd stories out of his past, argued raucously, and gave the impression that abstractly he was always aware of the plight of blacks in America but that he enjoyed his own existence and did not feel that ethnic complaints served either a personal or political need.

The Chiaromontes provided the bridge into the Italian scene. Miriam, who was American, met Nicola in New York in the early forties, when he had to leave fascist Italy. Nicola became a figure in radical circles in New York, writing for *Partisan Review* and, later, associating himself with Dwight Macdonald's political thinking and writing for Macdonald's new magazine, *Politics*. It would be difficult to pin down Chiaromonte's views, for he ranged over politics and the arts, and he was concerned mostly with the cultural and moral implications of politics. He was on the left, but anti-Communist. He questioned the moral basis not only of Soviet Communism but of Marxism itself, and he tended toward an anarchist rejection of state power and of centrally organized revolutionary parties. His writing was subtle and created an air of speculative resonance. In person, Chiaromonte had great charm and made his presence felt; he was generous and friendly, though usually in a manner that created a feeling of distance, and he was moody, often morose, and given to periods of silence especially with talkative people—a trait that reinforced the role of saint assigned to him by many of his friends. I myself was not aware of any particular qualities of saintliness in Chiaromonte and thought the reputation a disservice, for the presence of a "saint" always makes one uneasy, since it puts into question one's own purity. I suppose it might have been different with someone like Simone Weil, whose whole life was an exercise in self-denial, but it is difficult to accept the notion of saintliness in one who did not seem to reject the idea of intellectual or personal gratification. Miriam Chiaromonte was reserved, but always ready to put herself out for friends. Though she was clearly very devoted to Nicola, in an almost Italian pre-feminist way, there was no sacrifice of personal dignity.

As in France, the Italians with whom I felt the most rapport were the writers who were political and internationally minded. Soon after I arrived, I met Ignazio Silone at the Chiaromontes. (Darina Silone, his exuberant Irish wife, was in Ireland at the time.) Silone had been in exile during the dictatorship and, though he had become known in America, was cut off from the native Italian scene, and regarded almost as a foreign figure. This was due partly to the fact that exiles are often looked on as outsiders, partly because his clearly defined anti-Communism was not compatible with the blurring of distinctions on the left and the generally sympathetic attitude toward the Communist party after the fall of Mussolini. Silone was an impressive figure, but with a constant air of sadness and morbidity that seemed to reflect both his personal disgruntlements and hypochondria and his tragic sense of history. Like Chiaromonte, he would sometimes be animated by talking with people he liked, at other times he would sit in a room saying nothing, looking as though he were holding on to his wisdom, because he was bored, or sulking, or just unhappy.

I have always wondered why Silone was never a central figure on the international stage. He had all the makings of a large talent, with his easy control of the medium and ability to fuse theme and narrative. One can only speculate on the reasons he has remained a small though respected figure, on the periphery of the larger movements in fiction. Aside from personal factors, one reason might be the restriction of his subject, which, in turn, must reflect the narrowing of his thinking—a reversal of the usual development of major novelists. His first novel, *Fontamara*, a classically simple and compact work of great charm and extra-literary appeal, struck one as the effort of a mature writer limiting himself to a frame of modest proportions. The later novels retained the pastoral quality of *Fontamara* but shifted to the wider political concerns of anti-fascist and anti-Communist activity. But while these works did not lose the homely and moving effects of *Fontamara*, they did not break into the larger spheres where political and human currents cross. It was as if Silone's political experience had been transferred to the lives of the little people in the Italian countryside, with whom Silone had some affinity, and who apparently embodied Silone's ideas of human and political fatality. In speaking of Silone's later novels in these terms, I do not mean to diminish their stature; on the contrary, works like *Bread and Wine* and *The Seed Beneath the Snow* are masterful accounts of the intrusion of politics into ordinary existence. But I do feel that the dimensions of our political and personal fate, with all their complexities and contradictions, have not been sufficiently explored by Silone. And one cannot help but wonder to what extent Silone's clear-cut politics might have restricted his fictional vision.

This is not to suggest any lack of probity or artistic integrity, for in my knowledge of Silone he has been one of the most stubbornly pure figures I have known. One incident throws an amusing light on this aspect of Silone's life. Some years later, at a party at my house for him, he had been typically subdued, but he suddenly became agitated and came over to me later in the evening to ask me who that bearded man was in another corner of the room. That was Dwight Macdonald, I said, surprised that Silone had not known him before, and had not yet met him that night. Anyway, I asked why he wanted to know. "Because," said Silone, "he is unbearably rude. He said I worked for the CIA." What Macdonald meant was that he edited *Tempo Presente*, which was presumably subsidized by the CIA. I am sure that Silone's shock and anger reflected a genuine feeling that he, himself, had nothing to do with the CIA and that his whole life was a painful expression of his beliefs and his sufferings.

The Italian writers who left the strongest impression were Alberto Moravia, Elsa Morante, and Giorgio Bassani. Paolo Milano, who, like Chiaromonte and Silone, had left Italy during the Mussolini years, lived in New York and returned to Rome after the war. Milano was a strange mixture of Italian and American. He knew everything and everybody, was alert to every new trend, and, unlike Chiaromonte and Silone, had found his way back into Italian intellectual life. After a few years, Milano had acquired considerable influence on literary opinion as a drama and literary critic for Italian newspapers.

Moravia was something else. Very Italian in his suave intensity, he was also the internationally known and successful novelist, cosmopolitan in his mobility and adaptability, and, like his fiction, open and easy in manner. Elsa Morante, his wife then, later separated, was just the opposite. Though gracious and friendly when you got to know her, she was a brooding, reserved, intense figure, closed off from easy exchange. She appeared to be full of some dark, inner turmoil. Her early writing had the same brooding quality, sustained by a slow and carefully built up narrative—almost like a late Italian Gothic Brontë.

I saw her once, years later, in New York, after she had finally gotten a visa, denied for a long time because during the Fascist period she had been forced to join some group on the American blacklist. I chauffeured her on a tour of New York, as a minimal reciprocation for all the people who had shown me around Europe. I was disappointed that what she wanted to see included the standard itinerary of Harlem, the lower East Side, the Puerto Rican neighborhoods, and the various vistas New York has to offer. But then, what is there to see for a European writer here for the first time, especially when these are the aspects of New York that have been engraved on the European mind? The only surprise was her desire to see the cottage Poe lived in, which has been preserved in the Bronx. But then again, as we know, Poe has had some mysterious attraction for European writers since Baudelaire's celebration of him as the first American symbolist.

Bassani, an accomplished short story writer and novelist whom I first met for a drink in a restaurant in Rome, was sharp and spirited, as we exchanged the generalizations that make up the dialogue of people who barely speak or understand each other's language. Bassani talked in Italian and I in English, with both of us inhaling more than comprehending what the other said. What I remember most distinctly is Bassani's pronouncement on the nature of Italian women, which was inspired by two handsome young Italian women walking by us, their heads high, their waists elongated, their hips fashionably enlarged by long billowing skirts. "Italian women," he said, "are frauds. They remain virgins till they are married. Then they become liberated." Finally, I felt I understood chic Italian women, particularly those who paraded up and down the Via Veneto and stocked its cafés.

The most gratifying time was with Mary McCarthy in Florence.

Edna and I rented a car and drove up to Florence, stopping at Perugia and Siena, those cloistered towns that looked as though they had been preserved in a museum. We met Mary for dinner—a meeting that was actually a reunion. We had been on the outs since the publication of her novel, *The Oasis*, in which she satirized a number of New York writers, especially Philip Rahv. On a principle that could be defended only abstractly, for it was stupid when considered concretely, I felt she had betrayed some human code for the sake of fiction. And particularly in the light of my deteriorating relations with Rahv, I had begun to feel more and more that my reaction was senseless. (Sidney Hook complained that he took a stand against Mary McCarthy for using people she knew in her fiction, while Rahv, who was a victim, remained friendly with her.) So when Mary reminded me of some of the things I myself had said about Rahv, I was glad to admit that she was right. I was glad, too, to end the rift with Mary who, I always thought, was not only one of the most intelligent, but one of the most honest people I have known, and full of intellectual enthusiasm—a combination not found too often, though Mary was sometimes the victim of her honesty and her enthusiasms.

We had a marvelous time being taken around Florence by Mary, who had just written *The Stones of Florence*. She was an inspired guide, for not only did she have an awesome eye and memory for detail, but she loved the role of instructor and historian.

17

AN AMERICAN
IN LONDON

LONDON, where I thought I would be more at home, was last and seemed to hit me all at once. My introduction was stark and untypical. The first day, Geoffrey Gorer came to our hotel to see me. I had not met him before, and as I put out my hand he said sharply, "You have destroyed the monuments of Europe." "What?" I said, wondering whether he was mad or I hadn't heard right. He answered by reciting passionately all the sacred objects that had been marred by American GIs carving their initials, or names, or slogans. Even though I had been subjected to personalized anti-Americanisms in Paris, like snide remarks against Coca-Cola as the colonizing drink of American imperialism, I hardly knew how to cope with Gorer's totally gratuitous and far-fetched assault. Perhaps because I did not know how to reply, I answered angrily and crudely that the GIs kept Europe out of concentration camps. It turned out that my own bad taste put an end to his tasteless attack, and we went on to talk about the usual things visitors and hosts talk about: what's been happening in England and America, who is doing what, whom I should see, etc.

Shortly thereafter, I met what seemed to be London's literary establishment all in one place. It was at a huge reception for me and

Saul Bellow, with whom we had traveled to London from Paris. The room was filled with bright talk, which the English appeared to have invented, and the overall effect was a spirited cadence in a language that was both familiar and foreign. I must confess I felt like the mythologized American primitive abroad, lost in the sophisticated intellectual jungles of Europe. I did not catch the names of people I was introduced to; much of the time I did not know whom I was talking to; and most of the conversation was like an abstract verbal ballet one could admire but not always understand. At one point, Edna asked me whether I knew who it was who had invited us for a drink the next day. I had vaguely caught the name of York, but did not connect it with the novelist Henry Green, which was the literary name he used.

We arrived at five. Green whisked us into a small sitting room, told us apologetically in a whisper that he was expecting some steelmen from Chicago to close a big deal, and begged us not to say he was a writer for that would nix the deal. I remembered that under his real name, Henry York, he was in the steel business, and I imagined as he talked about it that his eyes looked like two small, hard steel balls. He seemed nervous and fidgety. He had obviously been drinking already, which did not surprise me, as I had heard he was a heavy drinker. After a few amenities I went to the bathroom, but when I got back I thought we had all gone mad. Green was talking passionately to Edna about football, while she looked as though she was responding. Now Edna is proud of her ignorance of all sports, so it was impossible to imagine how this conversation got started. I soon learned the secret, however. Edna had remembered that Green was a sports nut. He went from football to baseball, to water polo, to basketball, diagramming plays and generally exhibiting the inside knowledge only professionals have. Fortunately, I, too, am a sports nut; indeed America is full of amateur sports experts; hence we had a weird but pleasant hour talking like two typical Americans who have nothing on their minds but football in the fall and baseball in the spring. Suddenly, in the middle of this sportsfest, the bell rang, and as Green hustled us out I got a glimpse of two short, stocky Americans who really had steel eyes.

Unlike America, England had a genuine literary establishment. There is much loose talk in the United States of an establishment, mostly mythical and usually invoked by people throughout the country who feel out of it. But America is too big, too sprawling, the culture is too divided, and there are too many regional and academic centers for there to be a single reigning establishment. Not that it is monolithic in England, but the size of the country, the concentration of literary and intellectual life in London, and the proximity of Oxford and Cambridge, as well as the lack of competing cultures in the popular media and in the middle ranges of publishing—all of these compacting influences make for a more cohesive culture and at least the semblance of an establishment. Most writers and intellectual academics in England know each other, write for the same journals, and together they create the impression of a fairly homogeneous group that influences writing and intellectual currents in England. This produces a very civilized and sophisticated atmosphere, which I find most congenial, though the very concentration of the culture is said, even by the English themselves, to result in a certain amount of inbreeding and sterility. Another aspect of a unified culture that helps make one an Anglophile is the fact that leading businessmen, politicians, and writers mix easily and talk a common language. Political differences are also not so sharp or extreme as in America as left, right, and center intellectuals act as though they all belonged to the same club.

In America it would take years, but in London one scarcely had to go out of one's way to see those with whom one felt some affinity. My first visit was to *Horizon,* the English counterpart of *Partisan Review,* edited by Cyril Connolly and run by Sonia Brownell, who later became Sonia Orwell. Connolly had written a London letter for *Partisan Review,* and I had written some essays for *Horizon.* In addition, *Horizon* published an English edition of *Partisan Review.*

Connolly, whom I saw frequently on later trips to London, was a throwback to an eighteenth-century English man of letters. An accomplished writer, he was learned, very witty, and like so many earlier English writers he liked to live well. He was short and round and gave the impression of being jolly, though his tongue was cutting. As a critic, Connolly reminded me of Edmund Wilson in his literary range and his controlled sensibility; like Wilson, he was somewhat outside the more disciplined currents of modern criticism. Sonia, in comparison with the usual slow tempo of literary life in London, was a dynamo of social and literary activity, always tuned into intellectual and personal affairs on two continents. She was quick, extraordinarily articulate, and handsome, with her massive blonde head of hair swept back cleanly from her forehead. She was also rather dominating, as I discovered; she had to have her way. Years later, in 1957 when I was in Paris briefly, I ran into Sonia at the Hotel Montalembert. I had an appointment to see William Burroughs late that afternoon, but I had the flu and was on my way up to my room, hoping that a day in bed would cure it. When Sonia heard about Burroughs, she insisted that we both go, reinforcing her decision by giving me a letcure on hypochondria. Americans, she said, were by nature, or by cultural influences—I forget which—hypochondriacs, and the least I could do as an independent mind was to resist this insidious Americanism and take her to see Burroughs, whom neither of us had ever met. Out of either her strength or my weakness, I went. He lived on the top floor of a rundown house, and he welcomed us into a large room with a kitchen in it, which looked like a model of disorder. Sonia had a drink, I had some oddly flavored tea. I made an effort to talk to Burroughs, but my head was floating and my body sinking in waves of weakness, and what little strength I had left was not enough to compete with Sonia's manic articulateness. So I cut in and out like a fading radio, and after an hour I said I felt too sick to stay. We got into a cab to go back, I thought, to the hotel. But Sonia had other plans. We were going to dinner, she said, at a good, small, wholesome restaurant near the hotel. When I said I did not feel like eating, all I wanted to do was to fall into bed, she gave me another lesson on American hypochondria, and we landed at the restaurant. I had some chicken soup, and sat through a four-course meal, too tired to talk much, but I was amply entertained by Sonia who had never failed to be clever and amusing.

If London was dying intellectually, the symptoms were hidden, for its leading figures seemed very much alive to me. Some, like Stephen Spender, Isaiah Berlin, George Lichtheim, Richard Wolheim, Karl Miller, Noel Annan, and Frank Kermode, I saw frequently. I also saw a good deal of Dan Jacobson, Alan Sillitoe, John and Miriam Gross, Alfred Alvarez, Penelope Gilliat; less of John Osborne, Iris Murdoch, Arnold Wesker, Richard Crossman, Antony Crosland, and Kenneth Tynan. London was like a continuous cocktail party, very smart, with a touch of good-natured malice, which I suppose is part of the English genius. One has to remember that English intellectual life for centuries has been associated with the aristocracy and has taken on some of the manners of the upper classes.

Stephen Spender has been most friendly yet removed. I take this to be an expression of his person, which seems to require at the same time intimacy and distance. Thus he always appears to be involved and responsive, and yet totally cut off, as though his mind were somewhere else. Spender has contributed frequently to *Partisan Review* and has been for some time one of its consulting editors. My own feeling about his writing is that he is a major poet—a fact that is sometimes forgotten because he has not lent himself to an aura about his life and work, and because his excellent, sober cultural journalism seems to detract from the myth of the unfocused genius. Natasha Spender, high-strung, brilliantly alive, her large intelligence distributed among all her senses, has a kind of upper-class graciousness and concern for people, particularly for those who are weak and helpless, though, like most English people in literary circles, she is not above making fun of them.

I met Doris Lessing at the home of Wayland Young, now Lord Kellet, a very able English critic and journalist. The occasion was a party where I was to get together with the British new left, which meant most of the people around the *New Left Review*, plus some literary fellow-travelers. As I said in the opening of a London letter I started to write but was never able to finish, the new left in England fitted into a large living room.

Stuart Hall, the editor of the *New Left Review*, Janet Hayes, the managing editor, Charles Taylor, Mervyn Jones, Arnold Wesker, and Doris Lessing were among those who were there. Doris was shy and self-effacing, but she was the most magnetic figure. She was short, slightly plump, plainly dressed, with long black hair flowing down behind a soft, mobile face. Her eyes, which missed nothing, seemed to contain the strength of her person. I was particularly struck by her modesty, her apparent lack of any desire to display herself, and by her very un-English flat, low-keyed talk. Most English writers I had met were either themselves upper class or had adapted to the light, witty conversational manners of the aristocracy. Doris, on the other hand, perhaps because she had come from Southern Rhodesia, played up her plebeian personality and made clear her aversion to the gay, party-going literary life of London.

Doris Lessing was also more like writers who came from the working class in her directness, in the nakedness of her ambition, and in her radical views, which were uncharacteristically lacking in ambiguity or irony. For a writer of her intelligence and independence, she was strangely literal-minded in her leftism, which echoed the more fashionable European radical attitudes, particularly the anti-Americanism in European intellectual circles.

Once I had a knockdown quarrel with Doris about McCarthyism, when she insisted that no one was safe from the witch hunt and that all intellectual and academic freedom in the United States was shut down. She made America sound like Russia under Stalin. I tried vainly—and angrily—to make her understand that however bad McCarthyism was, it was slipshod and scattershot, and that most liberals, indeed most of the country, were only indirectly affected by McCarthy's and the House Un-American Activities Committee's campaign against real and imaginary Communists. I finally gave up, convinced it was hopeless. Having never been to the United States, she had absorbed the ideological picture of this country propagated by those who were not content to observe our real shortcomings but for obvious political reasons had to blow them up to monstrous proportions. However, she has long since moved away from her earlier left politics. The turning point was the Russian invasion of Hungary in 1956.

Her politics sometimes took a more amusing and almost refreshing form when it was personalized and transformed into an assertion of individual purity. For example, I took her one day to a reception by the American embassy for Mary McCarthy. Alan Sillitoe, a confirmed leftist at the time, and his wife also came with us. From the beginning, Doris could not contain her political hostility and contempt for the affair, which, I must admit, was a bit silly and pompous. There was a receiving line to meet Mary and the American Ambassador, David Bruce, and the lavish setting, with its almost imperial splendor, was scarcely in keeping with what Mary McCarthy stood for. But she graciously accepted the formalities of the situation while Doris Lessing, I thought, overreacted by fuming against capitalism in general and American imperialism in particular. While all this invective of the

class struggle was being delivered by the representative of the ex-
ploited masses, Mary McCarthy, the showpiece of the embassy, was
greeting her guests, mostly liberal to leftish English writers, with a
frozen smile, indicating her belief that on certain social occasions
gracious manners were more important than having the correct
politics.

But underneath Lessing's politics and personal style was a powerful
literary drive or, perhaps I should say, an enormous ambition, for that
is what seemed to come out in a very significant way. Once I asked, a
bit foolishly I realized afterward, what she wanted most to do. I had in
mind the kind of book she saw as her ideal work or the sort of life she
would like to live. Her answer stunned me so, I hardly knew what to
say. She said she wanted to conquer England, and she had already
accomplished that. I thought of all the conquerors who had preceded
her, and could scarcely find a basis of comparison with this small,
gentle, soft-spoken woman.

True, Doris Lessing has been enlarged into a heroic figure by the
feminists, but as she has said privately, she is not a feminist and has
been somewhat embarrassed by the attempt to coopt her into a
movement that is too one-sidedly ideological for her broad talents. I
suppose, too, she has had to resist having her effort to realize her gifts
blown up into a cause. Nor are her stories or novels feminist works,
unless any work by a woman whose leading characters are women is
to be taken as feminist writing—which is simply a tautology parading
as cultural or literary criticism.

In terms of criticism, the question, primarily, is how good or
important a writer Doris Lessing is, and, to a lesser extent, what the
meaning or impact of her work is. This is not the place to deal fully
with either of these questions and, as in the case of other writers with
whom I have been sympathetic, I cannot be entirely objective. But it
is clear that Doris Lessing is a fiction writer of considerable force, in
the line of the great naturalists. Although she does not have the brute
power of Zola or Dreiser or their ideological sweep, she does, like
them, build her narratives slowly, by accretion, brick by brick, as
though they were architectural structures. Her prose, like that of most
naturalists, lacks the grace of the more symbolic writers and the
inventiveness of the experimentalists. Except, perhaps, for the recent
semi-science-fiction novels, she is not a child of modernism. Her

themes are, of course, contemporary, and the fate of her characters is determined by the forces of the modern world, but her perspective is primarily social and does not draw heavily on the rhetorical and imaginative resources of the leading modernists. It is as a social novelist—as a post-modern writer—that Doris Lessing must be judged, and as such she is a dominant figure. After all, this was her credo: she herself argued that realism is the only literary mode for writing about contemporary life.

Recently, however, Lessing has made a remarkable switch, turning to the inventive and fantasy mode of science fiction as a vehicle for her social imagination. Thus there are now two literary Doris Lessings, though both her earlier and her later work express values and concerns. In any event, as a person as well as a writer, the honesty and directness of her vision—in both genres—are bound to have enormous influence on the way we see ourselves in our world today, both in fiction and in our lives.

Isaiah Berlin, whom I sometimes think of as the British Meyer Schapiro, combines a legendary erudition with personal sweetness. I once spent a charming week crossing the Atlantic with him on one of the *Queens*; unfortunately, he talks faster than most people can think, and my ear was not tuned in on his rapid-fire, heavily accented English speech, with a trace of some foreign origin and an idiosyncratic mannerism that resembles a lisp.

George Lichtheim was another writer I got to know, but, as with most of the others I met in London, I was never close to him. Partly, no doubt, this was due to his troubled personal life, which he kept hidden behind a façade of work. His Germanic seriousness and English reserve combined to put one off. We had many conversations and disputes, all very impersonal. But two personal encounters, very different from each other, stick in my mind. I decided one day to take my laundry to a laundromat because I was annoyed at the cost of the hotel laundry. After a careful search I discovered that London had one laundromat. So I left my clothes there one morning and came back to pick them up the next morning, just before a lunch date with George. The only trouble was that the laundromat had no dryer;

hence I had to take back the wet mess, wrapped in newspapers, and then spread it over my hotel room. When I met George, I still had not gotten over my annoyance, and though it was clear that the problem of my laundry was far below his usual concerns, I delivered a long speech on the backwardness of London. There was a very simple reason, I said, with the irrefutable logic of an American businessman, why New York was full of laundromats, all with dryers: the reason was that when one person found he could make money at something, hundreds of others tried the same thing. I could not understand, I went on, why the same natural law of human greed did not operate in London. George drew his German body to its full English height and said sharply, "We don't like too much commerce in London; therefore the Board of Trade restricts it."

The other incident was more personal and sadder. Susan Sontag, who was coming to my house one afternoon to talk about a manuscript, called to say that George Lichtheim wanted to come, too. He would sit in the living room with us, but would not disturb us. There he sat, without saying anything, for a couple of hours. Susan seemed tolerant but impatient, while all I could think of were those scenes in Kafka's fiction where some man is put in a humiliating position which he both resents and accepts. George's brain, however, appeared to be detached from his life. He had cultivated a cool, objective style and, in my opinion, he had one of the most astute and balanced political minds in this period.

Perhaps the most impressive English writer was George Orwell, whom I saw on a subsequent trip, in a hospital, shortly before he died. He had just received a *Partisan Review* award of a thousand dollars. I was afraid I was tiring him, but he wanted to talk, and I stayed for a couple of hours. Perhaps I was romanticizing a dying figure and reading the moral and intellectual dimensions of his writing into his person, but what struck me was the self-possession, the lack of self-pity, and the impression of utter seriousness, without any of the bright conversation one associated with men of letters in London. He was extraordinarily well informed, and even then, evidently at the end of his life, he wanted to know about everything going on in literature and politics. This is not the place to reassess his work, but it should be noted that the recent questions that have been raised about Orwell's work stem largely from the reaction of the new left to his strong anti-Communism.

My first contact with Frank Kermode was when a remarkable essay, "Poet and Dancer before Diaghilev" (1961), came to *Partisan Review* in the mail. I also wrote a preface on the publication of his first book in this country, saying he was one of the best of the younger English critics. I have admired particularly his earlier studies of romanticism and modernism, but all his work shows a wide range of scholarship and taste. Sometimes his writing has gone in too many directions, but unfortunately that seems to be the fate of critics whose writing is in demand. Though Kermode is part of the British literary scene, he seems almost un-English in his flat, low-keyed manner and his apparent lack of temperament—all of which makes for easy personal relations.

There were also the odd and revealing encounters, as with Kingsley Amis and Kenneth Tynan. We took the train to see Amis in Swansea. Since I had heard he shrewdly kept his cool while outdrinking everyone, I decided to reverse the situation. We started with beer, switched to Scotch, then to punch at a cocktail party given by two solicitous ladies who filled my glass after each sip, then back to Scotch before dinner, finally wine with dinner, and brandy after. I had noticed that Amis was disregarding his reputation and was drinking lightly, but I could no longer check my own momentum. By dinner, after I had reached the usual combination of good spirits and aggression, I got up to make a long, incoherent speech about how Amis was not all he was cracked up to be, which, I must say, he took rather well without trying to take me down. The next day I couldn't get up to make our morning train; only by evening was I able to drag my guilt-ridden head and sodden body to the station.

An evening with the Tynans produced a flashback into the thirties and a title for a book. We met Kenneth Tynan and his wife at that time, Elaine Dundee, at Teddy Sieff's house. We arranged to have dinner together a few days later and met at their house. Kenneth was already known as a drama critic, but he had not yet attained the dual role of left-winger and celebrity that later was a feature of the world where art and chic met. After a few drinks, we got into one of those arguments that, like some bureaucratic web, make you feel there is no escape. This one was about the social and class values of *Othello* in particular, and Shakespeare in general. Frankly, to put an end to a debate that had an elusive subject and woolly formulations, I said I could not continue because I could not remember the answers—the answers to those tortuous but simple-minded questions in the polemics that raged in the thirties about the class basis of art. Years later, remembering the answers became the title of a book by Nathan Glazer.

The argument over, we went to dinner in Tynan's Volkswagen. Elaine had said Kenneth could not drive, so I was surprised to see him behind the wheel, especially since he was drunk. I got very nervous, however, when I noticed that Elaine was working the brakes and clutch, and I said, as mildly as I could, that I thought she said Kenneth could not drive. "That's right," she said, "but he's a marvelous steerer." A few minutes later we crashed into another car. Everybody got out, and there was the usual dispute about whose fault it was, but it was instructive to see how calmly, almost matter-of-factly, the English settle such questions. We continued on to the restaurant, with Kenneth steering and Elaine doing the footwork.

The Americans I saw in London in 1950 and later were mostly people connected with *Encounter* and the Congress for Cultural Freedom. Irving and Bea Kristol were living in London, because Irving had been appointed editor of *Encounter*. They were already becoming more conservative, at least more than I was, but they had not yet gone all the way. Hence our disagreements were largely in tone and emphasis and most conspicuous in cultural matters. I have always thought it unfortunate that people like the Kristols and other neoconservatives should have moved so far to the right, for, at least in my relations with them, I have usually found them to be sophisticated in their awareness of intellectual matters and personally rather sympathetic. Bea has also been a superior student of history, though her bias may have distorted her reading of some issues and figures, especially in the nineteenth century, which is her specialty. Irving, though a bit cynical, is an excellent journalist and a fairly sweet and unmalicious person. English liberals, however, with their typical urban malice— and a faint touch of benign anti-Semitism—used to refer to Irving as the Tory from Brooklyn.

Somewhat later, I also met Melvin Lasky in London. But, unlike the other Americans with whom I disagreed, Lasky always seemed to me to have a career staked out beyond the limits with which I was accustomed to deal. In occupied Germany, he had been editor of *Der Monat*, which was sustained by the American military government, before he moved to *Encounter*. Lasky was always genial, glib, and self-assured. He suggested an intellectual as well as physical mobility. I am not implying that he did not believe in the causes and institutions to which he was attached, but his beliefs and affiliations did not clash as they did with so many people. Also, the fact that he moved from one official niche to another and was not responsible to any visible authority lent an air of mystery to his presence.

18

WRITERS IN THE FIFTIES

THERE has been an attempt recently to resuscitate the fifties, which for some time had been given up to the conservatives. It had been commonly assumed, at least by writers leaning to the left, that the literary side of the fifties paralleled the McCarthyite swing to the right. This was obviously too crude a view, too literal a connection of literature to politics—a hangover, perhaps, of the Marxist formulas in the thirties about the grip of politics on culture. As Hilton Kramer and other conservative critics who have been polemicizing against the new left version of the fifties as a conservative era have pointed out, the fifties produced a new generation of writers with an enormous wealth and variety of talent. As one looks back, the fifties seem less constricted than they did at the time. But despite the emergence of many good writers, there was a loss of the earlier focus, a lessening of the critical attitude toward existing society—in general, a shift from a radical sensibility to a more purely literary one. This shift was noted, and lamented, by a number of critics, including Irving Howe, Richard Chase, Philip Rahv, and me. However, the conservative literary spirit itself was deceptive insofar as it did not take an explicit and aggressive form, exhibiting itself mainly in a recoil from politics. And there were contradictions and such notable exceptions as Allen Ginsberg and the group around him, who actually were the forerunners of the free-wheeling, anarchic, communal, self-indulgent, leftish mood of the sixties. There was also the beginning of a black consciousness that was later to take more militant forms in novelists like Ralph Ellison and James Baldwin, even though they were later put down for not having extricated themselves from the dominant "white" literary traditions.

The fact is that the fifties were not of a piece, which permitted ideological polemicists to ride different aspects of the time and to disregard the obvious conclusion that fertile literary periods have not been necessarily politically radical ones. On the contrary, the point has been made over and over again that the large modernist figures were conservative politically, though the opposite position could be argued by citing Brecht, the earlier Malraux, the young Auden and Spender, Allen Ginsberg, Robert Lowell in some of his phases, Mailer, Aragon, Breton, Artaud, Sontag, and many others.

In any case, a new group of writers appeared in the late forties and the fifties, many of whom we published. Though it would be misleading to characterize them as conservatives, almost none retained the radical politics of the thirties, and few forecast the new left views of the sixties. As for the convulsions on the far right, summed up under the heading of McCarthyism, they had little direct effect on criticism or the arts; they were too manipulative and too demagogic in their appeal to the most mindless levels of patriotism to have much intellectual impact. With a few exceptions, one would have to characterize the new generation in literary rather than political terms.

It would be beyond the scope of this book to attempt to deal with the many writers across the country who came up in the late forties and fifties. Nor, in limiting my account to those who wrote for *Partisan Review* and with whom I had more than a professional relation, am I singling them out as the best or most important.

Isaac Rosenfeld, Robert Lowell, Irving Howe, Leslie Fiedler, and Richard Chase were first published by *Partisan Review* in the forties, but I think they came into their own in the fifties. I was least intimate with Lowell and Fiedler for reasons having to do, I suppose, with them as well as with me, though I have been aware of not being able to get close to people who are flamboyant, psychologically unpredictable, and alternately friendly and distant. Robert Lowell's ups and downs have become part of the history of poetry. But before the biography by Ian Hamilton it was less well known that in his manic periods, when he was drinking and not taking his tranquilizers and going into sanatoria, he became delusionary, often failing to distinguish between himself and God. It was also in these periods that he fixed his admiration on some "great" historical figure: at one time it was Hitler, at another Stalin. In the name of his art and his psychological needs, Lowell has been said to have done many reprehensible things. But I always found him gentle, sweet, and considerate—if somewhat wild. It has also become fashionable to downgrade his poetic achievements. But despite some falling off in his later work, I think he is one of the few contemporary poets with the verbal power and magic of the great nineteenth-century English figures.

Fiedler has shifted several times, but in each phase his views were expressed dramatically and brilliantly. Despite his obvious and large gifts, he seems to have been drawn, almost fatally, to unpopular and debated positions, sometimes following them to extreme lengths. When the Rosenbergs were tried and executed for espionage, he published a piece exposing their middle-brow cultural values. It was one thing to believe they were guilty, which many people, including myself, did, and Fiedler was probably right in his characterization of the intellectual world of the Rosenbergs, but to expose the values and the prose style of those misguided creatures who were being executed served, it seemed, to arouse some sympathy for them. More recently, Fiedler has swung the other way, to a repudiation of traditional art and to a celebration of popular culture. But even if one disagrees with Fiedler's dramatic and extreme stands, one does have to admire the originality of his thinking and his lack of caution in making his convictions public. On only one occasion, in my experience, did he not stick completely by an uncomfortable position. In 1948 he found himself in some academic difficulties as a result of a piece on Huck Finn he had written for *Partisan Review*, in which he made an interesting argument, but one that might have stretched the text, for a homosexual interpretation of the novel. This was not a very popular view in academic circles at the time, but Fiedler, understandably enough in that situation, did not then either disavow the piece or stand by it. Fiedler blamed his troubles on his association with the "radicalism" of *Partisan Review*.

Once, when I was on a panel with Fiedler at a Modern Language

215

Association convention in Denver, I felt there might be a clue to his personality in his delivery. He got up, looked off into space, and began to talk with the dreamy intensity of someone in a trance. He was remarkably articulate and resourceful in establishing his own intellectual tone.

Isaac Rosenfeld first wrote for *Partisan Review* in 1948. He had the kind of perverse and radical sensibility that would have flourished in the sixties. Unfortunately he died in 1956 before he realized his talents or found his literary place. As it was, he was cast in the wrong period, in a period, that is, when criticism was formal and narrow, and fiction was expected to be broad and naturalist, with recognizable human concerns and modes of narration. Rosenfeld's reviews and essays were involved in a form of social criticism that went back to the thirties and, at the same time, heralded the popular, media-oriented, and freewheeling counterculture of the sixties. His fiction tended to be abstract and allegorical, like an early version of Barth or Pynchon. He was also an anarchist before it became popular to be one, a premature Reichian, a prophet of the sexual revolution.

Isaac was short, stocky, roundheaded, bushy-haired. Usually warm and jovial, he had, however, a streak of rage that sometimes burst out at you. When seemingly under control, it showed itself in a curled and petulant lip, and I suspect that he was a competitive and angry man, envious of the greater success of some of his contemporaries. He was not a great talker, but a lively and eccentric one, and he loved to argue unpopular subjects and causes. He used to rail against the conservatism of the scientific establishment—he knew nothing about science —and go all out for Wilhelm Reich's orgone theories. And he went so far as to make an orgone box—it was cheaper to make than to buy one—that looked like a miniature telephone booth, in which he sat for hours, insisting that it rejuvenated him and restored his creative energies. I tried to argue with him about it at the beginning but soon gave up when I realized how much he had committed himself to this homemade therapy, and how much he was drawn to ideas that had something of the intellectually forbidden about them and were beyond the reach of reason and evidence. When he moved to Queens with Vasiliki, his wife, an attractive and energetic woman who indulged his eccentricities though it was not clear whether she shared them, he built a little pastoral orgone box to vitalize his vegetable garden. They had the usual suburban tomatoes, peppers, string beans, peas, and lettuce, but he kept the seeds in the orgone box before planting them, and he was sure that the orgone rays stimulated the growth of the vegetables. His Reichianism, however, was not just a fad; it was part of his thinking, and one could see in Isaac the process by which memories, ideas, neuroses, and fantasies were fused, as they were in tortured writers like Kafka or Joyce. But there was also the simple, homey side of Isaac, which displayed his Jewishness, his familial charms, his earthiness, and his deceptively mild humor and irony. His *pièce de résistance* was his translation of "The Waste Land" into Yiddish, which he would recite with the appropriate mixture of solemnity and impishness while everyone roared at the absurdity and folksiness of Eliot in Yiddish.

Rosenfeld was not only ahead of his time in his eccentricities, but he missed out by his early death on the rewards and seductions that came later to writers in the form of grants, university sinecures, advances, sales, magazine markets. At the end of his life he was beginning to move into the university circuit. Before then he was usually broke. The *Partisan Review* prize of one thousand dollars for his short novel, *The Colony*, published in 1954, was a bonanza. (Two other prizes went to Peter Taylor and George Orwell.) In 1945 I helped him get the munificent job of book editor of the *New Leader*, which paid, as I recall, fifteen dollars week. Though he was an anti-Communist, this was not his main concern, and his working at the *New Leader* could not be considered an act that was ideologically inspired.

Richard Chase, another writer who died young, also first appeared in *Partisan Review* in the forties but should be considered more properly a figure of the fifties, when he developed into a critic of the prevailing view. Chase's main work, *Democratic Vista*, published in 1956, was one of the few books that, in addition to having an unconventional outlook, were scholarly and critically sophisticated. The most distinguishing quality of his writing and his person was his affability and intellectual balance, which, I suspected, held together an interior volatility. He was tall, looking as though he had been stretched, with an oversized head, a shriveled arm that he carried loosely, mild and courtly in manner—a nice man who seemed to have to crank up to become polemical.

James Baldwin first appeared in *Partisan Review* in 1949, with a

217

piece on the literature of protest, "Everybody's Protest Novel," which was essentially an argument against writing bad novels in the name of liberation. Baldwin was right, but this kind of thinking stamped him as a black compromising with white values, and it put him in permanent disfavor with the younger, more militant black writers, particularly those who championed the idea of a black aesthetic. In this piece, Baldwin insisted that there was a common denominator in works like *Uncle Tom's Cabin*, Richard Wright's *Native Son*, and popular protest novels like *Gentleman's Agreement*, all of which made for bad politics because they perpetuated the political stereotypes on which the society was based, and for inferior literature because they reduced the complexity of human existence to these political stereotypes.

I emphasize Baldwin's critical thinking because I believe he is a first-rate essayist and that his main contribution has been to social and literary criticism. I do not mean to take down his fiction, which is deft and marvelously fluent; but somehow the personal drama on which his novels are built has not been able to engage fully those intellectual concerns that appear in his essays.

When I first met Jimmy Baldwin, he was intense, nervous, watchful, with an incredibly ingratiating charm, verging almost on camp, that came through his large mobile eyes and his disarming smile. We talked a lot, and I learned at firsthand what depths of anger, frustration, and ambivalence were buried in black life. For me, the main impact of his talk as well as his writing was to tear away the liberal clichés that satisfied white guilt and preserved white self-interest in dealing with racist injustice. Perhaps the most upsetting and most enlightening episode in our relationship was a confrontation we had in my house shortly after a weekend conference in June 1959, at Tamiment, the adult camp in Pennsylvania. Like most conferences, particularly on lofty moral or social questions, the discussion was both Olympian and banal, despite the fact that the participants included such intellectual performers as Hannah Arendt, Daniel Bell, Sidney Hook, and Harold Rosenberg. Baldwin's contribution was a long, earnest, passionate account of what it meant to be free, despite the heritage of slavery, that invoked the pathos both of freedom and of slavery. I did not say anything at the time, but when I saw him again I felt I had to tell him that his talk was sentimental and demagogic, unworthy of his gifts. Suddenly the gap between us widened and, almost snarling, he said to me that blacks never talk straight to whites, that they always present themselves to whites in a role that permits contact but conceals identity. It was useless to pursue the question, for aside from my feeling that I was lost in some personal and racial storm, it was clear that what I thought would be a candid exchange brought the kind of reaction that was, itself, impenetrable and symptomatic of the barrier Baldwin said was part of the black stance.

Allen Ginsberg was one of the fresh voices who had only a peripheral relation to *Partisan Review*. For though the magazine was open to new writing, the direction of the beat movement was not at the center of our literary concerns. And while I have admired some of the writers of the beat generation, such as Ginsberg and Corso, I have not had the same admiration for Kerouac. Still, the movement represented one of the few instances when we were not responsive enough to new talents. One day Ginsberg called to say he had a batch of work by himself and other writers that he would like to bring over for me to see. He came with his friend Orlovsky, and with a huge pile of manuscripts, to our dinky office on Union Square. Orlovsky was more talkative, Ginsberg more reserved yet sweeter, but both had a kind of old-fashioned friendliness that one did not normally connect with the wildness of the movement. Ginsberg, in fact, has always had a graciousness and politeness that one associates with more genteel figures and trends.

We talked about the things they brought, which Ginsberg spoke of as masterpieces, with the intensity and loyalty usually exhibited by leaders of new movements. But the literary exchange did not last long, for one of the women in the office said something that Orlovsky interpreted—whether correctly or not I never knew—as a reference to pot or to some other drug. The manuscripts were forgotten, and the rest of the conversation had to do with setting up an appointment to get whatever it was they were interested in. As for the material, I thought it was uneven but felt a generous selection should be published. I showed it to Rahv and to Katie Carver: she did not like it very much while he was dismissive of the whole thing. Nevertheless, we printed some poems by Ginsberg and Corso, and I now think we should have printed many more.

19

REALPOLITIK

I said that the question we grappled with in the thirties, as a small marginal group, later became central and occupied governments and whole societies. In a parallel manner, we too moved out of our intellectual ghetto and became more worldly. In my own case, my trips abroad had, I now realize, a symbolic meaning. My first trips to Europe, made possible by the Rockefeller Foundation, brought me into contact not only with European writers but with American government officials and diplomats, and signaled the end of the isolation and feeling of purity we had enjoyed as a dedicated intellectual minority.

In 1962 I made the big jump—what was called a world tour for the State Department. It was during the administration of John F. Kennedy, when the State Department Information Services crawled out of their bureaucratic shell and their ingrained habits of moderation and safety that made the cultural side of the State Department a haven for cautious people and policies. When I went to Washington for my briefing, I could smell the new atmosphere, which allowed for a little more freedom and chance-taking.

A Partisan View

Before leaving on my cultural goodwill trip, I was briefed by someone from the Australian desk, who said, with a convincing show
of modesty, that he could not tell me much, since he was not familiar
with the kind of intellectual matters and people I would have to deal
with. My assignment, as I understood it, was to start with a conference
of magazines in Sydney, and then move to India, Greece, Italy,
France, and England. I was to give some talks, but mostly see writers
and editors in each country. I felt compelled to tell the man briefing
me that, although the State Department was sending me and paying
for my trip, I was not a representative of the American government,
and that he should understand I would not talk as an apologist for our
policies. I might even criticize them, I added. Yes, of course, he said,
but he hoped that I might have some good things to say about my
country.

It seems never to occur to our superpatriots that writers and intellectuals are deeply attached to our country, but that we take our
attachment for granted, and find it offensive to flaunt it and to be on
the constant lookout for evidence of disloyalty in the intellectual
community.

Robie Macauley, who was then editing *Kenyon Review* and I were
making the first leg of the trip, to Australia, together. I met Robie in
Los Angeles for the long flight across the Pacific. I had never seen
downtown Los Angeles before, and my first impression, which is still
with me, is that it looked like an expanded Queens, flat, sprawling,
and undistinguished. Robie was a first-rate traveling partner. He was
gracious, considerate, reserved, and, above all, noncomplaining—just
the opposite of myself. He was the same way at the conference of
Australian literary magazines, which, in addition to the usual self-
congratulatory and windy nonsense of conferences, had its own
brand of provinciality and lack of sophistication, coming mostly from
an excessive admiration of all things American. Thus they failed to
distinguish the mass media and the commercial culture from the less
publicized writing and thinking in the United States. This is not to say
there were not some intelligent and charming people at the conference, but the overall effect was a litany of unexamined opinions. True
to my nature, I was constantly sputtering and criticizing, while Robie
took it all in stride, never letting on that he might not be agreeing with
the tenor of the conference. His composure was so much under

222

control that I began to wonder whether, indeed, he was at all critical. So one day I asked him how he could go along with what he knew to be nonsense. Robie shrugged in such a way as to maintain an aura of ambiguity and a suggestion of disapproval of my New York impetuosity. By the end of our stay, however, I felt we got to accept each other.

Australia, an odd offshoot of England, is a little raw, as America must have been a century ago. It impresses a casual visitor as a mixture of old English habits and American scramble for money and power. It is also, as many Australians said, provincial, which is not surprising for an island stuck away in the South Pacific. Australians complained that America did not think Australia was important enough to send front-line diplomats there, usually assigning businessmen who had to be paid off. Only, the Australians said, when it looked as though Australia was needed as a buffer against the Soviet Union did America upgrade its emissaries.

Robie and I stayed for ten days, then went off in different directions. I had gotten a small grant from the Ford Foundation to explore the possibilities of collaboration with writers in the Philippines and in Tokyo. So off I flew to Manila. I met some very nice young writers and editors there, but the cultural gap was too wide for me to cross in a few days. I also got the unfortunate impression that writers in the Far East thought of the United States as a source of handouts. And since I was not empowered by the Ford Foundation to make any grants or even promises, only a certain amount of goodwill—or so I think—came out of my most earnest efforts to establish East-West contacts. As for Manila, except for the climate, it struck me as an unattractive city, like an overdeveloped, overheated sprawling American frontier town. But what can you see in a few days, most of which are spent talking and drinking?

In Manila I could navigate because I knew some Spanish, and, besides, everyone spoke English. Japan was another planet. Tokyo looked like an anthill, bustling, swarming—the most organized chaos I had ever seen. Even after I had an interpreter, to whom I clung like a baby to his blanket, I had very little sense of where I was, whom I was talking to, what the cultural norms were. I found myself wondering how so many writers and journalists are able to write about the people, the politics, and the general mood of a country after a visit of a

223

couple of weeks. Perhaps, I thought later, the clue to Japan, as to India, was that the language and customs of the people are elaborate disguises for what they think and feel.

Maybe because Japan itself was prosperous, the political coloration of the intellectuals was different. Instead of looking for handouts from America, they appeared to be part of the anti-American propaganda mill. I had a meeting with a group of writers and editors who immediately asked me who had paid for my trip. When I told them it was the Ford Foundation, they replied aggressively, and with the purity that masks ideology, that the Ford Foundation was an agent of American imperialism. I denied this, and added that in the United States conservatives often accuse it of supporting subversive causes. But it was clear that they could not believe anything I said because evidently I, myself, was an imperialist agent.

USIA (the United States Information Agency) had been planning my itinerary and booking me ahead. So, although I was not officially in Tokyo, I dropped in at the embassy to check the rest of my trip. A woman in charge worked out arrangements for Hong Kong, Delhi, Beirut, Athens, Rome, Paris, and London. I was to give talks in Athens, Rome, Paris, and London, and she asked me for a list of people to invite in Paris so that she could cable ahead. Among those I suggested were Jean-Paul Sartre, Simone de Beauvoir, Jean Paulhan, Mary McCarthy, Manès Sperber, Raymond Aron. She asked me whether the cultural attaché in Paris would have heard of these people. I pointed out that they were fairly well known so that even a cultural attaché should have heard of them.

Hong Kong was a tourist interlude, a consumer's paradise. The only event that marred my stay was that I was told the hotel that had been picked for me was a center for Russian agents. I had visions of being abducted to Siberia, and tried to move.

But it was too late, so that night I barricaded my door with all the furniture in the room, and the next day I moved—probably to another center of intrigue. For, charming as were the city and the people, one had a sense of a mysterious underground in Hong Kong, which was undoubtedly part reality, part the image created by Hollywood.

When I got to Delhi, I had lost all connection with place and time. My hotel looked like an abandoned castle. I was told it had been a favorite of E. M. Forster and T. E. Lawrence, but its only signs of life were Indian boys moving silently through the long halls. I left as soon as I could and went to another, less grand hotel with a swimming pool. It was one hundred and twenty in the shade, and I immediately headed for the pool. I put my head under water and when I came up I felt like the movie line: "If it's Tuesday, this must be Belgium." I looked around, and could not remember what country I was in. So much for global travel.

I stayed a week in Delhi, had a car and chauffeur assigned to me, and did some cruising around the city and its outskirts. But India was not for me. I almost never lost the feeling that though the Indians spoke English, I could not understand them, for they used the language not as a system of signs but as a shield for what they thought and felt. The one exception was an evening with Ruth Jhabvala and some of her young writer friends. We talked about everything, as though things had a meaning and we understood them, and I forgot I was in India, as I do when I have a genuine exchange anywhere in the world.

Most of the time I kept my distance from the embassy, for Galbraith, who was then ambassador and whom I knew, advised me to stay away, since Indian intellectuals were suspicious of any American writers tainted by association with the American government. The only direct contact I had was when he asked me over to meet with some leading Indian journalists. What I remember most clearly is that Ken, as he is called by his friends, at one point asked his guests what they would do if China invaded India. What could we do, they shrugged, in a gesture that told the whole story of Indian apathy. You could resist, Ken said. What good would that do, they asked. Who knows, Ken replied, but at least you would not be giving up before you started. That, of course, is the way Westerners think. But one has only to see the absolute poverty and overpopulation of India to understand its passivity and resignation.

I got out of Delhi with difficulty. Some minor customs official could not grasp the fact that I was taking more money out of India than I came in with, because my tour was being paid for by the State Department. I argued, in a hot, bug-ridden room, until the minute my plane left, with meager strength; the night before I had had dinner at the home of a gracious architect and his wife who were insulted by my saying I could not eat anything uncooked. I finally gave in, and landed on the plane with aches, chills, and dysentery. I slept most of the flight to Beirut, which had been chosen over Instanbul because I thought it would be more restful. But suddenly I woke and remembered that some Arab countries do not admit Jews. However, I could not remember which ones they were. The stewardess did not know either, and indicated the question had never arisen before. She spoke to the captain, who also did not know. I became frantic, visualizing myself sick and stranded in the Beirut airport. I asked the stewardess whether she could get the captain to cable Istanbul, which was on the way, for a hotel reservation. She came back to tell me he couldn't. So, abandoned to my fate, I landed in Beirut, had no trouble, drove through the most incredible poverty in a landscape shaped by hovels, to a deluxe hotel on the Mediterranean. I slept for twenty-four hours in the largest and most luxurious hotel room I have ever seen.

In Athens, whose history-laden loveliness one cannot begin to absorb in three days, I was met by a Greek employee of USIA, a stocky, buoyant woman, who immediately told me that the embassy was impervious to the mood and the needs of the Greek people. I made her feel better by assuring her I was as helpless as she was. After a public lecture, which aroused no great enthusiasm or hostility, I left for Rome.

The rest of the tour—on home grounds so to speak—was not very eventful. In Rome, a new cultural attaché, who had just arrived, told me he knew no Italians and, in fact, did not know Italy. All he could arrange was for me to talk to his staff. He also could not manage a reception, so Darina Silone gave a party at which I could meet the Italian literary figures. In London I was asked to give a talk along with Melvin Lasky. I suppose that sharing the platform with Lasky was due to the fact that to some officials all intellectuals look alike. Actually, I was surprised to find that Lasky and I got along quite well as fellow speakers.

I did not go for my debriefing until a year after I got back. By then Kennedy was gone, Johnson was in, and the timid bureaucracy was back in control. I was asked to make criticisms and recommendations, which I did, in my usual crusading spirit, but it was clear that what I said would be filed away with all the other disturbing suggestions that are systematically ignored by self-respecting functionaries.

My next two junkets paid for by the government were to Sweden and Israel. I had met the Swedish cultural attaché, Ingrid Arvidsson, at a reception for her in Washington given by Roger Stevens. She turned out to be a remarkable woman, one of those educated and principled diplomats that only small countries seem to be able to afford—or to appreciate. She was herself a poet, at home in European and American as well as Swedish literature. She invited me and Edna to come to Sweden. I had no duties other than to meet with writers, editors, and government officials, to learn the ways of Swedish culture, and, I suppose, to engage in the kind of intellectual exchange that nourishes both countries. Sweden struck me as the only country I had seen or read about that is run with a sense of sanity and decency, though there was obviously an undercurrent of disorder, brought on perhaps by the long nights of winter. During the three weeks I was there, I cannot say I was able to fathom the Swedish psyche, any more than I could really grasp the nature of its culture. My general impression, when talking with—or reading—Swedish writers and publications, was that although there were common concerns and the common background of Western culture, the turns and complexities of thought and sensibility that were part of my experience were not there. These differences were most evident in the literary criticism in Swedish journals (the state of literary criticism is often a better index to the mind of a culture than the other genres). Swedish poetry, some of which is first rate, was almost completely international in its feeling. The novelists, I thought, were somewhere in between.

In 1972 we went for three weeks, as guests of the government, to Israel, a country that was the essence of all our hopes and dilemmas. It exposed the nerves of your beliefs, divided loyalties, contradictions, and sense of your destiny. It represents your tortured past and uncertain future and points up the split between the concrete facts of being an American and the abstract kinship with your people struggling in a distant desert that you face only when you land in Israel and see and feel the pioneer spirit of a country facing overwhelming odds. In a sense, all the difficulties and predicaments of modern history confront you directly in Israel. The conflicts of capitalism and socialism, the sabotage of democratic movements by the Communists, the real longings expressed by nationalist ideologies and their exploitation by demagogic Arab leaders, the conflict between East and West—all these forces create the almost unbearable strains of what often seems more like a settlement than a country. It is too small a country, situated

227

precariously, dependent on American good will, to take on so many of the problems of the modern world.

One often wonders why so few American Jewish intellectuals have chosen to live in Israel, and one reason might be that they prefer to confront these problems in their heads, not in reality.

Despite all my reading and talking about Israel, I did not know what to expect. Hence there was the constant excitement of discovery, mixed with fear, self-questioning, and ambivalence about its culture and its fate. I saw a good deal of the country since I was provided with a car and a chauffeur, and I talked to a number of leading figures. Many of them were impressive: the political and military leaders were tough and shrewd, the writers sophisticated and cosmopolitan. Yet the general impression, which I find hard to define or document, was one of provinciality. Perhaps this is inevitable in a small country, tucked away in another continent. Perhaps it is because the country is literally in a state of siege, a state that must constrict its cultural concerns. Perhaps it is because what we think of as not provincial is wrapped up in the perverse and decadent complexities that we identify with modern culture.

The most impressive and attractive figure I met was Amos Oz, who lives on a kibbutz not far from Tel Aviv. Despite his special work as a writer, Oz had no privileges. He took his turn in the kitchen and the dining room and shared all the other tasks in the kibbutz—something that compares favorably with the celebrity treatment of writers in the United States. We talked for hours in his small house, mostly about Israel, the Arabs, the "state of siege," not, I assumed, because that was his favorite subject, but because I was the inquisitive visitor. Oz revealed, in a sensitive and urbane way, very much in the terms we would cast such questions, the agony involved in the conflict between recognizing the legitimate claims of the Arabs and recognizing those of the Israelis. As he talked, one could see the insoluble conflict between his feelings of socialist brotherhood with his neighbors and the need for survival, the simple need to protect oneself against attacks, some of which he painfully described. The socialist dream of brotherhood was almost forgotten when his kibbutz was shelled and the children had to scamper into the shelters.

I am aware of the arguments by concerned figures like Chomsky and the Peace Now Movement that an Israeli intransigent nationalism alone cannot solve the problems of Israel or of the Near East as a

228

whole. But neither can they be solved, it seems to me, solely by Israeli concessions. True, Israel is far from an ideal state, and many of its positions are not defensible, but we cannot expect this little, beleaguered state to be the only country in the world to behave in an ideal moral fashion. We cannot demand that an ideal democratic or socialist state be built in one small country, surrounded by hostile nations whose irrational and aggressive policies are justified on the grounds of nationalism, which masks their true purpose, the destruction of Israel.

I also met a number of other writers, theater people, students, and politicians. All had that hardened, purposive intelligence that one associates with a pioneer spirit, though some were a bit too conservative for my tastes. The political and military leaders seemed extraordinarily intelligent and tough. The students, naturally, were more speculative and dreamy, but I was impressed by the fact that their radicalism did not take the form of hostility to their country; on the contrary, they were clearly, like everyone else, ready to defend its existence.

My own naiveté or perhaps I should say my own habit as a Westerner, of chewing every political question instead of simply acting on it, was embarrassingly revealed when I met with General Dimitz, who was second-in-command of the occupied territories. I was taken by an officer to an army building, where we had to clear several security barriers. When I began to talk with the general, I suddenly realized that I was cast in the wrong role. Israeli politicians and generals were obviously accustomed to talking to journalists, and I was clearly but mistakenly assigned to that category. Now, journalists do not usually engage in discursive and speculative conversation with a general who has given them an interview. They are supposed to know what has been happening and simply ask further questions about current situations. I had no such skills or background, so I began to talk about "the problem" of the Arab occupation, and to raise questions about the reliability of America's—and Nixon's—support of Israel. General Dimitz, who obviously knew things I did not know, was in no mood for probing historical possibilities and government motives. Hence the "interview" limped along until I felt it was time to go. Then, to salvage the situation, I said to General Dimitz that I was delighted to talk with him, and that Israeli generals are more intelligent and sophisticated than American generals, which is probably true. He was not a kind man, for he snapped at me, "What American generals have you talked with?" I got out as fast as I could.

I had said I wanted to talk with some Arab writers to get their side of the story. I was told there were none of any importance in the occupied West Bank, but that arrangements would be made to meet with some local Arab leaders in Nablus. In part, my interest was a matter of intellectual curiosity. But it was also, I must admit, an expression of my belief in the omnipotence of argument and reason. Unconsciously, I must have thought I would make the Arabs see the light. We were picked up, with another couple, by a bilingual Israeli student of Arab culture, who apologized for our not being taken alone, but there was no other car and guide available. Our companions were William Davis, the editor of *Punch*, and his wife. He was an amiable fellow who kept complaining that Israeli jokes were not so good or so abundant as Jewish jokes in New York. Also, unlike some of his illustrious countrymen, he was afraid of the Arabs and Arab food. We stopped for lunch in a small restaurant and he ate only the bread, which he must have thought of as international food, and therefore safe.

The Arabs we were to see were leaders of local Palestinian groups, and one was a small banker. There were five of them, three women and two men, in a modest but comfortable cottage, with a typically small living room. There was a good deal of rambling talk, which the English couple encouraged. But I was determined not to have the day wasted in chitchat, so I kept barging in and insisting that we talk about the Israeli-Arab conflict. They replied by complaining about the Israeli occupation of their homeland, by which they meant all of Israel, while I argued that that was past history. I tried to stick to the very simple point, that neither cold nor hot wars were to their interest, anymore than to the Israelis', and that a permanent peace could bring prosperity to the whole area. But I got nowhere. They brought out a copy of a paper that had been written by some members of the American new left, a crude document that defended the views of the Arabs with primitive Marxist arguments and blamed Israel for all the trouble. They waved it triumphantly at me, as if to say the fact it had been written by Americans proved the Arabs were right.

Up to then they had been very restrained and polite as they hospitably served some very exotic cake and coffee. But when I dismissed their American text they became more shrill, and told me that I had

230

been brainwashed by Nixon. Apparently, they conceived of the United States on the model of the Arab countries, with a leader and a controlled press that brainwashed everyone. Finally, their true opinions came out when, in the heat of the argument, one of them shouted, "Why don't the Jews go back where they came from?"

I also had a few short flings at real politics on the home front—politics, that is, that was not just intellectual speculation and agitation. In the thirties, people talked about political reality (a pseudonym for Marxist analysis), which presumably penetrated the ideologies and rationalizations, the "false consciousness" concealing the real meaning of political movements and events. But as we left the Marxist orbit, some of us strayed into occasional political acts that had to do with the forces and people that ran the country. Perhaps some of us strayed too far, but that is a matter for historical controversy. At the time, one felt like doing something immediately useful, instead of always thinking about basic and ultimate questions.

My first fling was to support Robert Kennedy. I had indicated to Joan Cooney of "Sesame Street," a remarkable woman who had once worked for *Partisan Review* and was now on its advisory board, that I was for the Senator. She spoke with Thomas Johnson, who was active in the campaign, and he, in turn, told Carter Burden, who was also working for Kennedy, of my interest. I met with Burden, and we arranged for me and George Plimpton to set up a committee of writers for Robert Kennedy. Despite the allegiance of liberal intellectuals to the memory of John Kennedy, getting support for his brother was not as easy as I had expected. Many writers—including Norman Podhoretz and Diana and Lionel Trilling, surprisingly—were for Eugene McCarthy, who had a more radical image than Kennedy. And Senator Kennedy's political past clung to him. But a number of people, including Norman and Diana, told me the day before Kennedy was assassinated that they were turning toward him. If the atmosphere at campaign headquarters meant anything, Kennedy would probably have been elected, for the campaign was incredibly high-powered and efficient.

There were some amusing testimonials to Eugene McCarthy's appeal, such as the reaction of John Berryman. I phoned Berryman one day to ask him to sign up for Kennedy. He was most sympathetic

231

and genial but sounded drunk and spaced out. Sure, he said, he was for Kennedy. A few days later, however, when one of the volunteers called him to corroborate his being for Kennedy, he said he would never support that son of a bitch. Still, we got a fairly large and impressive list of writers for Robert Kennedy, and shortly before he was killed several more told me they would switch from McCarthy.

I had been asked to come to California to make some speeches, but I did not feel competent to go into all the issues. All I could say was that everything Kennedy stood for was a lot better than his opponents. I was, of course, quite shaken when I heard he had been shot, and I was annoyed at my modesty and dislike of speaking, not shared by most writers, which had kept me from going to California. That weekend Edna and I went to our place in New Jersey. I had heard of the train to Washington, and I felt it would have provided the catharsis I needed, but I had not been invited, I thought. On Sunday, however, a telephone operator reached me to tell me that people were trying to find me to let me know about the train, which was then moving slowly through Philadelphia. We might have caught it, but neither of us had anything to wear besides our rough country clothes.

In 1961 I had a mini-fling with New Jersey politics. Richard Hughes, a Democrat, was running for governor. The Republican candidate was campaigning on a reactionary platform, one of his main planks being an assault on Rutgers University for its tolerance of radicals. A big point was the student demonstrations at Rutgers University, but the Republican candidate had also fastened on the so-called Genovese case. Eugene Genovese, a well-known Marxist historian, had indicated at one point that a victory of North Vietnam was a lesser evil than a continuation of the war. I myself thought this was politically perverse and wrong. However, President Mason Gross and the administration wisely and coolly defended Genovese against the cries for his resignation. Sandman and the American Legion were blowing up the matter. After all, it was not the end of the world, not even the end of Rutgers.

The least we could do was to support Hughes. My small contribution was to organize a writers' committee for Hughes. I was helped by Carla Lynton, the wife of Ernest Lynton, who was then a professor of physics at Rutgers. She was lovely and efficient. But we soon discovered that not many famous writers lived in New Jersey. We got about fifteen, the most eminent being Glenway Westcott. My biggest rebuff came from John O'Hara who told me, in an irritated tone, that I was calling him at the wrong time, and, besides, didn't I know that he was a Republican.

My political insight was clearly demonstrated when Hughes was elected governor by a landslide.

Another small excursion into real politics was my marginal involvement with John Lindsay's campaign for mayor of New York in 1966. Elizabeth Holtzman, whom I supported when she ran for Congress in 1972, asked me to come to a meeting of writers and to help form a committee for Lindsay. It seemed clear that Lindsay, though obviously superior to his opponents, did not fire the intellectual community of New York. The idea was for me to co-chair the operation with Bennett Cerf who, presumably, was to provide the popular touch, while I was to add the serious one. The trouble was that Cerf objected to my sharing things with him. I could not tell whether he was acting out of vanity or thought that I came out of the intellectual ghetto, far from the chic world he wanted to recruit. Liz insisted I stay, and I helped get up an array of serious writers and celebrities. The history of New York puts into question the value of my efforts, but I still think Lindsay was probably more honest than his opponents, and certainly a man of goodwill.

The latest sally into non-Utopian politics was to support Jimmy Carter, the barefoot boy from the Georgia establishment. This time I reasoned that, despite my apprehensions about his outdated populism, Carter was at least a fresh and intelligent voice and a man whose mind had not been honed in the conventional politics of corruption. The country had had enough of Nixon and Ford and politics as usual. I volunteered my services. Bob Montgomery, *PR*'s attorney and member of the advisory board, knew the Ted Sorensens, both of whom were close to Carter, and Bob spoke to Gillian Sorenson, who was in charge of "the arts" at Carter's New York headquarters. I met with Mrs. Sorensen, and got George Plimpton, who knew everybody, to co-chair a writers' committee for Carter. A surprising number of writers refused to support Carter, either because they did not like or did not trust his populist talk. But we got a respectable list, only to discover at the end that the Carter organization did not have the money to run an ad in the *Times*. Just before the election, I phoned a few wealthy people who, I knew, were for Carter, to try to raise several thousand dollars for an ad. Some said they couldn't give or raise any more; a few shockingly said it did not matter who won the election, so why waste money at the last minute. One person complained that I did not involve her in the original thinking about the committee, and called her only at the last minute for money.

I learned two lessons from the Carter campaign: that the vanity and self-interest of some wealthy people often conflict with their ideals and that Carter's campaign, in New York at least, was so sloppy and disorganized that it was a wonder he won the election. Compared to the Kennedy campaign, it was kid stuff. For example, I was put on a Carter task force for the arts, but I was never asked to a meeting, nor was I consulted about anything. Also, unlike the Kennedys who, in the midst of grief and confusion over the assassination, remembered that I had helped, the Carter administration forgot right after the election that George Plimpton and I had, as they say, been part of the team. As for my political wisdom, events have made it highly questionable. I also discovered that my true talent for politics seemed to lie in organizing writers' committees.

20

WRITERS AND POLITICS

PERHAPS the largest, wildest, least focused talent that came into our orbit in the fifties was Norman Mailer. He is also probably the most difficult to understand and evaluate, because of his contradictions and because he has sprawled in so many directions, his commitments ranging from the radical, experimental world of the little magazine and the anti-war movements to the chic arena of the large media, with their earnestness, their topicality, and their opportunities for self-advertisement. He is clearly a writer who has not realized his enormous gifts—although he is one of the most, if not the most gifted, writers in the country. In this respect, as well as in his protean qualities, he is, despite his ideological interests, very American, very much in the line of all those writers who have not had an easy relation with the culture and the country. The accepted notion has been that American writers tend to burn themselves out; my own view is that the literary tradition has not been strong enough to keep writers with general appeal from being pulled in too many popular directions.

Yet, in some miraculous way, Mailer has both responded to the pressures of the period and maintained his own core, perhaps because his own core has so many sides. Mailer is essentially a magician, a superb literary athlete, whether the medium be fiction, or journalism, or television, or the conduct of his life. Perhaps it is for this reason that his essays represent his very special virtuosity more than his fiction does. Fiction, like poetry, dredges up those parts of one's being that lie below the surface of one's literary mind. But the basic quality of all Mailer's writing is a brilliant surface, full of improvisations and multiple effects. Mailer has always seemed to me, in my own relation to him, to be too tangled up in himself to be able to get close to another person. And perhaps his peculiar and appealing combination of sweetness and wildness was both the expression of his ambition and his protection against over-involvement with other people. In any case, I have always found him to act correctly and reasonably, but firmly, keeping an appropriate distance. The only time there was any difficulty in his relation to the magazine was when he wrote a piece about Norman Podhoretz's *Making It*. In his usual manner, he moved in all directions like a fighter, feinting with his body before the deadly hook, and in the course of his digressions, Mailer made a few remarks about Rahv and me that had the innocent but cutting effect of candid camera shots. As a typical image of Rahv, Mailer had him biting into a corned beef sandwich, while he pictured me in a tweedy jacket. I thought this was all within the limits of literary license and fun, but Rahv objected and invoked his rights as an editor—which he was constantly doing when something did not please him. (This was not the least of Rahv's contradictions, though it was a particularly striking anomaly for someone who presented himself as a radical intellectual to be so quick to assert his legal rights.) I could not persuade Rahv not to take the matter so seriously and that it was petty to insist on deleting the reference to him, so I called Norman and explained Rahv's reaction. Norman was at first naturally reluctant to let himself be censored. I told him he could leave in the reference to me—but he soon good-naturedly decided to take out both remarks.

Two incidents—or events (incidents become events in Mailer's life)—illustrate the whackiness and the charm, and the constant sense of himself and his audience that characterize his life and work. In 1965, *Partisan Review* was in need of money, and it occurred to me that Norman Mailer might have some suggestions. He had always been available, and he seemed to know everyone. I phoned and asked him if he could do anything. He said he would think about it and call me back, and soon after he decided the thing to do was to talk to Marion Javits about it, preferably over lunch.

What seemed at first to be a simple project turned out to be most complex and bizarre, for it became clear that for Mailer everything he did took place on a stage and therefore had to be carefully rehearsed. There were a number of phone consultations to pick just the right restaurant. I was clearly an amateur way over my head in this aspect of social activity, and Norman finally had to make the decision. At first he leaned toward an odd, campy restaurant on Fifty-seventh Street where Tennessee Williams often came, but finally he said the right place for this occasion was El Faro, a tiny Spanish restaurant in the village, with just two or three tables, famous for its gazpacho, where a reservation had to be made long in advance.

Lunch was like a symphony, with its prescribed movements, rhythms, and themes. Norman was the conductor. We started off with several drinks each, and with the most general conversation, made up of small talk and big subjects approached obliquely. Then we finished two bottles of wine. Next we started on brandy, and finally were able to begin talking about *Partisan Review*. My head was swimming, and both Norman and Marion Javits sounded as though they had taken off. After much jockeying, they agreed that what was needed was the right kind of gathering, with the right people, at the right place—and the perfect sponsor. There were a number of suggestions, none of them exactly right. All along, I had been more of a spectator than a participant in this social ballet, but at this point I came out with what I thought was the magic name that would make it all go. How about Jackie Kennedy, I asked. Marion Javits looked at me as though I didn't belong, and said scornfully that if I thought the delicate affair we had been plotting could be held at Jackie Kennedy's, then there was no point in proceeding any further. There was some unrelated talk, as though the question had never arisen, and Norman drove off with Mrs. Javits in an enormous chauffeured black limousine. I dragged myself home, wobbly, to sleep off the alcohol and the muffed assignment. The subject was never alluded to again by Norman or me.

The other event put on display Mailer's narcissistic charms, perversities, moral scruples, political contradictions, and his incredible drive to dominate—all together. It was in 1968, at Norman's house in Brooklyn Heights, a gathering of writers, some wealthy people, a few celebrities, and an assortment of Mailer's eccentric collection of fighters, journalists, adventurers, drifting women, put together to raise money for Students for a Democratic Society. Three SDSers from Columbia came down to sell their cause to this mixed group of liberals, radicals, and conservatives, half-friendly, half-hostile to the militant tactics of SDS, but waiting to be convinced that they should support some radical group of whom they disapproved so that their guilt could be dissolved and moral principles kept intact. After everyone, especially Norman, got sufficiently boozed up, which took a long time, impatient people not accustomed to the leisurely warm-up shouted at Norman to get started. But he kept walking around with a glass in his hand and a benign smile, which did not conceal his determination to have his way. After it had gotten almost too late to start the speeches, we sat down in rows of straight chairs facing a speakers' table, like a symposium at one of our *Partisan Review* discussion evenings or an amateur theater performance. The main difference, however, was that most people were drunk, and Norman, who was the moderator, the master of ceremonies, the main speaker, still could not be gotten to start the meeting. Finally, Norman, glass in hand, weaving like a boxer without a knockout punch, began to talk. He talked and talked while his captive audience became more and more restless. Slowly and deliberately, he covered all his favorite themes: sex, anality, peace, God, writing, America, the Kennedys, cancer, etc. He went on and on, with his amazing articulateness and rhetorical improvisation, emphasizing each word and each idea, clipping his syllables for extra accentuation.

Finally, as it was becoming clearer that there would be little or no time for SDSers to speak and for the actual fund-raising pitch, some students came up to the table where Norman was swaying with the rhythms of his peroration, and began to yell for Norman to shut up and sit down. Norman shouted back for them to shut up. One student, a black, shot back at Norman, "Fuck you, whitey." Norman stopped as though he had been shot.

It was the first time I had seen Norman silenced by anything.

Obviously, given Mailer's machoethnicity, particularly in his White Negro piece, this was a low blow by the black student. But it had the effect of getting to the main purpose of the evening, and the SDSers were each given a chance to talk. Unfortunately, they were impressionable kids, and, taking their cue from Mailer, they began to talk about fucking and cocksucking and trips of one kind or another. I was sitting next to Barbara Walters, who had been a student of mine at Sarah Lawrence, a very bright and engaging one, and she said to me, "Is this what we came for? Do they think they are shocking us? Who do they think we are?" This really summed up all the misapprehensions and the false staging of the evening. I think very little money was raised. I had the impression that some of those who gave money gave it partly as a matter of principle and as a protest against the way the meeting was run. Edna gave a donation—why, I do not know.

Robert Brustein, Hilton Kramer, Michael Harrington, Steven Marcus, and Norman Podhoretz began to contribute to *Partisan Review* in the fifties also. I had some influence on Brustein, who has developed into an experimental director, a solid theater and social critic and upholder of traditional standards. He had asked to write about the theater, and over lunch one day he explained his credo. He said he wanted to write in such a way that playwrights would learn from his criticism. For example, if he were reviewing a play by Inge, he would expect that Inge would become a better dramatist as a result of Brustein's advice. I was taken aback by such a simple, unsophisticated view of the theater critic as teacher, and I found myself educating the educator, as we argued about the role of the critic. There was a sane and rational streak in Brustein that responded to my dismissal of his naive pedagogic ideas about the relation of art to criticism—at least as evidenced by his later writing. We have had other disagreements over the years, mostly political ones, but we have taken them in stride.

Hilton Kramer's first piece for *Partisan Review*, in 1953, was a polemic against Harold Rosenberg's earlier essay on art as action, but its main characteristic was its ambivalent attitude toward the value of the new abstract American painting. Up to now this has remained Kramer's position, though he has praised David Smith and other modernists. His tastes and values might best be described as eclectic, which is a somewhat unusual stance, for most contemporary art criticism has been identified with some movement or set of artistic principles. What is significant is that, unlike that of many art critics of this period, his taste has run toward realism, and he has questioned the monopoly of the abstract expressionist school. Among the modern Americans, it would seem that those he has singled out for praise were the less abstract and the more lyrical painters, like Motherwell and Helen Frankenthaler. Though one might disagree with many of his judgments in politics as well as in art, he is one of the few who bring a knowledge of literature and politics to art history. He is actually a cultural as well as an art critic.

From the beginning, Kramer has had reservations about the abstract painters. Once at my house in the fifties, a brawl was barely averted when Kramer told some exponents of the new art, including Gottlieb, Baziotes, Newman, Tomlin, and Ferber, that the reason the abstract expressionists were becoming famous and being publicized by the Luce publications was that they represented the drives of American imperialism. What he seemed to be referring to was the fact that a recent issue of *Time* had a reproduction of a painting by Jackson Pollock—upside down.

Recently, Kramer has taken a neoconservative turn, which has led him on occasion to talk about *Partisan Review* as though it had been kidnapped by the counterculture. And like other neoconservatives, he has been engaged in some rewriting of cultural history, most recently in a review of *The Truants* in *The New York Times* of February 7, 1982, which put down *Partisan Review* and those of us who did not get on the neoconservative bandwagon.

Kramer's recent venture, *The New Criterion*, supported by conservative foundations, has become a vehicle for his neoconservative ideology, which he was able to pursue only sporadically as an art critic for *The New York Times*. But it also has become an organ of shrill polemics against all the people Kramer regards as not conservative enough or too liberal. His views on art shuttle between his attempt to reconcile his liking for realistic art and his antipathy to the democratic and progressive aesthetic tendencies favored by the left.

Perhaps there are some vestiges of an earlier misunderstanding. When Delmore Schwartz, in his paranoia, accused Kramer, and made all kinds of threats against him, of having an affair with Delmore's wife Elizabeth, Kramer called me to enlist me on his side of the quarrel. The story is that Delmore, drunk and wild, went to Kramer's room at the Hotel Chelsea, banged on the door, and threatened to kill him. Kramer allegedly called the police, who came and took Delmore to Bellevue, where, after a few days, he charmed the doctors and impressed them with his being a poet, and was released. I told Hilton—in a friendly spirit—that I believed him to be innocent and Delmore to be mad. But I said that I did not want to line up against Delmore, since his stability and sanity were so shaky.

John Hollander was one of the best poets and critics emerging in the fifties. Like Randall Jarrell, Allen Tate, Robert Penn Warren, he was urbane, sophisticated, educated, a poet with a critical mind. Also like Auden and Schwartz, Hollander was both quirky and scholarly, with a wide range of interests and knowledge. Large, awkward, birdlike in his mental quickness, he reminded me of Delmore.

The two younger writers I became closest to were Steven Marcus and Norman Podhoretz, who started out on parallel careers, then moved far apart. They were students together at Columbia, in a class that included Allen Ginsberg, John Hollander, and Jason Epstein; both were favorites of Lionel Trilling; both went to Cambridge. Then Marcus stayed in the academy while Podhoretz moved into the world of literary and political affairs and became the editor of *Commentary*. Marcus remained a liberal, while Podhoretz moved further and further to the right. Both were among the brightest and ablest of the younger critics.

What impressed me most when I first met them was that they seemed to represent a new breed of critics, learned, well trained, thoroughly grounded in the tradition of the earlier epoch, and already skilled in a type of criticism that combined the close study of the university with the generalizing flair and historical sense of the non-academic social and literary critics. Also impressive, though odd, was that they seemed to have memorized everything in *Partisan Review*.

Their first pieces in *Partisan Review* were remarkable for their historical sweep and for their grasp of the central issues. Marcus, reviewing Van Wyck Brooks's *The Writer in America* in 1953, was one

241

of the first to point out the provinciality of Brooks's sense of the American past and its place in the tradition of progressivism. Podhoretz, in a review of a book on Southern writing and one on symbolism, exposed the historical provinciality of the Southerners and the literary myopia of those who tried to reduce the meaning of the European symbolists to their formal innovations. There were essential differences between Marcus and Podhoretz that suggested their very different later developments. Marcus's body was lean and square, Podhoretz's round. Marcus, though articulate, was restrained, controlled when he talked; Podhoretz was flamboyant, enthusiastic, argumentative.

Marcus's development has been fairly even and steady, with one foot in, one foot out of the academy. He is not an innovator or improviser, like Bloom or Rosenberg, but probably sounder. He is extraordinarily intelligent and scholarly; perhaps his main quality is his stability of taste and judgment applied to a broad range of concerns, from politics to psychoanalysis. Though we have disagreed about many things, mostly about politics, and particularly about Israel, he has been on the board of *Partisan Review* since the fall of 1960.

Norman Podhoretz's relation with me and with *Partisan Review* has been more uneven, though I still find it hard to think of him and of Midge Decter, his wife, as adversaries. There were times when I was to the right of Norman, others when I was to the left of him, and who knows what alignments and shifts the future will bring. Despite our differences, we usually refrained from joining each other's opponents. One evening years ago, for example, when Norman was in his left phase but younger and less secure, Lionel Trilling criticized Norman for his leftish views. It was a very disturbing situation, particularly for Norman, and I tried to mediate because Norman lacked the assurance and poise to cope with it. I thought Lionel uncharacteristically stern, but, on the other hand, I did not agree fully with Norman.

I should say of Midge, too, that though her conservatism has carried her to extremes in her opposition to women's liberation and other radical movements, I have always admired her intellectual quickness and her fearlessness in saying and doing what she wants or believes in. I was able to see some of these qualities close up when she worked as

242

an editorial assistant at *Partisan Review* for a short time in the late fifties. Recently, her political turn has seemed to affect her judgments, and that, I suppose, is the reason all ideologies have become suspect. She has also written for the magazine, and after I had worked with her on her first review, in 1958, of Caitlin Thomas's *Leftover Life to Kill*, she very graciously said to me that she learned more about writing from me than from anyone else.

Everyone wants to know the reasons for the conversion of Norman and Midge, and I have been asked many times whether I knew the secret—the assumption being, of course, that there was some mysterious agent or motive buried in their personal lives. I think there is only a small psychological component. Like many liberals, Norman has reacted to the retrograde leftism that has led many intellectuals to support Communist-inspired liberation movements, for instance, or to take the side of the Arabs against Israel, in the name of some distorted Marxist principle, and, generally, to follow a double political standard in judging left and right regimes and causes. But the question is why Podhoretz has swung so far in his opposition to what he considered the mindless and dangerous ideas on the left. Why has he been unable to maintain a critical attitude to American and European society of the kind other liberals have maintained, along with his criticism of their softheaded and fashionable radical attitudes?

In addition to the normal difficulties of maintaining one's political equilibrium through rapidly changing and often provoking situations, there seems to be some force driving otherwise rational and intelligent people to extremes. It is difficult to understand why writers as politically sophisticated as Podhoretz have failed to see that the politics of conservatism cannot be counted on to fight the battles and save the values they think the radicals have betrayed. Nor has it been true, as many conservatives have claimed, that radical propaganda has been responsible for all our difficulties, either at home or abroad. Neither the gains of the Communists in Asia or Africa, nor the aggressive acts of the Arabs, for example, are solely the doing of the left. At first, Podhoretz's rationale for his ideological polemics was that on the cultural front the main enemy was the radical intellectual, which was partly true. His argument more recently has been that America is losing its will to defend not only its values but its very existence. In the larger perspectives of history, this may well be true, but history should also have taught us that the morale of the nation will not be lifted by conservative rhetoric or political pep talks, or by railing against homosexuality, or crime on the streets, or the excesses of the liberation movements. All this does is to bolster mindless nationalism and vague reactionary thinking.

The process by which valid criticism becomes transformed into a total indictment of the liberal catechism, and, in effect, of one's own earlier thinking, is also cultural and constitutes a response to the vast cultural shifts of our era. Two incidents might serve as illustrations. In 1959, before the counterculture had set up shock waves in the old culture, Edna and I went to see *The Connection* with Steven Marcus and his first wife, Jean. I became quite upset by what appeared to me the first signal of a new sensibility and new set of values. I saw the foreshadowing of what later came to be called the counterculture, and I was shaken by the idea that all the assumptions on which I thought and wrote and on which the magazine was based would be destroyed by a new generation with few ties to the past. My own world was crumbling, and I felt like a refugee in an alien world. Steven and Jean did not share my apprehensions, and we argued about what the play represented. But our disagreements served only to aggravate my feelings of loneliness and uprootedness, of being an outsider.

A few years later, I had one of my few arguments with Norman about this new culture. Norman was putting down the younger writers as a group, insisting, among other things, that they were lazy and spoiled. Since, as chairman of the Coordinating Council of Literary Magazines, I had met dozens of young writers throughout the country, I said his characterization was not accurate. These writers, I maintained, had many faults, including a lack of literary education and an attachment to a cult of regionalism that rationalized a primitive anti-intellectualism and a defensive hatred of the "eastern establishment." But they were not lazy. If anything, they were too busy, too energetic, too zealous in promoting themselves and their prejudices. They were also a mixed bag, I said; many substituted activity and grass-roots ideology for solid work, but some were promising poets and novelists.

As happens often in such situations, the facts became irrelevant to the argument. So I shifted gears and said to Norman something I had been feeling that I thought might be a bond between us. This is a new generation, I said, a new world, which will sweep away those of us who belong to the old world. Never, he shot back at me, never will he permit himself to be swept aside by young radicals. It struck me at the time as a very vivid and disturbing example of the conservative impulse to preserve the old order against the new barbarians, to preserve moral values, aesthetic standards, and social order. This is the impulse that moved such different conservative figures as de Gaulle, Irving Babbitt, de Tocqueville, and it lay behind even the more moderate conservatism of Matthew Arnold. But such a posture must be modulated, particularly in literary matters. If it is carried too far, one is removed from the real and immediate problems of the contemporary scene and is converted into a Utopian of the right, that is of the past, as against a Utopian of the left, that is of the future.

In Norman Podhoretz's case—as in many others—the polemics with the left exacerbated the situation, pushing both sides to further extremes. The leaders of the counterculture became more aggressive against Podhoretz, and he, in turn, denounced liberal views he might normally have been sympathetic with. It became a holy war on both sides.

Podhoretz's own account of his intellectual history in his political memoir, *Breaking Ranks*, published in 1979, which was intended to explain and justify his political shifts, does not make them more acceptable or attractive. Unfortunately, he justifies more than he explains. The drift of his argument in defense of his present position is that he has come to see not only the USSR but the entire left as a threat to America and to all civilized values, which seem to be identical.

Now there would be little disagreement and no need for high-powered polemics if all Podhoretz were saying was that in the present situation the United States is better than the USSR and worth defending or that a part of the liberal left supports backward and dictatorial regimes and movements in the name of humanity and progress. But this is not all that he is arguing. Podhoretz is also against alienation, the Beats, bohemians, hippies, affirmative action, the women's movement, homosexuals, abortion. To be sure, there is no lack of nonsense on the political and cultural left, but idealizing the norms of respectability is scarcely an attractive or viable alternative, or one that solves anything.

Such is Podhoretz's credo at present. Even that could be respected as an honest difference of opinion about the state of the world if his account of his political development were less self-righteous and more balanced. He seems always to have been right, always "ahead of his time." When he was a radical, it was because of the failings of American society. As for Vietnam, he was against it from the beginning, unlike those bandwagon intellectuals who rode the tides of opinion. He was anti-Stalinist early on, though he did think some anti-Stalinists went too far—as they did. In the end, he came to see how most progressive intellectuals betrayed their country, their civilization, their liberal faith. By his own account, he was always right—something almost nobody else claims for himself. He rationalizes his shifts into a steady course of thinking by claiming that he was always against "liberal orthodoxy," against "established liberal wisdom," earlier from the left, more recently from the right. Hence he was always breaking ranks. Unfortunately, this picture of intellectual heroism does not always correspond to the facts and involves a certain amount of self-inflation. His anti-Stalinism was indistinguishable from the politics of the community he grew up in, as was his attempt to hold on to a radical position.

In the sixties he fell for the politics of the new left more than most of us did, though in his latter phase he accuses some of us of having succumbed to it. Like many of us, he was against Vietnam, for political, not for moral reasons, though he claims to have had a unique attitude. Nor is his latest turn distinctive: his conservatism is neither a minority stand nor an unpopular one. Being out of step with one group means being in step with another.

Further, Podhoretz's defense of his own shifting views is weakened by his misrepresentation of the views of those who have not always agreed with him. Thus he singles out Norman Mailer, Lionel Trilling, Irving Howe, and myself as betrayers of the anti-Communist faith. Our motive, he says, has been fear, fear of criticism by the left. The evidence seems to consist of our unwillingness to take the extreme positions occupied by Podhoretz and his fellow neoconservatives. It does not seem to have occurred to him that Trilling was drawn to modulated views; he shunned extreme and shrill ones. Or that Howe has his own mind, and has always tried to maintain an anti-

Communist politics within a radical perspective. Mailer is Mailer, and he cannot be defined by the usual left-right, Communist-anti-Communist categories. As for myself, Podhoretz has a small point, but a distorted one. It is true that I have had some fears, but they have been fears not of criticism by the left, but of being boxed out by ideological commitments from a relation to the contemporary scene—a fear, one might say, of living in some imaginary idyllic past or in some futuristic dream. Still, one would never suspect from Podhoretz's polemical portrait of me that I have always been accused of being too anti-Communist, and a cultural "elitist" to boot, nor that I have been very critical of the contempt for quality and standards rampant these days.

Podhoretz says he could not understand and cannot remember what I said to him about *Making It*. I said that his critics were inflating its faults into a criminal act. But I also said the book was off key in that it gave too much importance to the drive for success. I thought he took literally Rahv's diatribes and exposés of the grubby motives of his fellow intellectuals. And I said Podhoretz's so-called "family" was driven more by literary and intellectual ambitions than by the desire to "make it." Hence *Making It* had the wrong emphasis and tone; in the same way *Breaking Ranks* has the wrong tone. It is too full of speculations and revelations of people's motives and of their greedy push to get ahead, and too comfortable with its discovery of the worship of success in this country.

Sometimes I feel that Podhoretz has been created by the left. His almost ritualistic conservatism is a response to the foolishness and irresponsibility of the left—and is justified by it.

Too bad. Some of my best pieces were written for *Commentary*, and actually solicited and encouraged by Norman. And when Norman had to make a decision years ago whether to become the editor of *Commentary* or go into academic life, he told me I was one of the few who supported his decision to stay at *Commentary*. Many people, according to Norman, strongly advised him against it.

The recent invasion of Afghanistan by the Soviet Union, and the subjugation of Poland, as well as the general growth of Soviet power, have not only startled established opinion into a reconsideration of the idea of détente with the USSR and of American foreign policy as a whole, but have also bolstered the position of the neoconservatives and given a certain amount of credibility to their strong anti-Soviet and anti-radical stand. Many liberals who spend their lives wobbling between radical and conservative views have been leaning toward the tough talk of the neoconservatives, which combines an appeal to patriotism, with the ideals of freedom and human rights, and with the seductive logic of *realpolitik*. It is an almost irresistible appeal, until one begins to examine its political content and strategies—most of which boil down to the old rhetorical bluster about using American military and political power. But the question still remains as to how to use that power effectively.

In my opinion, neither Podhoretz nor the other neoconservatives address the real problems and difficulties that have so far stymied American foreign policy. For one thing, it is certainly no secret that America does not have a foreign policy: what goes under that name is a succession of ad hoc, contradictory, shifting moves. There is no enduring and clear-cut estimate of Soviet power or intentions, or for that matter, of any other country, whether friendly, neutral, or hostile. Nor is there any accepted idea of the national interest, beyond the assumption that Europe, and maybe Israel, are to be defended.

There are many reasons for this weird mixture of empiricism and anarchism in our handling of foreign affairs. But the main one is that America is made up of such a conflicting melange of interests that it is almost impossible to get a consensus except in time of war. Big business wants maximum profits and low taxes, small business worries about its own ledgers, and both are more interested in carrying on as usual than in gearing themselves to a long-term policy that may not be economically advantageous to them in the short run. Labor wants higher wages, even at the cost of losing out to foreign industry on the world market. Politicians have to satisfy their constituency at home with a piece of the pork barrel. The minorities want more. The ecologists want to curb big business. Big business is against both. And so on. And how do the conservatives propose to cope with these obstacles? The truth is that they have no program for consolidating or overriding these powerful forces generated out of self-interest. In fact, the neoconservatives never challenge the very system of self-aggrandizement that is unable to generate a consistent and rational foreign policy.

There are other serious difficulties to which the neoconservatives do not have an answer, and the nature of their position precludes an answer. Even if we assume their basic premise—and it may be correct—that the survival of American and of Western democracy depends on thwarting Soviet or Communist expansion in Africa, Asia, Latin America, and Europe, they have no means for solving the political problems inherent in such a policy. Again, the difficulties lie within the American system and our way of thinking, to which the neoconservatives are committed. Iran presents a typical example of what America is up against. If we back regimes like that of the Shah, we are put in the position of supporting a government that cannot withstand popular revolt, whether with or without Communist military or political assistance, unless we are prepared for all-out military and political intervention. On the other hand, we cannot ally ourselves with radical movements, hoping they will be anti-Communist and pro-American. For one thing, they do not trust us. But more important is that we carry with us the ideology of a business civilization, while the Russians supply indigenous forces of revolt with a revolutionary ideology and a corps of organizers.

Nor is domestic policy free of the same contradictions as foreign policy, and the two are not disconnected. For the loss of American power and prestige, which the neoconservatives decry, is due mainly to the decline in productivity, for which they have no solution. Nor can they have one, for they are not sufficiently critical of the society and the culture that make a rational solution impossible.

I am not suggesting that liberals or the left have any better solution. In fact, most liberals and radicals do not even admit the existence of the problem, at least in the terms we have been discussing it, in terms, that is, of the ability of America to cope with growing Soviet power and its manipulation of nationalist movements in Asia and Africa. Many people of goodwill still think that moral and restrained behavior on our part will act as a model for the rest of the world, including the Russians. There are, of course, knowledgeable liberals, like Stanley Hoffman, who advocate a sophisticated use of politics in the Persian Gulf and other critical areas. But he leaves unanswered the question of how a country steeped in the ideology of private enterprise, which atomizes us into competing units of self-interest, can pursue a radical political policy abroad or can ally itself with nationalist movements—movements that are born out of the myths as well as the realities of liberation and opposition to American capitalism.

Such are the dilemmas of American politics.

21

THE SIXTIES

THE sixties were a trying period for me, for *Partisan Review*, for those of us who had our roots in earlier eras and traditions. It was also full of contradictions, crosscurrents, dead ends, new starts, fake avant-gardism, real talent, genuine liberation trends, and their *reductio ad absurdum* into crackpot movements. The period seemed to be dominated by the new left and the new conservatism, and by a polarization between these two. What was actually going on, however, was a reshuffling of cultural forms on the surface that both reflected and concealed the basic shifts of consciousness that had been developing for decades. But these shifts were not fully visible until the seventies.

At the center of the stage, spotlighted by the media, was the combination of attitudes and movements gathered together under the heading of the counterculture. It was a true melting pot, into which was poured a revival of radical moods, a reaction against the so-called old left, a rejection of traditional Marxism, a sympathy with anarchist tendencies, an emphasis on youth culture, a general loosening of old prohibitions, a conglomeration of liberation movements ranging from the self-evident to the self-caricatured, and a variety of experimental literary works, some genuinely innovative, some trading on the idea of the avant-garde.

Morris Dickstein, in *Gates of Eden*, has made an exhaustive study of the main figures and trends of the sixties, with many original observations, noting the numerous contradictions and crosscurrents. Occasionally, however, Dickstein's analysis is somewhat one-sided, for despite his awareness of the complexities and his attempt at detachment, he is himself, to some extent, a child of the decade. The sixties were the formative, liberating years for Dickstein, and the basic values of the counterculture, or those associated with it, are the standards by which Dickstein occasionally judges earlier ideas as well as contemporary ones.

Of course, we are all products of a specific time and cultural moment, and only people without a core can identify with every old and every new tendency or fashion. Ideally there must be some dialogue, some play, between what one is and what one becomes; otherwise a sensibility formed in one period can never relate to new images of ourselves. As T. S. Eliot and others have pointed out, there is a fragile and indefinable balance between continuity and change that only those minds that are both sufficiently open and partially closed can negotiate.

As has now become apparent, the sixties were not all counterculture, and what one took to be the counterculture represented the working out of cultural forces that were deeper and part of a larger change over a longer period. But, at the time, the counterculture became a primary concern. One felt assaulted not only by the contempt for the past on the part of the new radicals, but by the cultural fragmentation that made tradition look like an outdated custom, and I felt uneasy about the ability of *Partisan Review* to steer a proper course between the claims of the past and the trends that spoke in the name of the future. Concretely, this meant a constant exercise of discrimination between genuine advances and the new forms of avant-garde kitsch. It also meant discrimination between authentic political movements and their distortions to serve special ideological interests. This was not easy, for the application of older values and standards was itself being questioned, and the notion of novelty was elevated into a value. To resist in any way the artistic and intellectual

252

nonsense that was flooding the market and being celebrated by the media was dismissed as a sign of reaction. And to add to the confusion, the earlier distinctions between serious and commercial art, between art and entertainment, which served to keep some kind of order though they were not foolproof and were often used to bolster conservative prejudice, were now being put down as relics of the past.

The attempt to wipe out these distinctions obviously served the interests of the cultural media and the general commercialization of art, both directly and by adding to the general chaos. Even serious critics, such as Susan Sontag and Morris Dickstein, argued against excluding popular movies and the popular arts from the pantheon of art. Presumably, they reflected a more general tendency to adapt to the realities of the new situation in the relation of popular to unpopular art.

The pendulum seems to be swinging again, and while there is not a clear return at present to earlier distinctions, there are signs of recognition that the blurring of distinctions helps to promote the chaos of the marketplace.

Another difficulty was the difference in attitude toward the idea of tradition. Most of us who were associated with the development of *Partisan Review* had been brought up on the idea of central Western traditions. The classic statement of this view was made by T. S. Eliot, and the extreme one by F. R. Leavis. Eliot, it will be recalled, had an organic, almost a biological, conception of tradition and the emergence of new writing—a conception related to the organic sense of literature advanced by Coleridge and later elaborated by the New Critics. It was essentially a poetic principle but it pertained, more loosely, to all of literature and, presumably, to the other arts. Leavis, who applied it to fiction, narrowed the tradition to four novelists in the English language, Jane Austen, Joseph Conrad, Henry James, and D. H. Lawrence, a lineup so schematic and provincial as to mock the whole idea of tradition. (I do not mean to disparage all of Leavis's work, for, in my opinion, he is one of the best of modern critics.) But even Eliot's picture of tradition, however intellectually suggestive and seductive, and however useful for explaining the relation between old standards and new works, leaves out too many side currents, and is too authoritarian in its legislation of the mainstreams in the tradition.

The belief in a central tradition also brings one into conflict with the large variety and plurality of figures and trends that both make up and define the nature of American culture as distinct from that of Europe.

The sixties transformed the sense of multiplicity into an active principle of creative and critical thinking, and explicitly challenged the earlier assumptions about lines of artistic tradition. Naturally this new climate, geared to novelty and cultural permissiveness, came into conflict with the attitudes on which we had been nourished. It was not the new work as such, much of which was original and good, that was challenging; it was the principle of immunity from literary and intellectual judgment. The problem could not be solved purely theoretically or purely practically, for it involved a combination of aesthetic judgment and a willingness to take some risks by plunging into the sensibility of a new era. So as the magazine became part of the current scene we published the new talents and argued with the new attitudes—which is the way the present has always become part of the past.

Insofar as the problems of confronting—or relating—to a new era can be approached consciously, though the process is mostly a matter of literary sense and practical judgment, *Partisan Review* did not go in for large pronunciamentos for or against the new scene. Instead, we continued the basic policy of presenting the best and most interesting work and discriminating between seminal and trendy ideas. Several new and younger people became associated with the magazine. Richard Gilman, Morris Dickstein, and Peter Brooks, critics open to cultural innovation, joined our board, along with Susan Sontag, Christopher Lasch, and Richard Poirier, who may have flirted too much with the counterculture.

The neoconservatism of the seventies was germinating in the sixties, and the old and new politics highlighted a conference we held in 1968 on "The Idea of the Future" at Rutgers University, funded by the Ford Foundation and co-chaired by Daniel Bell and me. Originally I was to chair it, but Bell thought that since the funding was part of a project he was directing for the Ford Foundation, he should be involved in both planning and chairing.

The main point of dispute at the conference was whether any form of socialism, however anti-Communist, was acceptable either as a theory or as a goal, and it focused on Edward Shils' central theme in his paper on "Costs of the Future": that a drastic change, particularly one brought on by revolution, was likely to produce a society worse than the one it was supposed to improve. Aside from bloodshed and dislocation, Shils argued, there was the danger of a repressive regime. I replied that Shils was right about the risks of revolution, but that his equation was one-sided because it ignored the costs of maintaining the status quo. Lines were quickly drawn, with Bell, Hook, Kristol, Lasky on one side, and Marcus, Poirier, Marcuse, Gertrud Lenzer, and myself on the other.

I can now see that the question was formulated too abstractly by all of us. For risks always exist in the concrete political world, and it is now clear that when we talk of revolution, we cannot separate it from Soviet-dominated movements. Perhaps this is what those who emphasized the risks had in mind.

One of the dramatic moments came when Gertrud Lenzer made some criticism of American society and politics, and Edward Shils and Sidney Hook responded. Hook said that because she was a European her knowledge of this country was bound to be limited and distorted. Gertrud began to cry, presumably because of her personal history and feelings about fascism and her German origins. I felt impelled to defend her with a rambling account of how, as a young man who was constantly warned by my elders about the danger of new, rash ideas, I had resolved that when I grew older I would never turn the same arguments against a younger generation. (I should add that I have failed to keep my resolve.) My noble message, which was not very political, vanished into the air. George Lichtheim, whose forthrightness I had never had reason to question before, tried to stay neutral, and it was clear that his sympathies were divided. Perhaps he saw the complexity of the issues more concretely than I did. How we all stayed friends after the conference was a miracle of American intellectual life—maybe we had too many enemies already.

Susan Sontag first wrote for *Partisan Review* in 1962; it was a review of Isaac Bashevis Singer's novel, *The Slave*. I met her at a Farrar, Straus and Giroux party. If she had published anything, I did not know about it, and I had never heard of her. She walked up to me and said, "How do you write a review for *Partisan Review*?" I said, "You ask." "I'm asking," she said. "O.K.," I answered, "what do you want to do?" I do not know whether it was the whiskey or the fact that my guard was down or that there was something immensely attractive and impressive about Susan. I prefer to think that I was open to new talent and that I was mesmerized by the intelligence one could detect in her eyes and in her face. The review was not epoch-making, but it had those qualities that distinguished her later work: it indicated a sophisticated knowledge of modern thought and modern literature, and an ability, unfortunately quite rare, to get quickly to the heart of the question being discussed. After a few more reviews, she phoned me one day to say she would like to write a piece on Camp. I could pretend to the shock of instant recognition, but it would be nearer the truth to say that what she wanted to do was not entirely clear to me. I asked her to tell me more about it, and while I was still not sure of the exact nature of the piece, I began to see what it was about. I told her it sounded good to me. When it came in, I thought it was exciting and original, one of these distinguished pieces of thinking that come along once in a decade, even though its views and its approach to the subject were somewhat alien—and disturbing—to my own sensibility and my own way of thinking.

"Notes on Camp" brought to a head many problems that had been troubling me that constituted the predicament of the magazine in facing a new cultural situation. Susan Sontag was coming to terms, if only obliquely and somewhat playfully, with a world of popular taste and entertainment. To be sure, she was exploring the juncture between the serious and the frivolous, not simply appropriating or sanctioning the latter. Still, it meant the end of the old adversary attitude to the products of popular and commercial culture. Such a stand obviously dramatized the dilemma of the magazine in determining the relation between its traditions and the new outlook. In part, but not completely, and certainly in a biased way, Susan Sontag's piece was an answer to the dilemma, for it transcended the simplest and most conventional terms of the opposition, and it was not just another effort at conciliation, but had its own force and its own justification as a new way of looking at the objects of our culture.

Original creative and critical works tend to resolve problems that polemics only exacerbate. It was probably this aspect of her earlier writing, this capacity for surmounting the ordinary terms of the arguments that led me to play down my own reservations about the position itself. After all, it was significant that "Notes on Camp" swept the world of chic culture and made Sontag an international celebrity overnight, yet it was rarely mentioned that it had appeared originally in *Partisan Review*. Nor were the sales of the issue containing the essay substantially increased. It was as though the piece were the result of an immaculate conception. And its appropriation by the culture of the media only attested to the division the essay presumably denied.

Most of Susan Sontag's other early essays, collected in the two volumes *Against Interpretation* and *Styles of Radical Will*, were just as bold in breaking through conventional categories, though less sensational. But, like the essay about Camp, they had their roots in the prevailing mood of the sixties, in the peculiar combination of a freewheeling radical assertiveness and the pressures of the media to wipe out the distinction between traditional and popular art. In commenting on the new styles of art and behavior, Sontag drew on the classic definitions of modernism of Ortega y Gasset, particularly on his emphasis on the element of play in the modern imagination, though she obviously rejected his distinctions between popular and unpopular art. Recently, however, she seems to have abandoned her earlier views, not explicitly, but by moving to other subjects and more traditional attitudes. Her long essay on photography, for example, is an analysis of the effect on all the arts of the tradition of realism, with its emphasis on reproducing the look and feel of objects and on "objective reality," whatever that may be.

My own dilemmas and conflicts in relation to the cultural changes of the period affected a piece I wrote about Susan Sontag's work in the 1969, number 3, issue of *Partisan Review*, in which I was so concerned with defending her against her hostile critics that I failed to distinguish properly, as I now see it, between her own contributions and her reflection of current moods and ideas. It was not a good essay. Still, she is one of the few younger writers to emerge in the sixties who combine the openness and speculativeness of a younger generation with the generalizing capacity and the feeling for tradition of earlier cultural critics.

22

FRIENDS AND ARRANGEMENTS

SEVERAL things important to the history and fate of *Partisan Review* happened in the sixties, one being our move to Rutgers University, another my meeting Lou Cowan and his association with the magazine, and a third, the founding of the Coordinating Council of Literary Magazines.

I met Polly and Lou Cowan in a very indirect way, in 1959, and both became associated—Polly immediately, Lou later—with the magazine and remained close friends until they died in a fire in their apartment in 1976. It all came about because of the difficulty of getting competent people for the magazine. First-rate managers, copy editors, even secretaries, are either highly paid or dedicated. Unfortunately, our staff was badly paid and only partially and sporadically dedicated; hence the solution, I thought, would be to find a highly capable person who did not need the money and could be trained. I had met June and Jonathan Bingham in Albany through some friends, Naomi and Harold Mager. Jonathan Bingham was Governor Harriman's right-hand man, and Harold Mager a special assistant.

A Partisan View

We had had dinner on New Year's Eve at the governor's mansion with the Binghams, the Magers, and the Harrimans, and there were several amusing incidents during the course of the evening. At dinner, the Governor, who had apparently been briefed—but not enough— asked me whether he could do a sports column for *Partisan Review*. I said sure, without even asking about his knowledge of sports. After dinner, the men retired for brandy, while the women went to the powder room. Over brandy, the Governor asked me what Adlai Stevenson had that he lacked. (Stevenson had beaten out Harriman as the Democratic candidate for President.) Harriman went on to say that he understood the Russian question much better than Stevenson, which was true, and he wondered why intellectuals went for Stevenson. As tactfully as I could, I tried to explain Stevenson's intellectual charisma, but since I, too, had some reservations about Stevenson's fitness for the presidency, aside from his chances of winning, I was able to be honest and diplomatic at the same time.

Anyway, it occurred to me that June Bingham had done some writing, and might want to work at *PR*. She was working for Humphrey, and she asked me whether I had any great idea or slogan for his campaign. I said he should say the country was in trouble and explain exactly what stringent measures were necessary: in other words, tell the public the political truth. Oh, June said, that would not be politic. (Some time later, I was pleased to see that John Kennedy ran on a rhetoric of crisis talk.) I spoke with her about coming to *PR* as an editorial assistant or a managing editor, but she finally said she had better not do it, because of a possible conflict with her husband's activity as a Congressman. I did not agree, but it was not my decision. However, June introduced me to Ellen Straus who, she thought, would be good and might want to work at the magazine.

After several lunches with Ellen Straus, it became clear that her interests and abilities lay elsewhere. (Soon after, she started a program of community aid, "Call For Action," at WMCA, the family radio station.) But Ellen had me meet her friend Polly Cowan, who, she felt, would be just right for *PR*. Polly and I liked each other immediately, and though she had not had any editorial experience, she began working at the magazine. Years later Polly's interest lessened, as Lou became more involved in *Partisan Review*. She usually had to move out, she once explained, when Lou moved in. In addition, she realized that she was meant for social causes, like black and women's liberation, in which she made some important contributions.

Polly was a wonderful woman, one of the nicest I have ever met; she was organized, responsible, dedicated, forthright, loyal, utterly without guile, or malice, or envy. And she was enormously helpful. She read manuscripts, proofread, got ads, and pitched in whenever needed at all the miscellaneous tasks of a magazine. The only problem was that for reasons of office morale we did not advertise the fact that she was driven to work at our dingy offices by a chauffeur.

I did not get to know Lou well until years later. He was president of CBS when we first met, and if I had ever had any doubt about my fitness for business or corporate management, it was dispelled when I saw the toll it took on Lou. We visited them once at Martha's Vineyard. Lou flew up and back for the weekend in a chartered plane, and almost every minute was spent on the phone. It was only after Lou resigned from CBS that he became interested in the affairs of *PR*. (He left CBS at the time of the scandals surrounding "The $64,000 Question," which was one of his ideas. But he told me he knew nothing about the rigging of the program, and I believed him.) Lou joined the advisory board—later he served as its chairman—and became interested in all the activities of the magazine. In the world of intrigue, self-serving, and doubledealing dominating business, politics, and the media, Lou, like Polly, stood out for his decency, loyalty, and honesty. Like Polly, too, he was modest and self-effacing, but where Polly always maintained the integrity of her own person, Lou was always questioning himself and sometimes denying his own person—a trait that visibly annoyed Polly. On the whole, he was an invaluable member of the board, and his suggestions and contributions on more than one occasion literally saved the magazine.

Shortly after Lou joined the board, when he discovered that *Partisan Review* was in a hole, he asked me how much money we needed, and handed me a check for twelve thousand dollars; he continued to make comparable contributions whenever a crisis arose. We saw each other constantly, and he served as an adviser, a listener, a moral supporter. If anything, he had too many ideas in too many directions, but that, I believe, is characteristic of many people, particularly those with wealth, who do not have to work and do not have one driving intellectual bent, hence are open to all the attractions and seductions of our culture. He was a large, angular man whose movements were forthright and decisive, and such big blunt men are never scheming nor nasty. Lou's almost naive modesty more than made up for his cultural diffusion, and it was a sad day when he died so senselessly.

Roger Straus was the first friend of the magazine outside its inner circle of writers and professional intellectuals. A bluff, energetic, strong-willed man with a good deal of macho charm, he was also very sharp and quick to size up people and problems—qualities that enabled him to build one of the best of the independent publishing houses. I had met him first, but Rahv, as he tended to do in such situations, became more intimate with Roger and his wife, Dorothea, a shy and sensitive writer. Rahv had a way of surrounding people; so as he got closer to Roger, I found myself pulling back. Anyway, Roger, with his practical instincts and his worldly experience, was immensely helpful. At one point Rahv said Roger was interested in publishing the magazine, and Rahv had some scheme for bringing in Robert Silvers. I liked Silvers and thought him very able, but this did not seem to be his metier, and the whole thing fell through, perhaps because it had too many components and calculations. But Roger helped to put us in touch with some worldly people, though, as one would expect, not all contacts were fruitful.

Once we had a board meeting at Ben Sonnenberg's house with the expectation of getting some assistance from him. Ben was a wealthy, self-made public-relations expert with a strong interest in the arts, and he had one of the few remaining salons in New York in his lavishly and meticulously appointed house on Gramercy Park. He was articulate and witty, but the most striking thing about him was that he looked as though he had been designed for his role. He was short, stocky, with a large head, made larger by the putty pallor of his face, and an enormous, upturned waxed mustache. At the meeting, Ben was sitting near a window, and at a point when the meeting was floundering, when Ben had either planned or had the instinct to take over, he began to deliver a professional speech that sounded like a mixture of scolding and exhortation. The gist of it was that we had endless opportunities waiting to be seized by us, but we had not, for whatever reason, taken advantage of them. The climax was reached when he pointed to the window and said that the world was out there, all we had to do was to open the window.

The meeting petered out after his talk, for nobody knew exactly what followed from it. I left with Lou Cowan, and I said to him that I did not understand either the point or the value of Ben's remarks. Lou said that Ben got five thousand dollars for delivering the same talk to a meeting of businessmen, which only strengthened my feeling that American capitalism was based on an enormous amount of wasted money and energy, though I did not doubt Ben Sonnenberg's shrewdness and ingenuity as a public-relations man.

Recently, Joanna Rose has been the main force on the advisory board. A large, handsome, driving woman, she seems to be in motion all the time. She is unusually intelligent, and completely without malice or cunning—an unlikely combination—and she has made many valuable suggestions, editorial and financial, in her role as chairman for a number of years. Her husband, Dan Rose, one of the new breed of sophisticated and educated businessmen, has also been very helpful (particularly in reminding us that the world is bigger than ourselves).

A decisive event was the move to Rutgers University in 1963. It worked until 1978, when a new administration decided to end the relationship in a rather unpleasant fashion. The support of the university, though only partial, helped the magazine, and the university felt there were definite benefits in the association with *Partisan Review*.

It all happened like this. In 1962, Merlyn S. Pitzele suggested that since Richard Poirier was coming from Harvard to build up the English department at Rutgers, it might be to everyone's interest to have the magazine there, too. I met with Dick Poirier, who was enthusiastic, and he spoke with Richard Schlatter, the provost of Rutgers, who discussed it with Mason Gross, its president, both of whom liked the idea. I then talked with Dick Schlatter to make the final arrangements and had lunch at the Harvard Club with the outgoing chairman of the English department, Rudolph Kerr, who wanted to see me—pro forma, I suppose. He struck me as a gentleman of the old school, of the kind that dominated English departments of universities earlier in the century, with their intellectual hobbies and eccentricities. One of his eccentricities showed up in the form of a large suitcase he was carrying. When I asked him casually whether he was on his way somewhere, he said no—when he came to New York he brought his clothes to be cleaned and pressed as New Brunswick had no good cleaners.

Arrangements proceeded fairly smoothly. In fact, there were only two hitches, one involving Poirier, the other having to do with Rahv. When we got to discussing Dick's precise role and title, he said I had agreed that he would become an editor. I had no such recollection, and the confusion came, I thought, because I had indicated that he would become a member of the editorial board, which Dick took to mean a full editor. But we had agreed about everything else, so I finally accepted his version instead of going on bickering. The main difficulty was that it was not entirely fair to Steven Marcus, who had been an associate editor for years. Steven was angry, but graciously accepted the situation.

Rahv, who was not so gracious, created more of a problem. When I told him about Rutgers, he sounded as though it were a tragedy to be avoided at all costs. He was agitated and used every conceivable argument and ploy to forestall the move. He could not deny the advantages to *Partisan Review* as well as to Rutgers, but his sophistical objections seemed to indicate that he thought the move would not be in his own interest. As my co-editor, he used his presumed rights to stall for time and to cast around for any possible alternative. At one point, he told me that Roger Straus had spoken with someone at Wesleyan, and asked that we delay until he heard. Why Wesleyan was better than Rutgers was not at all clear, unless it was better for Rahv. Wesleyan fell through, however, and Rahv had exhausted all his delaying tactics and arguments, not the least of which was a continuous criticism of Poirier's character and abilities.

The arrangements with Rutgers were simple and considerate of the rights and responsibilities both of the university and of the magazine. We were to be associated with Rutgers but would maintain our own identity. Hence the university would not be responsible for either our finances or our policies, while we would have complete editorial autonomy and freedom. There was no contract, no time specified.

The association could be for one year or ten years, or more. What the university provided was office space, a secretary, and several teaching assistants (assigned to the magazine). Later, a managing editor, who gave a course in the English department at Livingston, was added. I became a member of the Rutgers English department, with release time for working on the magazine. No money was to be given to us to help cover our costs, which remained our own responsibility. This relation obviously had its advantages but also its disadvantages, not the least of which was the fact that we had to raise money constantly to meet a deficit. But it was, on the whole, a viable form of cooperation and one that avoided the kind of entanglements and interference that sometimes accompany institutional support of publications. Until the brutal end, which was a betrayal of everything that went before, differences could be worked out. Mason Gross and Richard Schlatter were scholars and enlightened administrators, as was Henry Winkler, who became vice-president of Rutgers, and is now president of the University of Cincinnati. There was never enough money for added services, but this was compensated for by a civilized relationship with the university. After Gross and Schlatter left the administration, bureaucratic and budgetary controls, particularly from Trenton, were tightened, and though Edward Bloustein, who succeeded Gross, was a sophisticated man, one had the feeling that power was passing to the politicians, the functionaries, and the mediocre educators.

Several members of the English department—Tom Edwards, George Levine, Dan Howard—also became contributors to the magazine. But Dick Poirier and I were closer, at least superficially, despite our literary and temperamental differences. He had a sympathy with recent cultural developments that often clashed with my more traditional attitudes. At the beginning there were arguments, as we both probably pushed each other to extremes, but later we usually assumed our differences. One of our conflicts arose out of Dick's sense of his own interests, modulated often by his urbanity. Another arose from his bias against New York literary life, which I never could entirely understand since he was not averse to participating in it. Perhaps the anti-New York stance was an extension of earlier rivalries with New York and Columbia that he felt at Harvard and came from a feeling that New York represented a "family" from which Harvard had been excluded.

I recognized that my sense of tradition might be too narrow, though it was ingrained in me as part of my literary development; but it did serve as a restraint—or corrective—on the use of the idea of pluralism to destroy traditional standards and to justify all new adventures in the arts. Poirier, who actually was very critical of most people and things, was nevertheless more easily impressed by new cultural events. Too open, many people thought, as evidenced, they said, by his piece on the Beatles, which argued that the apparatus of criticism was as appropriate to the Beatles—who were geniuses—as to the work of, say, T. S. Eliot.

The founding of the Coordinating Council of Literary Magazines in 1967 benefitted the entire magazine community. Roger Stevens, a knowledgeable and fair-minded man, who had just been designated by President Johnson as chairman of the National Endowment for the Arts, appointed Carolyne Kizer as the program director for the literature program, and both wanted to do something new and useful. Carolyne talked about helping literary magazines, and CCLM was born at a lunch meeting that included, besides Carolyne and me, Reed Whittemore, the poet, James Boatwright, editor of *Shenandoah*, Peter Caws, who taught philosophy at Hunter College and later became the first treasurer of CCLM, and Caroline Herron, managing editor of *Partisan Review*. The name derived from the aim of setting up a new council to coordinate the existing organizations of literary magazines. Reed Whittemore had been chairman of the Association of Literary Magazines of America (ALMA), modeled on a trade union, to which most literary publications belonged, and I was chairman of the Council of Literary Magazines (CLMA), made up of *Kenyon Review, Hudson Review, Sewanee Review, Poetry,* and *Partisan Review.* Thus we were presumably to unite the plebeians with the elitists, the unionists with the professionals. Our purpose, expressed in our charter, was simple and direct: to help American literary magazines with money, advice, and general support.

The first year, we received a grant of fifty thousand dollars from NEA. We formed a board of directors, set up an office in Washington, and we were in business. We rented some space and the services of a secretary in the offices of the National Institute for Public Affairs, whose president was Carl Stover, a friend of Reed Whittemore. The board of directors included Whittemore, Boatwright, Jules Chametsky of *Massachusetts Review*, Robie Macauley of *Kenyon Review*, Caws, Stover, and myself as chairman. We soon found we needed an executive director and a New York office, as our work grew and meeting in Washington regularly became difficult. But Stover, whose motives I never understood, opposed this move.

I could never figure out, incidentally, what his organization did, though it seemed to be well financed. Ostensibly, it educated government workers, but I could not understand why they needed education any more than anyone else.

The showdown came at a meeting of the board in New York, at which Stover alternately tried threatening and cajoling us, while his assistant kept adding milk to a glass into which Stover was pouring whiskey. At one point he seemed to forget that I was the main obstacle to his apparent desire to run our show, or he thought he would win me over, as he delivered a long, stuttering tribute, which sounded like a eulogy, to my gifts as a writer, editor, and chairman. His performance did not help his cause, although some of the members of the board were sentimentally reluctant to remove him. Finally, Stover indicated that he would resign at the request of the chairman and permit the office to be moved completely to New York.

When CCLM was started, I thought it was going to be easy to run: all we had to do was to look at applications from magazines and award grants to the needy and the qualified. As for need, all magazines were broke. And quality was something we all knew how to recognize. The only trouble was that we soon discovered there were not fifty but a thousand literary publications in the country, of varying sizes, policies, and quality. Moreover, we soon realized that we were not a private foundation, exercising our own tastes, which, though we believed them to stem from the highest literary standards and traditions, did not necessarily represent the vast, sprawling, variegated world of the small literary magazine. And since we were dispensing government funds we were supposed to take account of a number of considerations besides abstract quality, such as representativeness, regional interests, and quality within a certain category. We also had to consider claims to represent black writing, women's writing, and other political-literary movements. Not only was our volume larger than expected and rapidly growing as little magazines across the country learned of this new source of funds, but the political pressures kept creeping up on us until, in the end, they transformed the organization. The creeping process was so slow and insidious, however, that I was not aware of its destructive power until it was irreversible. At the beginning, it seemed to me that our board was much too narrow and unrepresentative of the range of magazines. Hence we began gradually to expand the board, while some older members dropped off.

We also created an auxiliary board of consultants, which included a number of young editors and writers from different parts of the country. Almost from the beginning, however, we were subjected to a chorus of criticism for not being democratic, by which was meant two things: one, our board was not elected; two, some magazines that wanted a piece of the pie did not get a grant. To meet this criticism, while retaining the centralized control we thought made for continuity and responsibility, we soon transferred the grant-making powers to partially elected, partially appointed grants committees. But, of course, nothing we could do, short of handing over CCLM to our critics—who would then fight among themselves and with their critics—could satisfy them.

Who were our critics? In addition to the usual quota of disgruntled editors, born oppositionists, and wild men, they were mostly editors and writers connected with the smaller publications, mainly in the mid and far West. Basically, they were acting out of self-interest in their hostility to CCLM and to the larger, more prestigious of the little magazines they felt it represented. The more reasonable—or more diplomatic—ones demanded a larger share of the kitty; others boldly and nakedly insisted that none of the better known magazines, which included most of the quarterlies and those attached to universities, should get any support. But this dollar diplomacy from below was usually enveloped in a regional, populist credo that celebrated smallness and grass-roots ideologies and pitted itself against a mythical establishment in New York and the East, presumably running the rest of the country. By the establishment, they did not mean *The New York Times, Time,* NBC; they meant *Partisan Review, Paris Review,*

Antaeus, Massachusetts Review, etc. As for facts, they argued that the biggies of the littles got the lion's share of the grant money, even though the reverse was true. For a few years a California organization dominated by the little littles, called COSMEP, led the assault on CCLM and on the quarterlies, but recently COSMEP itself has been accused by a new group of littles of going soft. There are always new small publications coming up, ready to trump the existing ones, by claiming to be more radical, more democratic, less elite, closer to the soil and the people. Once a myth has been generated, there are always new sects being born to carry the banner to more and more absurd extremes. And, of course, when polemic fails, they appeal for support to rural and provincial politicians, who have their own reasons for claiming a larger portion of the pork barrel.

If the issue had been simply the proper distribution of government funds, it could have been settled quite easily and reasonably. For a balance between the better known and the smaller ventures was constantly being adjusted by the board of CCLM. What the critics really wanted was to cut off all funds from the larger magazines and to take over CCLM. And they had going for them a number of forces. Not only were the "democrats" more numerous, but they also seemed to have plenty of time for infighting. In addition, because the main source of funds was the NEA, they could resort to all kinds of political appeals and maneuvers. Their biggest ally was right in the NEA, in the person of the literature program director, Leonard Randolph. He supported the most aggressive, the most provincial, and the least talented editors and writers in and around COSMEP. Hence nothing we did could appease our critics who felt they had support in the NEA.* Under pressure from Randolph, we added representatives from small magazines, regional groups, and minority movements. The result, finally, was that the ideological criticism that originally came from the outside gradually found its way into the organization, and meetings were often taken up with banal discussions of represen-

*At a panel discussion in Boston in 1982, sponsored by the Associated Writing Programs of America, Michael Straight, chairman of NEA under Carter, acknowledged that the endowment exercised pressure on its panels and on CCLM to spread its funds over the country regardless of quality.

tativeness versus quality and of the virtues of smallness. (God knows we were all small and poor enough.) The political irony is that this populist drift of the administration began under Nixon.

I do not mean to play down the good work of CCLM. On the contrary, it was the first and the only organization to undertake to assist the nonprofit literary magazines of America, and there is no question in my mind that it has not only lifted the morale of the magazine community but has helped countless magazines to survive. I have been emphasizing some of its problems only to indicate the difficulties involved in government support of the arts in this country, where the myth of mass participation in the arts is so strong. As for my own role, after seven years as chairman of CCLM, a time I regard as paying my debt to my country and my culture, I was kicked upstairs, and I basked in the glory of being the first president emeritus of an organization that opposed its original principles—and of having many of my own magazine's requests for grants turned down. (Recently I severed my connection with CCLM.) In the last few years, CCLM has been mostly oriented to the smaller, regional, and ethnic magazines, giving only occasional and token support to the larger, better known publications.

The fate of the Coordinating Council of Literary Magazines was sadly illustrated at a meeting of the board of directors and consultants in Winston-Salem, North Carolina. I was present as the newly elected honorary chairman, after my years in the trenches. Ishmael Reed, the new chairman, was presiding over a discussion of candidates for the board. Ishmael was pushing hard for someone who shared his third world and ethnic views, and his populist program for CCLM. Several people disagreed with Ishmael, but Trudy Kramer, a consultant, argued harder, questioning the qualifications of Reed's candidate. Reed almost instinctively lashed out at Trudy, accusing her of racism, the most deadly charge in liberal circles, and insisted, besides, that as an employee Trudy had no right to talk. Trudy left the room crying. I launched into a criticism of Reed's tactics, probably illegally, for it was questionable whether I had the right any longer to speak up. But, of course, when the vote was taken it was unanimous for Reed's choice—presumably to maintain the unity of the organization.

23

COEXISTENCE

IN the sixties, my relation with Philip Rahv, which had been bad for a long time, came to an end. It is an unpleasant story, difficult to tell, and up to now I have talked about it only to a few friends. But it is central to the history of the magazine, and there has been so much inaccurate gossip about it that I feel it must no longer be treated as a badly kept family secret. Obviously, I can write about it only from my viewpoint—but as objectively as possible.

From the beginning, Rahv was not easy to work with. He was aggressive, flamboyantly assertive, and domineering, and he instinctively put his intelligence at the service of his need to dominate. Still, at first we did get along, at least enough to collaborate, or I thought we did. We were constantly arguing, sometimes violently, but there was sufficient basic agreement for the arguments to be settled by persuasion or compromise, or by a shifting of terms—a tactic at which Rahv was a master. He usually ended up on the same side as I did on most literary and political issues, so this, too, served to mask the friction between us. However, I do not know whether Rahv's behavior, which led to later explosions, was better or under control in the early years, or whether I was blind to what I saw later as his ruthlessness and disloyalty. I did become aware early on that he would claim most of the credit for finding new writers and for other achievements of the magazine, at the same time that he maneuvered me into handling the less glamorous aspects of the magazine, leaving him free to deal with contributors and publishers and thus to be in on the more visible and the more rewarding activities. He was able to do this mostly by preserving his incompetence in the financial and other practical aspects of *Partisan Review*—and by my tolerance of this division of labor. He also would get up very early, beat me to the mail at the office, and handle those things he thought more important to him. To tell the truth, I was both annoyed and indifferent, an ambivalence that did not make for any resolution of the problem, but in general I had a distaste for his almost reflexive reaching for the limelight and what amounted to a constant push for power. However, I felt it was more important to have the magazine run properly than to carry on a power struggle. What was in Rahv's mind I cannot even try to guess, for he was very close-mouthed about his own life, though loose-tongued about other people's, constantly speculating about their motives, which were always reduced by him to the most crass and materialistic basis. In fact, I often said of him that he was a Marxist mainly in his analysis of people's psychology. He also had the instinct of a politician.

It was not until much later that I had an inkling of the extent of Rahv's disloyalty. Signs of his ruthlessness kept multiplying. Either I was waking up or Rahv's guard was being lowered, but it was becoming clear that he had his eye constantly on his own interests. Once during the fifties, when we were working as consultants to Criterion Books, he told me he was thinking of shifting to another publisher. I said I did not think it was a good practical move, and, in addition, he would be turning his back on friends. He looked contemptuous, and shouted at me, "That's stupid, you believe in friendship." Later Criterion turned out to be unsuccessful, but that was something neither of us could foresee.

When we made up the guest list for *Partisan Review* parties, we would quarrel about whom to invite. Anyone who did not have a reputation, or power, or some form of glamor, he would dismiss as a "nobody." Rahv made up his guest list for his own parties more carefully than the President chooses his Cabinet. Rahv also became more and more savage in his diatribes against most of the writers we knew or worked with—behind their backs. To their face he usually overwhelmed them with his friendliness and charm. The number of his targets grew from year to year, and by the time I last saw him, in the early seventies, they included Hannah Arendt, Lionel and Diana Trilling, Norman Podhoretz, Norman Mailer, Susan Sontag, Clement Greenberg, Harold Rosenberg, Daniel Bell, Irving Kristol, Lionel Abel, Delmore Schwartz, Alfred Kazin, Irving Howe, Sidney Hook, William Barrett, Elizabeth Hardwick, Mary McCarthy, Robert Lowell—and all the conservatives. Few people, however, including his supposed friends, escaped put-downs and snide remarks. Nor was it always clear why he bad-mouthed any particular person. Sometimes it was for political, sometimes for literary, sometimes for personal, reasons. But on the whole the chief motive seemed to be competitiveness and bad temper. Once, when Mary McCarthy asked me why he was going after someone, all I could think of was that he was following some principle of rotation.

A boiling point was reached in the spring of 1946, in what we called the "confrontation." I had been dimly aware that his campaigns, secretive as well as open, against almost everyone we regarded as a friend were intensifying, and it had come back to me that he was talking against me in a way that surpassed normal criticism or exuberant rhetoric. Everything came out of the closet when Delmore Schwartz said to me one day that it had gotten so bad he felt he ought to tell me that Rahv was saying nasty things about me and trying to undermine me everywhere. I said I knew something, but apparently not the full extent, and I told Delmore that he was doing the same thing to him and to almost everyone else. I had heard that Rahv was belittling me at Dial, where we had been consultants, but I did not know that he was running down almost everything I did. Delmore also said that Will Barrett and Clement Greenberg were upset about Rahv. Delmore, Barrett, Greenberg, and I talked about it, and decided to tell Rahv he must stop tearing down and playing off against each other people with whom he was working and pretending to be friendly.

We met for lunch at Ratner's Dairy Restaurant on Second Avenue and Sixth Street. I had expected one of the others, Clem or Delmore, to open the subject, but they all waited for me. So I finally plunged in, and they followed with their complaints and evidence. Rahv stiffened, turned white, and his hands began to tremble. Since Rahv was not known for his heroism, we were not surprised by his collapse and his squirming to get out of the situation. In fact, at first I felt sorry to see him put in such a helpless position. But my sympathy was quickly dispelled, for the first thing Rahv said in reply to our accusations was that people talked too much, meaning, of course, that there would be no problem if people did not repeat what he had said. He then tried to deny some of the charges, but when that did not work he resorted to one of his usual tactics to avoid anything unpleasant—try to play the whole thing down, get it over as soon as possible, and change the subject. I suppose he succeeded in dismissing the affair, for there were no sanctions we cared to apply. The only visible effect was that Rahv became more cautious, but eventually that wore off, too.

After the confrontation, we had an armed truce. Rahv tried to act as though nothing had happened, while I was on my guard. But Rahv continued to pretend to be involved in the nonliterary side of the magazine, while really concentrating on the more public aspects. After 1957, however, when he went to teach at Brandeis, he began to do less and less, though, as usual, he would make a show of holding up his end. He wrote pompous letters, giving long-winded opinions about manuscripts he insisted be sent to him, saying either irrelevant or obvious things, often about pieces that had already been accepted or rejected. He would come in every few months for a day, interrogate me and the women in the office, spend most of the time gossiping, then disappear again.

To keep the record straight, I should say that, in addition to reading the key manuscripts, he occasionally suggested or arranged for a piece. But this was hardly enough for a co-editor and far less than his work in earlier years. We had many fights, usually when, without knowing or seemingly caring about what was going on, he would try to assert his authority or tell me I was not running the magazine properly. No doubt I was far from saintly in my treatment of Rahv, but I always felt put upon and angry at his claim to equal status and authority, amounting almost to veto rights, when he left all the financial and editorial concerns of the magazine to me.

Nor were the disagreements purely personal or organizational. We were beginning to drift apart intellectually. For one thing, Rahv was becoming more and more cantankerous: nobody was any good. The established writers were overrated and had sold out, younger ones were phonies—so who was left? Most of his editorial thinking was devoted to figuring out who could attack whom—which was what he concentrated on later in his own magazine, *Modern Occasions*. More important, however, is that in his later years Rahv's ideology hardened. His early Marxism was born again, but narrower and almost more rigid. It was a kind of Marxism in one head, as no one else was radical enough or good enough to meet his revolutionary standards. But it was a radicalism without a goal, without a movement, without a policy; in fact, without a politics. It was a Marxism used as a moral weapon to expose the corruption and pretensions of everyone and everything. Of course, since there is no shortage of stupidity or venality, Rahv was not always off the mark. But his abstract ranting about radicalism and conservatism had little applicability to the needs of the magazine. In addition, as Rahv moved left politically, he became more conservative in his literary views. No doubt there was a good deal of nonsense produced in the name of modernism and experiment, but Rahv went in for a wholesale dismissal of any writing he was not accustomed to. Again, as in his new radical politics, but in reverse, ranting was a substitute for criticism and discrimination. True, he had not lost entirely his shrewd sense of political and literary diplomacy, so that he was careful not to go as far publicly as in his private harangues. But this ideological and personal self-indulgence did not make for easy or fruitful editorial collaboration.

After the move to Rutgers the situation became worse. Rahv contributed nothing to the daily running of the magazine, very little to the editorial side. And the less he contributed, the more he dwelled on his authority, his status, his rights. He even demanded a desk all his own in the office at Rutgers, although we were cramped and there was no possible use he could make of the desk. In fact, in all the years at Rutgers, while he was still an editor, he came out only once to see the place, and then he had to have Steven Marcus drive him out and back. At Rahv's insistence, we met every month or two for lunch with Marcus and Poirier, usually at the Hotel Dorset.

To tell the truth, I must say we all thought Rahv was getting senile. He could not remember what he had read or what we had already

275

discussed, and he would continue to rant about the neoconservatives and the new left, but the ranting was like the dance and comedy routine of an aged performer. It was sad and funny, and, as always, Rahv's outrageous demands on us and his wild attacks on everybody else would stifle our sympathy or our sorrow at seeing an extraordinary intelligence breaking down and losing itself in tired rhetoric and spite.

The end, I am sorry to say, was petty, unsavory, and absurd. Dwight Macdonald once said that the relation of Rahv and myself was the only marriage held together by a magazine. Well, the divorce finally came after a shameful legal hassle, and Rahv's putting out his own magazine in which he had his revenge on us and all his other opponents. In the fall of 1965, the editorial board voted to list me as editor-in-chief in keeping with what was clearly my role and my responsibilities. Rahv objected strongly and instituted a lawsuit against me, which turned out to be an ugly charge that wasted everyone's time, ours and the lawyers' and raised unanswerable questions, for all such suits are based on the assumption that there are contending claims to property that is profitable and has a marketable—that is a sales—value. I do not believe there has ever been a lawsuit about a nonprofit literary magazine, and only an intransigent revolutionary mind, deeply immersed in the traditions of Marxism, could have thought up such a parody of capitalist property relations and litigation turned on their head.

Actually, to call what went on a lawsuit is misleading, though it was just as aggravating. My attorney, Robert Montgomery of Paul, Weiss, Rifkind, had a number of meetings with Rahv's attorney, who, incidentally, complained that Rahv did not listen to him. After months of haggling, a settlement was reached that was mostly face-saving. Instead of editor-in-chief, I was designated chairman of the editorial board. Rahv was to see all manuscripts being considered, and decisions were to be made by a vote of the board. He was to have visitation rights to the office. It was stipulated that if either of us started another publication, that would constitute a conflict of interest and would amount to withdrawal. Not much was changed, since Rahv was not really working actively as an editor, and he was demanding nothing more than symbolic and abstract rights. But the relation of Rahv not only to me but also to Poirier and Marcus became more bitter, and it was inevitable that working with Rahv meant listening to the raving and bitter rhetoric to which he was entitled in the new agreement. In the fall of 1969 Rahv resigned to start his own magazine. But before then I had seen him several times alone in Boston where we had lunch together. The old cunning was there, as he alternated gestures of friendliness, almost affection, putting his arm on my shoulder, and talking about old times, or giving me a choice bit of gossip, like a candy, and, at the same time, making little threats, thrown out casually to give me a jolt. But I felt that Rahv was coasting on his native intelligence and political instincts. His body was shot from emphysema, high blood pressure, gall bladder trouble, aggravated by chain smoking, sleeping pills, and whiskey. It was very depressing, despite our quarrels, to see him falling apart. Though it was clear that we could no longer work together, and that even the pretense of friendship was long gone despite the fact that some of the forms of the earlier intimacy persisted, I found myself wishing it had been different. Why could we not have collaborated without the hate that comes from professional competitiveness and the scramble for power? After all, the invasion of literary life by the kind of competition and power struggle that dominated business and politics was absurd. There was no power, or fortune, to be gained on a literary publication—one that presumably had no use for the values of power and money.

When Elizabeth Hardwick called in 1972 to tell me that Philip Rahv had died, my first reaction was that all the fighting was so unnecessary; then I felt this was the end of an era, which was a way, I suppose, of impersonalizing myself and personalizing history, a way of masking feelings that resist definition. I assume that the story Rahv must have told was different. I know, too, that many people found him charming, and entertaining, and intellectually impressive, although few were blind to the negative side of his character. Perhaps when he was not in the close, competitive relation that he was with me, one could laugh off as foibles or eccentricities things he said and did that might otherwise be intolerable.

In any event, I do not want to be understood as denying those qualities that made him an outstanding critic and editor in earlier years. He had an original, resourceful mind, though he did soak up ideas around him, and he was unusually sensitive to the changing intellectual climate. As a critic, Rahv was better at theory than at text, but at his best he was innovative and able to see literary works in a new historical light. In his most original work, his Marxism served as a basis for historical criticism—one that avoided the reductionism and the tone deafness of most Marxist criticism. He was also endowed with an enormous, restless energy. He could not even sit still. When, in the beginning, we wrote several pieces together, we would both talk as we tried to formulate sentences, but he had to do the typing as he was a better typist than I was. There were constant interruptions, however, for he could not stay put at the typewriter for more than a few minutes at a time, and he would pace the room, waving his pencil like a weapon. When he wrote in longhand he would stand at the fireplace and write on the mantelpiece.

Part of Rahv's later misanthropy and disgust with the world probably came from the fact that he found himself outside all the prevailing currents. Rahv was always insistent, often overbearing. Earlier, when he was part of a group that shared many assumptions about literature and politics and was embattled against other cultural voices, his own drives blended with those of the loose grouping of writers around the magazine. Toward the end of his life his Marxism was a badge of political purity. Norman Podhoretz tells of a taxi ride with Philip Rahv and Theo, his wife at the time. (She later died in a fire in their home in Boston.) Rahv, in one of his negative, declamatory moods, was lashing out at one of his favorite targets, capitalism, because the stock market had suddenly dived. Theo, who was not very sophisticated in these matters and certainly unable to distinguish between radical rhetoric and practical considerations, said, "Philip, maybe we should sell all our stock." "Don't be a fool," he said, "this is just theory."

As he failed to adjust his theories to a changing literary and political situation, he became a more dogmatic editor. Earlier, Rahv's biases acted as a kind of critical direction, especially for younger or less ideological writers; later, as writing and thinking became decentralized, Rahv's forcefulness was transformed into editorial bullying.

In his person, Rahv always struck me as having the physical traits and the psychology of an immigrant. He reminded me of my father in his awkwardness and his detachment from his body. He had no idea how a car worked, or what specific medicines were for. He once asked me what aspirin does. And he was almost killed when a wheel came off while he was driving; he had not known that a car had to be greased. He could not throw or catch a ball, ride a bike, play any game, or swim. He did not even seem to know that you can drown if you go in over your head. One summer when we had a house in Peekskill, Rahv came to visit and we went to swim at a nearby pool. Rahv flopped in, came up, gurgled, and went down again. He would have drowned if I had not jumped in and pulled him out. Fortunately, I had worked my way through school as a swimming counselor and lifeguard. He also had an immigrant's fear of authority; he literally trembled at the thought of the law, the police, going after him. But he became thoroughly Americanized in his sense of the practical world, quickly learning where power lay, and how people jockeyed to get ahead. In fact, the main fault of Norman Podhoretz's book, *Making It,* was that it took Rahv's worldly sensibility, perhaps unconsciously, as the model for an entire generation. He was a model, an extreme one, only in one sense, that he exemplified an articulate, polemical, politi- cized generation that came from nowhere and had as much trouble handling its success as its alienation. Though we thought of ourselves as dissidents, we always complained that we were not sufficiently heard and understood, even when we were having our greatest influ- ence. In this respect, Rahv was a symbolic figure, an insider and an outsider at the same time. A story told me by one of our editorial assistants, Jane Richmond, a woman with a strong sense of all our ironies, seems to me funny, sad, and representative. Rahv was in the office dictating a letter to her, pacing up and down as usual, and she asked him to sit down. "Why?" he asked, "Does it bother you if I walk around." "No," she said. "I don't understand you. I'm lipreading."

24

D-DAY

ANOTHER event that has been fogged by false rumors and inaccurate stories, some innocent, others inspired, was my leaving Rutgers in 1978. A couple of years before then, knowing that I would be reaching retirement in 1978, I began to talk to several people about the magazine and my staying on. I talked first with Richard Poirier, whose goodwill I never questioned, and who had the ear of the administration. (Poirier had resigned from the magazine in 1971, saying he needed to have more time to write.) He got in touch with Henry Winkler, acting vice-president (Edward Bloustein was on leave), who said he thought arrangements could be made. Things dragged until the spring of 1977 when Robert Montgomery, our attorney, and I met with Paul Pearson, the new acting president, and Kenneth Wheeler, the provost. As I recall, Clyde Szuch, an attorney for Rutgers, was also present. I particularly remember the meeting, as Bob Montgomery drove us to Rutgers, and I was so busy talking that we missed our exit and found ourselves at Trenton. I remember also that the Rutgers people were strangely noncommittal. They asked me about my intentions, to which I said that I would like to stay at

Rutgers, and that when I was ready to give up both teaching and the magazine, I would be disposed to leave the magazine to Rutgers, perhaps with a designated committee taking over. They said there was one hitch: the board of governors would have to approve, but they were hesitant to bring it up before them, as that would reveal how much money had been spent on the magazine. The implication was that the sum had been kept secret from them. At the time, this consideration seemed strange. But later it seemed even stranger, as we discovered that a secret analysis of the costs of the magazine had been made on orders of Provost Wheeler. (The figures were used at the subsequent trial.)

I heard nothing more, except undecipherable rumors, until the fall of 1977. All this time Poirier had an air of diffident optimism, but he had nothing concrete to suggest. In November 1977, I had a call from Kenneth Wheeler, asking me to meet with him at his office. We spoke for ten minutes, just long enough for him to tell me a decision had been reached not to support the magazine beyond June 30, 1978. The reason: it cost too much. I suggested we raise some of the money. He said they could do that with younger people. The meeting was over.

I left feeling I had been mugged. I had heard that Wheeler was not known for his courtesy, but in all the years at Rutgers I had always been treated graciously. A few days later a brusque note arrived from Wheeler, confirming what he had said, and notifying me that no one from Rutgers could be employed by *Partisan Review* after June 30, 1978, and that our premises were to be vacated by then. I told Poirier about the conversation with Wheeler, and he shrugged as though to suggest he knew nothing about it and had no power in this situation.

I was upset by the rudeness and impatience with which I had been brushed off. But there was nothing else to do but look for another home for myself and the magazine. I entered into negotiations with about ten universities, all of which showed varying degrees of eagerness to have us. By the spring of 1978 the field had narrowed to four that were seriously interested. The negotiations were difficult because there were many factors to consider: convenience, money, compatibility, terms, etc. Hence the negotiations dragged out.

As the summer got nearer, the pressure to get us out built up. There were calls every few days from the provost's office and the office of real estate, reminding us that we were to evacuate by D-day. Finally they moved someone into part of our office, and we had to consolidate in the remaining space. Unfortunately, we could not settle things by June 30, so I had to call the real estate people and the assistant provost to tell them that we would be out in a few weeks.

Finally, by the end of July we were ready to move. Arrangements had been completed with Boston University, and only one detail remained. B.U. had indicated it expected the *PR* files to come there with the magazine. I called Richard Schlatter to ask how I should go about getting Rutgers to release the files that had been stored in the library. He reminded me of a letter I had forgotten, written to me by him as provost in 1963, in which he said among other things that it was understood the files would be deposited in the Rutgers Library. The letter, dated March 20, 1963, contained the following statement about the files: "It is to be understood that in coming to Rutgers you will bring with you the files of the *Partisan Review* to be deposited in the Rutgers Library. You will have to work out an agreement with the librarian about what files are to be opened, if any, to the public, and what are to be closed for the time being." But he thought there should be no difficulty and suggested I call Paul Pearson to get the library to release the files to us. Pearson was polite but noncommittal, suggesting that he was not familiar with the situation, and would have to get the advice of Schlatter, Poirier, Tom Edwards, the overall English chairman, Daniel Howard, the Rutgers chairman, and Wheeler. Pearson also referred to the 1963 letter, and offered to give me a copy.

From this moment things moved with a dizzying confusion, compounded by stalling, evasion, and double-talk. And all this time Rutgers was pressing us to get out. I called Schlatter, Edwards, and Poirier several times; each time they assured me they would recommend to Pearson that the papers in the library be released to us as soon as we were ready to move.

Apparently, the administration had already decided to keep the papers, and the justification was based on the fateful letter of 1963 from Schlatter to me, and on Schlatter's and Poirier's belated recollection that I had intended to give the files to Rutgers. Much of the subsequent legal hassle revolved around the meaning of the word "deposit," which to me meant simply to deposit temporarily as one does with money in a bank. Subsequent consultations with librarians, publishers, and lawyers all corroborated this interpretation of the word.

We decided to move to Boston University, with which we had finally concluded an agreement, without the files, assuming that this question could be settled later. We had packed many of our things earlier, and we planned to finish packing and to engage a mover on the weekend of August 4.

At eight-thirty on Friday morning, August 4, 1978, I arrived at the office with Edith Kurzweil, an editorial associate, expecting Linda Healey, our managing editor, shortly after. But my key would not open the door. Thinking that someone had jimmied the lock, I called William Richardson, at the department of real estate, telling him we could not get into the office to complete our moving arrangements. He came immediately, agreed the lock had been tampered with, and entered the building through a loose window. After about a half-hour, Wheeler arrived, waving a piece of paper, accompanied by a cop. The paper was a statement signed by Pearson, proclaiming that Rutgers was impounding everything in the office. (He was annoyed at Richardson, who had not been told about the plan to seize the office, for letting us in.) Wheeler also ordered a trucker, who had come to pick up back copies we had sold weeks earlier, to unload everything in his truck and put it back in the garage, where it had been stored.

What followed was a rapid succession of orders, counterorders, seizures, releases, threats, legal maneuvers, attempts to salvage enough of our material to continue publication—all in a melange of confusion in an atmosphere ruled by the presence of the police. It is impossible to reconstruct just how many police were present at any moment, but throughout at least six to eight cops were coming and going, while one or two were always present to see to it that we did not take anything out of the office. At first, I was so stunned by the police occupation of our office—something all my liberal experience and faith in my country had taught me could not happen here, unless the country went fascist—that I thought I was going to have a heart attack. Not only could I not cope with this kind of action, but I could not comprehend it, and, in addition, I kept thinking that Rutgers was killing the magazine. How could we continue to function without our files? Edith suggested I take some meprobomate, which calmed me a bit.

As though the appropriation of all our files were not highhanded enough, they also took all the original manuscripts, some of which, as we tried futilely to point out to them, did not even belong to us. No matter how one interpreted the word deposit, it never included manuscripts. As for the files themselves, consisting mostly of correspondence with authors and a variety of miscellaneous documents of varying interest, the procedure, which was very informal and irregular, was to send back files over to the library every few years, keeping in the office the correspondence of the last several years because it was essential to the daily function of the magazine.

Even more outrageous was their impounding all my personal papers, some of which were kept in a special drawer marked personal, but most of which were locked in a closet upstairs. I had kept these papers at home, but had brought them to the office recently as I was writing this memoir and wanted to have them sorted out. My own papers included purely personal correspondence and a variety of documents that had nothing to do with the magazine, many being completely nonliterary. But I could not touch them, and they insisted on examining me when I left the office—to make sure I was not sneaking out some of my own papers.

The majordomo of this police operation was the assistant provost, John Salapatas, who made no secret of the fact that he was just acting under orders. One of the more frustrating, and I suppose amusing, aspects of the situation, if we were disposed to be amused by having everything we had worked for all our lives confiscated, was that we had to give a quick course in magazine publishing to Salapatas, who had to make decisions without the slightest knowledge of literary publishing.

Our only immediate recourse, however temporary, was legal. Hence we called Robert Montgomery as soon as possible, and he arranged a three-way conversation with the Rutgers attorney. We agreed, obviously under duress and with no other choice so long as the police kept us from our files, to have Rutgers copy for us to take to Boston University files defined as necessary for continued operation. I thought at the time that under our system it was a worse offense to interfere with a business than to seize one's property.

Naturally, everything was mixed up. Salapatas, out of his vast store of literary and publishing ignorance, kept trying to decide what was essential. Edith, Linda, and I kept insisting on what we needed. But

285

our objectivity was under suspicion because we were not disinterested and because we were upset by goings on we had never experienced. Edith was the only one who had ever seen anything like such an arbitrary police action, for she had been a young girl in Vienna when the Nazis were taking over.

Distressing as this event was on its own, it also had some unpleasant revelations about the nature of friendship. The entire Rutgers case, such as it was, rested on the testimony of Schlatter and Poirier, both of whom claimed to recall that I had told them that I meant to donate the files of *PR* to Rutgers. And both were my friends. Even more disturbing was the discovery during pretrial testimony of a memorandum to Wheeler by Poirier, Edwards, and Howard—all my friends—indicating that they had met, and recommending not only that support of *PR* be discontinued so long as I remained the editor but also that they try to seize the magazine from me when I found no other home for it and had to accept their terms. This memo was written just before I got my notice from Wheeler in November 1977. From then until July 1978, I had many conversations with other universities, and throughout Poirier played the part of my friend, confidant, and adviser. He would ask me the most minute details of all the negotiations and offer me what I thought was advice, some of which I found hard to understand at the time.

After we moved to Boston, we sued Rutgers for the return of everything they took, including all my personal papers, plus damages. The trial itself, which took place in December 1979, was the peak of all the tension that had been building up. But at the same time it was an anticlimax.

The trial took place at the county court in New Brunswick, presided over by Judge David Furman, a very intelligent and honest judge, who seemed to note from the very beginning that the Rutgers lawyer, Ronnie Leibowitz, went in for diversionary tactics to hide the fact that they had no case. She tried unsuccessfully to prove that we did not own the magazine, hence had no claim to the files; that Rutgers deserved the files because it had put a good deal of money into the magazine; that I might have claimed a deduction on my income tax for donating the files—which was not only untrue but impossible because the papers did not belong to me—etc.

Hence they had to fall back on the central issue of the case, namely whether deposit meant give or deposit, and whether I had promised the files to Schlatter and Poirier. On the meaning of the term they had no argument, since it was generally understood in the legal and library worlds that if the intention is to donate then the words give or donate are used and not deposit. Rutgers put an uncertain librarian on the stand, who started out by saying he understood the files were given. But on cross-examination he could not explain the basis of his "understanding," and he ended up by acknowledging that donated files are processed in a way different from the way ours had been handled. Albert Besser, our attorney, who tried the case brilliantly, also established on cross-examination that the notations on the cards in the library, referring to our files, were not the original ones, having been added later, and that the Rutgers librarian failed to produce these records during pre-trial discovery.

All that was left then of the Rutgers case was the testimony of Schlatter and Poirier, both of whom began by saying I had told them I was giving the files to Rutgers and ended by saying they could not remember what I had said. Poirier also admitted that he had told me that Rutgers had a moral right but not a legal one to the files. Under cross-examination, Schlatter and Poirier took back things they had said earlier and contradicted themselves constantly. There were also some funny moments in their testimony that did not help the Rutgers case. At one point, Schlatter was asked by Albert Besser, our attorney, whether he did not think it significant that a letter I wrote him outlining the advantages both to Rutgers and to *Partisan Review* did not mention the files. Schlatter answered that the letter also did not refer to heating and janitorial services. And Poirier, in explaining toward the end of his testimony why what I told him about the files was not clear, said I did not approach questions frontally. "You know," he said, "William approaches things from the side. It is a likable trait, and is found in most literary men."

After two days of a trial that belonged to the theater of the absurd, Judge Furman called the attorneys to the bench and told Ms. Leibowitz that her case was hopeless and that Rutgers could at least save face by settling. After some skirmishing on her part, a settlement was reached, which gave all the magazine files and my personal papers—everything Rutgers had seized on D-day—to me, but Rutgers was permitted to microfilm the files for its own library. In fact, the settlement was precisely what we had offered Rutgers originally, partly out of generosity, partly to avoid the anguish and expense of legal proceedings. I was concerned with getting back to my own work and with putting out the magazine after the pain and distraction of a trial.

Throughout the trial, Boston University was very supportive. President John Silber was particularly strong and sympathetic, and Vice-President Gerald Gross was helpful.

Perhaps the best commentary on the whole affair was made by Bob Montgomery. One day at lunch, shortly after the trial, I said to him that I guessed people who deal with big business are used to this sort of thing. "No," he said, "big business would think it unethical."

25

THEN AND NOW

SO thorough has been the rewriting of history by both left and right that one scarcely recognizes one's own past in these versions of earlier periods. It is as though one looked into the mirror and saw somebody else.

A recent example of remodeling by the left is the introduction by Francis Mulhern to Regis Debray's *Teachers, Writers, Celebrities*. Debray's book itself is a strangely academicized tinkering with literary history from a Marxist point of view. And the short account of *Partisan Review* in the introduction illustrates the steady erosion of truth on the left. Distortions breed further distortions, which are then canonized into official left history. Mulhern simply takes it for granted that *Partisan Review*, driven by its anti-Communism, became more and more conservative, to the point even of accepting the political premises of McCarthyism.

Another instance, not directly related to *Partisan Review*, is Garry Wills's book, *The Kennedy Imprisonment: A Meditation on Power*, which turns the legend of the Kennedys upside down. This is surely a strange phenomenon, this transformation of the Kennedys from heroes into villains, and surely it has something to do with the current tendency on the left to denigrate any concern with American national interest and security as reactionary.

The only study I know of the early history of *Partisan Review* that is faithful to the facts and the spirit of the period is James Gilbert's *Writers and Partisans.* Unfortunately, the book does not go beyond the forties. But it uses the resources of scholarly research to recreate what the editors and writers for *Partisan Review* actually said and did.

The latest alteration from the right, after Norman Podhoretz's *Breaking Ranks,* is *The Truants,* by William Barrett, a reminiscence about some of the people and events in the history of *Partisan Review* that deserves serious attention. The book is engagingly written and is to be commended for its cool tone and its many shrewd observations. And I cannot complain about most of his references to me, which show considerable affection and respect, as I always had for him. Still, the entire portrait does not seem right. There is something about the book, not simple to pin down, that is somehow distorting of the total picture, though it is accurate and perceptive in many of its details.

William Barrett was an associate editor of *Partisan Review* from 1945 through 1955. It was a time of many changes, some noisy, some quiet. McCarthy was scalping Communists in public, Vietnam was building up, intellectual radicalism was on the wane, the media were invading the arts, mass and middle culture were on the rise, new writers were coming up. But Barrett only touches on most of the political and cultural forces of the period, which were very complex and contradictory. Instead, he concentrates on the lives of a few people, Trilling, Rahv, Schwartz, and myself, which he does cleverly, but much is left out. The major issues Barrett discusses are what he calls the two M's, Marxism and Modernism, treating them in terms of ideology, and neoconservatism, which Barrett now espouses, and through which he now sees the past. This bias leads, in my opinion, to a certain amount of distortion.

It would seem from Barrett's memoir—even more from Hilton Kramer's review of it in *The New York Times*—that we were all up to our necks in Marxism and Modernism and that we are now in a more enlightened phase because these twin fallacies have been abandoned. But the fact is that none of us was any longer a Marxist at the time Barrett writes about though we retained some of the historical sense with which Marxism is endowed. As for Modernism, we did not go over then to the antimodernists who were endorsing a more popular and more wholesome idea of culture, but we were aware that the modernism of Joyce and Kafka was becoming a thing of the past.

I think the main distortions in Barrett's account come from two sources: his neoconservative ideology and his intellectual design, which requires a representative figure. Barrett singles out Hannah Arendt, Mary McCarthy, and Harold Rosenberg as possible representative figures, but rejects them as insufficiently representative. Yet his choice of Philip Rahv as the representative figure makes the picture even more askew. For, as I have indicated, Rahv was not representative either in his personal traits or in his politics. At his best, he was a very good editor and critic and very intelligent, when he was not out on some rhetorical limb. However, his personality and behavior were certainly distinctive. He was extraordinarily flamboyant and overbearing in his talk, especially when he felt safe. But, as Hannah Arendt once said, he was basically timid and needed approval for all his stands, from me and others he worked with. Hence in practice he was most compromising and adaptable. He was even less representative politically. Except for the anti-Communism that he shared with all of us, his rhetoric often carried him to extreme positions, from which he had to pull back later. And his movement to the left, to the "radicalism of his youth," which began in the sixties and grew stronger in the last years of his life, was certainly not typical. Nor was it then the policy of *Partisan Review*. Nor is it now. In fact, I do not know of any other person close to *Partisan Review* who had either Rahv's personal traits, which Barrett makes out, himself, to be quite objectionable, or his swerving politics, which Barrett condemns. It is Barrett's ideological bias that makes Rahv's late reconversion typical— typical of the failure of what Barrett characterizes as the politics of the truants, of those, that is, who played hooky from reality. But not even Rahv played hooky; he played with ideas. And if Barrett wants to depict Rahv as a truant, then the question is whether his original leftism, his later anti-Communism, or his final radical reversion was the expression of his truancy. And how were the rest of us truants? Barrett suggests our truancy consisted in our critical attitude toward the quality of modern life.

An example of Barrett's ideological inflation of small incidents is his report of a silly encounter between Harold Rosenberg and Philip Rahv. According to Barrett, Rosenberg asked Rahv how *Partisan Review* could have published a supposedly "bourgeois" piece by Trilling. This kind of banter and political baiting was not uncommon at the time, as we were all shifting and watching each other's shifts. And Rahv considered it worse to be *accused* of moving an inch to the right than of having betrayed a friend, which involves only sentiment. But this was only talk. Rosenberg was obviously posturing and using the occasion to indicate his superior editorial nose and the purity of his politics. And Rahv was also posturing and protecting his left flank without having to do anything about it. For the fact is that Rahv's genuflection to the left did not reflect editorial policy, and Trilling was welcome to publish in *Partisan Review* and did so.

Ideology makes not only for strange bedfellows but for strange divorces. It is part of Barrett's thesis to claim that the editors of *Partisan Review* and those close to them did not follow the logic of their position and end up as neoconservatives. Now this is based on the assumption that all anti-Communist roads must lead to neoconservatism. As Trotsky once said of Stalin: Barrett assumes what he has to prove. Barrett puts Trilling somewhere in the middle, as one who foreshadowed neoconservatism but did not go all the way. This reminds one of the Podhoretz argument that Trilling, like a few other anti-Communists, including myself, pulled back from neoconservatism out of fear of being ostracized by the left. However, as I have said, neither I nor Irving Howe nor Lionel Trilling was afraid of becoming a neoconservative. What was there to be afraid of? We were always being criticized by the left. And now, after all, the neoconservatives have been riding high. The fact is that Howe and I have been critical of neoconservatives on political and cultural grounds though we both grant that they are right in some matters. And Trilling, aside from his political convictions, did not like extreme positions of any kind. As I said earlier, I recall Trilling one evening telling Norman Podhoretz and Midge Decter that he felt *Commentary* was becoming too ideological and too predictable.

I cannot leave the subject without noting that Barrett assumes attitudes now that he did not have earlier. Where others revise history, Barrett also revises himself. Why, for example, does he now glamorize Mary McCarthy and Hannah Arendt? And, aside from ideology, it is hard to understand Barrett's personal reasons for inflating Rahv's role on the magazine and in the intellectual community as a whole. Nor can I comprehend why he dedicated his book to Rahv and Schwartz, unless it was meant ironically. For, if the truth is to be known, Rahv was bent on putting down Barrett—like everyone else—and I was kept busy defending him. On the other hand, Barrett himself was always critical of Rahv's mind and character. Barrett's feelings about Schwartz are more understandable. They were those of a devoted friend—perhaps, in the beginning, too devoted—and though Schwartz lost no opportunity to exploit that relationship, there was a bond between them until Schwartz's madness made any relation impossible. Could it be that Barrett is retroactively putting himself in the same relation to Rahv? If so, the ideological reason would be clear, but the personal one remains obscure. It seems to me that in placing himself now in this relation to Rhav, Barrett not only distorts Rahv's role and character, and hence some of the history of the magazine, but also does himself an injustice. For in inflating Rahv, Barrett diminishes everyone else, including himself.

Hilton Kramer's review of *The Truants* follows Barrett's script, but, lacking Barrett's personal memories, it is necessarily even more ideological. Kramer, of course, has had ambivalent attitudes to modernism, and is well known as a spokesman for the neoconservative politics that dominate a number of publications in this country and command the allegiance of many writers and social commentators.

My own experience has been more complex and not so easily categorized. I have been asked by younger writers what the thirties were like as compared to the present. It is difficult to make the comparison as the face and spirit of the country have changed so much. Neat cultural divisions no longer exist. We no longer have "our" culture and "their" culture. Communism then meant their propaganda and our gullibility. Now fewer people are taken in, but Soviet power has led to accommodation. Then one protested the Moscow trials; now it is Afghanistan and Poland. There is a feeling that America is going down; but earlier radical impulses have been supplanted by the mushrooming of cults, breeding an optimism of political and psychological self-realization. The early dream was of socialism, later liberation—women, the third world, blacks; now it is simply peace.

Recently, most disaffection has been channeled into a movement against the bomb. These shifts and dislocations have had their effect on everything from styles of living to intellectual fashions. Writers have moved from the WPA to the academy, from cold-water flats to high-rise apartments. In the thirties, nobody talked about popular culture, or about movies—except for a few avant-garde experiments and some Russian epic film makers, like Eisenstein—as though they were a part of serious culture. And there was no television to inflate into art. It was all so high-minded and highbrow, and nobody worried about being elitist. Now what one feels most strongly is that there is no central idea in our culture, no leading tradition, no main direction, only divergent themes and visions, expressing the chaos of modern life. And into the chaos the neoconservatives have tried to bring a sense of order and purpose and moral values. But it is arbitrary and imposed from outside, and it supports the ideal of free commercial and intellectual enterprise, and of self-aggrandizement, that has produced the anarchy neoconservatives lament.

New York in the thirties was like the other side of the moon. Perhaps some of the atmosphere of the period can be conveyed by remembering that we were all broke, that we were lifted momentarily by false hopes, that we enjoyed the benefits and the disadvantages of being out of the mainstream of the culture, that I was a kid, which meant that I looked at the situation from the perspective of someone who still had his way to make and saw it as a painful but adventurous way of learning and growing up. It was a world where ideas were important: it was bounded on all sides by such figures as Eliot, Valéry, Marx, Miró, Ortega y Gasset, Proust, Kafka, Freud. Whatever else it was, it was the only world I knew.

I was a member of five minority groups. I was a disaffected writer and an editor of an against-the-grain publication. I was a Jew. I believed in modernism, which at that time was outside the dominant culture. I had become an anti-Communist after a brief flirtation with the party, which was not very fashionable. I tried to hold on to some radical politics and socialist ideals, however vague and Utopian they really were, and compromised by the Soviet regime, when the swing was clearly to the right.

Literary life in New York in the thirties for me and the writers around *Partisan Review* seemed marginal to the main concerns of the city and the country. We felt completely outside the literary as well as the political establishment. Our favorite hangout was not the Algonquin but Stewart's Cafeteria on Sheridan Square, where for a dime you could get coffee and cake and sit for hours, arguing and solving the problems of the world.

But it was not only poverty that the great depression brought. It brought an air of restlessness, uncertainty, and drift, somewhat like the present—with this difference, however, that the drift of young people today has an element of middle-class self-indulgence and antipathy to the idea of work, and is not without a measure of affluence. Most young writers and painters were on the WPA writers' and artists' projects. The painters were paid twenty-three dollars and eighty-six cents a week to paint. But the writers' project was mostly a symbol of meaningless work. It was perhaps one of the most typical experiences of the time, in that one had no past, no future, and one was rewarded for not using one's talents. Some writers wrote useful state guidebooks. Others catalogued old books in dingy, dust-ridden, underground storerooms. I had roving assignments that were indistinguishable from busy work. One assignment, for example, was to write a report of a trial in a law court. Another was to describe the weather station in Central Park.

We used to sign in at nine o'clock, four days a week, and then leave for the day. Rahv and I usually got to the *Partisan Review* office by ten. But the union that represented the writers and painters was Communist controlled and was constantly looking for grievances and ways of demonstrating its militancy. There was a small Trotskyite opposition, but it was easily throttled. Joe Gould, the oral historian, who defended them, used to say the Trotskyites had as much right as the Stalinists to make fools of themselves.

Finally, the union found an excuse to strike. It demanded shortening the four-day week to three. So we went on strike, a sit-in strike, which would be more dramatic and get more publicity than an ordinary one. We stayed all night at WPA headquarters until the police were summoned in the morning to get us out. The veterans of labor warfare showed us how to fill our hats with crumpled newspapers to soften the expected blows on the head by the cops' clubs. Wives and husbands and friends gathered outside to shout the slogans of class war and to bring us food, which we hoisted up with improvised boxes and ropes. Finally the cops came. Rahv and I, who thought the strike was absurd and were not eager to become labor heroes, stood in back as far from the cops as we could get. After about ten minutes of snarling on both sides, the cops went away, apparently ordered not to force us out. We soon left, victorious, our skulls intact, now having to punch in only three days a week. Such were some of the pleasures and rewards of having principles in the thirties.

Principles and commitments change, but in my case, at least, Utopianism persisted for some time. Years later, my own Utopianism, which by that time was intellectual, not social, led me several times to try to reconstruct the intellectual community, which had fallen apart. My rationale was that what we had in common was greater than our differences. I should have known better. The first time, in 1969, my efforts were bumbling. It was in the midst of the political wars of the sixties, between the new left and the old left. I thought I could bridge the gap by bringing Jack Newfield and Nat Hentoff together with Norman Podhoretz, James Gilbert, and Mike Harrington. They met at my house for sandwiches and beer. It was a disaster from the start. Newfield and Hentoff were sweet but entrenched within all the assumptions of the new left and the counterculture, and suspicious of Podhoretz. Podhoretz was slightly patronizing and contemptuous of Newfield and Hentoff, whom he regarded as political innocents, particularly in their lack of concern with the evils of Stalinism. After two meetings, it was clear that I was trying to mate lambs and wolves.

The next attempt was on a grander scale. There were two meetings. The first one, in 1970, included Lionel and Diana Trilling, Irving Howe, Susan Sontag, Steven Marcus, Robert Jay Lifton, and Peter Brooks. Mary McCarthy said she would come but could not make it. If such veterans of conferences and discussion groups, one thought, could not manage a civilized exchange, then discourse was impossible.

Well, the first meeting was a fiasco. Somebody mentioned that he would like to go to China, which brought out all the passions that had been nurtured for years about Communism, anti-Communism, soft and hard liberalism, intellectual freedom, etc. I tried to keep the peace, but that only put me in the role of compromiser, which both sides spurned.

I tried once more, chalking up the failure of the first meeting to having started on the wrong foot, so to speak. But this time it was harder even to get people to come. The Trillings felt it was hopeless. Irving Howe said he was so charmed by Susan that he forgot she was his political adversary. I pulled a boner by forgetting the new etiquette engendered by the women's movement. On the card reminding people of the time and place, I said it was not a social evening, therefore no wives. It was all I could do to make amends by explaining that I meant it was a meeting, not a party. But it was clear that my blunder served as a means of disposing of my noble project, which everyone recognized as dead anyway. What I failed to realize was that polarization was growing and that ideological divisions could not be bridged by talk.

One occasion in the seventies, which was not an attempt at community rebuilding, nevertheless should have demonstrated how fragmented literary life in New York had become. It was a dinner party at my home, a small one, with Diana and Lionel Trilling, Stephen Spender, Donald Barthelme, Marian Knox, who is now married to Barthelme, and Edith Kurzweil, at the time one of our editors, now executive editor, and Paul Zweig and his wife. The Trillings had been encouraging Spender to tell stories about English writers, which he did with great charm and wit. But Barthelme, who had been mellowing from a few drinks, suddenly indicated he was bored with this in-talk about an earlier generation. To change the subject, Diana mentioned that *The Middle of the Journey*, Lionel's novel about the thirties, was being reissued, but that not much was being written about it. Donald said that it was not a good novel, whereupon Diana told Donald that it was better than anything he had written. Marian added some fuel by accusing Lionel of ignoring the question of feminist writing in all his criticism, which Lionel made no attempt to answer. I tried to be a peacemaker, at which I was not very good. But everyone was civilized enough to calm down, and the evening went the way of so many literary evenings: knowing chitchat within an armed truce.

The latest attempt to create a sense of community by bringing people together has been in Boston, since the magazine moved to Boston University in 1978. But its purposes were different, having more to do with sinking roots into a new community than with reconstructing one by obliterating old feuds. Hence we set up what was originally called a planning committee but has become a discussion group, which seems to be a natural habitat for academics.

Yet one has to recognize that intellectual life in Boston has been at the opposite pole from New York, particularly New York in the thirties. The ideas both of conflict and of community are vastly different. In the thirties, when New York literary manners were developed, we were a brawling community, everyone trying to impose his views on everyone else by sheer force of logic and rhetoric, which was often merciless. We had not yet learned the academic mode of ignoring or accommodating to ideas we found repugnant. Boston, however, is above all a university town, perhaps the largest in the world, and its impressive concentration of academic talent exhibits dramatically the gap between the noisy, intolerant, freewheeling intellectual and the quiet, tolerant scholar.

The city of Boston, which has been called the Athens of the West by cultivated Bostonians, has acquired some of the smooth edges of a university. It is a soft city, like Paris, Vienna, San Francisco, and Athens itself, unlike New York and London, which are hard cities. Life is easier in a soft city, especially for one who has been brought up in the intellectual jungles of New York. It almost makes you forget that the world is in a bad way, and that it is not improved by ideological warfare and by mindless movements of the left and the right.

If we survive, and I suspect we will, despite our gloomy predictions, it will be because our civilization, with all its cracks, seems to be able to outlast the intellectual efforts to prop it up or to destroy it. Even though the terrible events and crises of this century have given us enough ground for pessimism, there is one reason for optimism. I think the very destructive power of the bomb and the build-up of nuclear armaments by America and the Soviet Union, which the antiwar movement insists make the use of the bomb more likely, have just the opposite effect. Though it cannot be proven, they seem to me to make nuclear war more unlikely. Contrary to the fashionable notion that governments, particularly ours, are itching to use the bomb, I think that, whatever else might be said about them, neither the Soviet nor the American leaders are insane. Clearly, missile strength is coming to be used more and more as a political, not a military, weapon.

One of the uncertainties is public opinion, which can change like the wind, but keeps repeating itself. The last few years have been distressingly reminiscent of the thirties in the proliferation of "left" ideologies and movements whose motives and aims are questionable. The disarmament unilateralists, the Greens in Germany, the anti-Israelis, the supporters of the PLO, for example, exploit the credit of the left. But they have little to do with traditional socialist ideals, and they represent non-socialist national interests. Nor are they simply a revival of Stalinism, for these new groupings include many anti-Soviet people. But they resemble the earlier Stalinists in one respect—their combination of innocence and ideology, the proportions of which are almost impossible to fathom. To be sure, since nothing lasts very long these days, this new phenomenon may be transformed into something else—either better or worse—or it may simply subside. In the meantime, one cannot help feeling that political naiveté and bad faith are back again.

In this age of uncertainties, all we can be sure of is that we are on the verge of large historic changes. For the politics of both the West and the East, not to speak of the Mideast, are based on a precarious adjustment to unsolved problems. I say this not with any equanimity, since I have found change of any kind to be traumatic, and often for the worse. Such ambivalence about change would appear to be a sign of split intellectual personality—of having one's head in the clouds of theory while one's psychology is that of a tree that does not want to be moved. Perhaps, too, this resistance to change is symptomatic of the division between our ideas and our feelings, which makes people more conservative or more radical than is warranted by their experience. It is one of the sources of ideology.

In any event, as this epoch draws to a close, one has to be consumed by curiosity about the future. The fear of death is not to be underestimated, but I can think of no better reason for surviving than to see how it all turns out, if by some miracle of human persistence, the world should become a nicer place to live in—how awful not to know about it.

It is perhaps more realistic to assume that all one can hope for is that things do not get worse—that the status quo is maintained. What a contradiction one has finally arrived at: to have been brought up on the necessities of history and now to be drawn psychologically and politically to the stability that exists only outside of history.

299

INDEX

Index

Index

Index

311